Arkansas

ADVENTURES IN TIME AND PLACE

TOM GREER
Anthony Professor of the Humanities
Ouachita Baptist University
Arkadelphia, Arkansas

LAVELL COLE
Associate Professor of History
Ouachita Baptist University
Arkadelphia, Arkansas

THE LOVELY OLD STATE HOUSE IS IN LITTLE ROCK. COMPLETED IN 1840, IT SERVED AS THE CAPITOL BUILDING OF ARKANSAS UNTIL 1911. TODAY MANY PEOPLE VISIT IT TO SEE WHERE OUR STATE'S FIRST LEGISLATURE MET.

Macmillan McGraw-Hill

New York   Farmington

PROGRAM AUTHORS

Dr. James A. Banks
Professor of Education and Director of
the Center for Multicultural Education
University of Washington,
Seattle, Washington

Dr. Barry K. Beyer
Professor Emeritus, Graduate School of
Education
George Mason University
Fairfax, Virginia

Dr. Gloria Contreras
Professor of Education
University of North Texas
Denton, Texas

Jean Craven
District Coordinator of Curriculum
Development
Albuquerque Public Schools
Albuquerque, New Mexico

Dr. Gloria Ladson-Billings
Assistant Professor of Education
University of Wisconsin
Madison, Wisconsin

Dr. Mary A. McFarland
Instructional Coordinator of Social
Studies, K-12, and Director of Staff
Development
Parkway School District
Chesterfield, Missouri

Dr. Walter C. Parker
Professor and Program Chair for Social
Studies Education
University of Washington
Seattle, Washington

NATIONAL GEOGRAPHIC SOCIETY
Washington, D.C.

CONTENT CONSULTANTS

Marie McNeal
Supervisor of Social Studies
Little Rock School District
Little Rock, Arkansas

Carrie Vee Wilson
Member, Quapaw Tribal Council
Fayetteville, Arkansas

GRADE-LEVEL CONSULTANTS

Pat Coyle
Third Grade Teacher
Langston Elementary School
Hot Springs, Arkansas

Vicky Logue
Fifth Grade Teacher
T. G. Smith Elementary School
Springdale, Arkansas

Pate Neely
Fifth Grade Teacher
Carnall Elementary School
Fort Smith, Arkansas

Sue Tackett
Fifth Grade Teacher
Jones Elementary School
Hot Springs, Arkansas

Donna Wright
Fifth Grade Teacher
Jones Elementary School
Hot Springs, Arkansas

ACKNOWLEDGMENTS

The publisher gratefully acknowledges permission to reprint the following copyrighted material: "Take only what is needed . . ." is excerpted from CREEK MUSIC: OZARK MOUNTAIN BALLADS, by Diane Taylor. Copyright © 1985 by Diane Taylor. Reprinted by permission of August House, Inc. Excerpt form "Flatrock Creek" by Dorothy Jones, from "Native" by Rosa Marinoni, and from "Creation of the Earth" by John R. Swanton from ARKANSAS VOICES edited by Sarah Fountain. Copyright © 1989 UCA Press. All reprinted with permission of UCA Press. Excerpt from AUTHENTIC VOICES *Arkansas Culture 1541-1860* edited by Sarah Fountain. Copyright © 1986 by UCA Press. Used by permission of the publisher. Excerpt from a poem by Joe Page from ARKANSAS *A People and Their Reputation* by David M. Tucker. Copyright © 1985 by Memphis State University Press. Reprinted by permission of the publisher. Excerpt from "We're Coming Arkansas" from SONGS OF THE OZARK FOLK by Leo Rainey. © Leo Rainey, Olaf and Orilla Pinkston. Published by Mountaineer Books, Branson, Missouri and reprinted with their permission. Excerpts from A DOCUMENTARY HISTORY OF ARKANSAS edited by C. Fred Williams, S. Charles Bolton, Carl H. Moneyhon, and LeRoy T. Williams. Copyright © 1984 by the Board of Trustees of the University of Arkansas, The University of Arkansas Press, Fayetteville, Arkansas 72701. Used by permission of the publisher. Excerpts from I KNOW WHY THE CAGED BIRD SINGS by Maya Angelou. Copyright © 1969 by Maya Angelou. Reprinted by permission of Random House, Inc. Mary Medearis quote about Arkansas is reprinted with her permission. Excerpt from BITTERSWEET EARTH edited by Ellen Gray Massey. Copyright © 1985 by the University of Oklahoma Press, Norman, Publishing Division of the University. Reprinted by permission of the University of Oklahoma Press. Other sources consulted: EYES ON THE PRIZE *America's Civil Rights Years, 1954-1965* by Juan Williams. Copyright © 1987 Blackside, Inc. Viking Penguin Inc. New York, New York.

Macmillan/McGraw-Hill
A Division of The **McGraw·Hill** *Companies*

Macmillan/McGraw-Hill
1221 Avenue of the Americas
New York, New York 10020

Printed in the United States of America

ISBN 0-02-147079-0/4

3 4 5 6 7 8 9 VHJ 05 04 03

CONTENTS

UNIT 1 Studying Arkansas   8

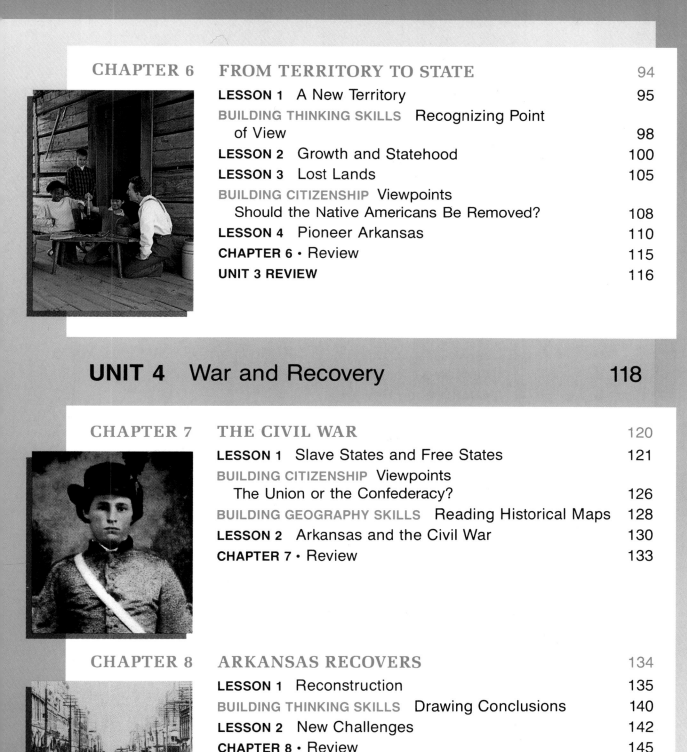

REFERENCE SECTION

Building Citizenship

Building Skills

Charts, Graphs, Diagrams, and Time Lines

Maps

WHAT IS AN Arkansan?

Dear Student,

Look at the photographs on the opposite page. These people live in different areas of our state and lead different lives, but they have one thing in common. Like you, they are Arkansans.

Throughout this book you will learn about the different areas of Arkansas in which these people live. You will learn about what makes each part of our state special. What does it mean to you to be an Arkansan? As you read this book, keep that question in mind.

You will read about the mountains, lakes, rivers, and plants found across Arkansas. You will learn about the rich history of our state—about the people who lived here thousands of years ago, and about the people who live here today.

In the end, it is the people who make our state special. And it is you and your classmates who will continue to make Arkansas a strong, growing state.

When you finish this book, you will know more about Arkansas. You will also have some new ideas about what it means to be an Arkansan.

Sincerely,

Tom Greer and Lavell Cole

Arkansas

the official Arkansas state song
words and music by Eva Ware Barnett

I am think- ing to-night of the South- land, Of the
'Tis a land full of joy and of sun- shine, Rich in

home of my child-hood days, Where I roamed through the woods and the
pearls and in dia- monds rare, Full of hope, faith and love for the

mea- dows, By the mill and the brook that plays; Where the
stran- ger Who may pass 'neath her por- tals fair; There the

ros- es are in bloom, And the sweet mag-no- lia too, Where the
rice —— fields are full, And the cot- ton, corn and hay, There the

jas - mine is white, And the fields are vio - let blue, There a
fruits of the field bloom in win - ter months and May, 'Tis the

wel - come a - waits all her chil - dren Who have
land that I love, First of all dear, And to

CHORUS

wan - dered a - far from home. Ark - an - sas, Ark - an - sas, 'Tis a
her let us all give cheer.

name dear, 'Tis the place I call "Home, Sweet Home;" Ark - an -

sas, Ark - an - sas, I sa - lute thee, From thy shel - ter no more I'll roam.

1

USING YOUR TEXTBOOK

Your textbook contains many features that will help you read, understand, and remember the geography, history, and people of Arkansas.

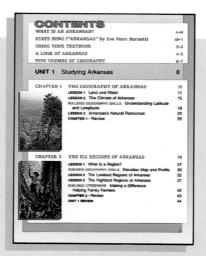

TABLE OF CONTENTS
Lists all parts of your book and tells you where to find them.

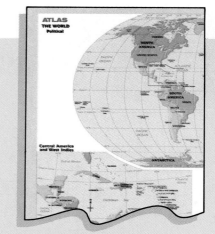

ATLAS
Maps of the world, the United States, and Arkansas.

LESSON OPENER
Important vocabulary, people, and places introduced in the lesson

Lesson introduction

Asks you to think about what you already know from your book or your own experience

Question you should keep in mind as you read the lesson

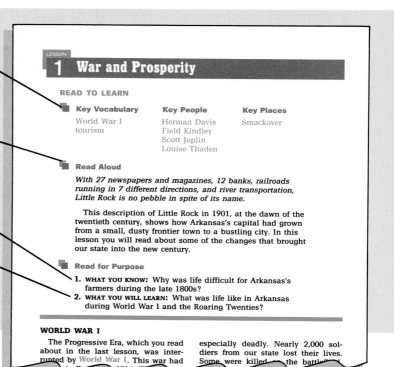

LESSON

1 War and Prosperity

READ TO LEARN

Key Vocabulary
World War I
tourism

Key People
Herman Davis
Field Kindley
Scott Joplin
Louise Thaden

Key Places
Smackover

Read Aloud

With 27 newspapers and magazines, 12 banks, railroads running in 7 different directions, and river transportation, Little Rock is no pebble in spite of its name.

This description of Little Rock in 1901, at the dawn of the twentieth century, shows how Arkansas's capital had grown from a small, dusty frontier town to a bustling city. In this lesson you will read about some of the changes that brought our state into the new century.

Read for Purpose

1. **WHAT YOU KNOW:** Why was life difficult for Arkansas's farmers during the late 1800s?
2. **WHAT YOU WILL LEARN:** What was life like in Arkansas during World War I and the Roaring Twenties?

WORLD WAR I

The Progressive Era, which you read about in the last lesson, was interrupted by World War I. This war had ... in ... 1914. The ... tral ...

especially deadly. Nearly 2,000 soldiers from our state lost their lives. Some were killed ... the battle ...

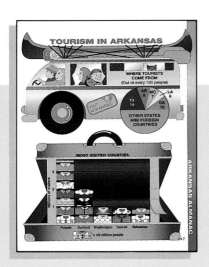

ARKANSAS ALMANAC
Interesting facts and information about Arkansas

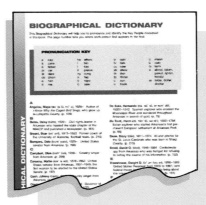

BIOGRAPHICAL DICTIONARY
List and pronunciation of important people discussed in your book and the page where each is introduced

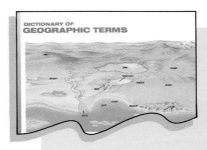

DICTIONARY OF GEOGRAPHIC TERMS
Definition, pronunciation, and illustration of major geographic terms

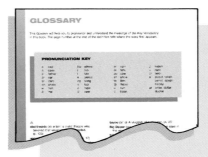

GLOSSARY
Definition and pronunciation of all Key Vocabulary and first page where each is introduced

GAZETTEER
Location and pronunciation of major places discussed in your book

INDEX
Alphabetical list of important people, places, events, and subjects in your book and pages where information is found

NATIONAL GEOGRAPHIC

A Look at Arkansas

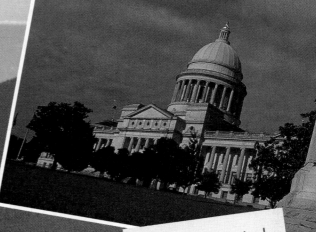

The State Capitol building rises over Little Rock, our state's capital and largest city.

The Ozarks invite everyone to sit and enjoy the sights.

The poultry business isn't chicken feed to Arkansas's economy.

Fabulous fishing attracts tourists and locals alike to the Buffalo National River.

Most people want to test the steaming mineral waters at Hot Springs fountain.

NATIONAL GEOGRAPHIC

Five Themes of Geography

Location
How do people know exactly where things are?

Place
What makes Arkansas different from other places?

Region
What are some things that help make the Ozarks a special region?

Movement
How do people travel from one place to another?

Human/Environment Interactions
How have people changed the landscape?

UNIT
1

STUDYING ARKANSAS

WHERE WE ARE

The state that we call home is in the part of the United States known as the Southeast. In our state you can dig for diamonds, listen to a symphony orchestra, or go canoeing in the white water of the Buffalo River. You can also catch a glimpse of our state's history at the Ozark Folk Festival or at the Arkansas Territorial Restoration. Let's find out about Arkansas—its land and its people.

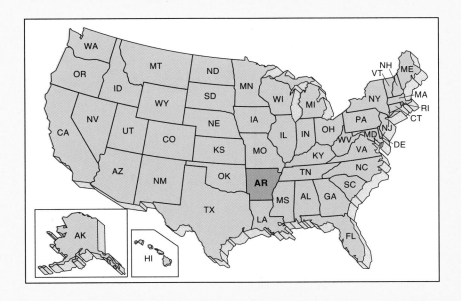

CHAPTER 1

THE GEOGRAPHY OF ARKANSAS

FOCUS

We're coming, Arkansas,
We're coming, Arkansas.
Our four-horse team
Will soon be seen
In the hills of Arkansas.

These words were sung long ago by people coming to our state. Today, the car or airplane has replaced the team of horses. But travelers keep coming to "the hills of Arkansas" to visit or to stay. This chapter will help you to understand why Arkansas is a special place to live.

READ TO LEARN

 Key Vocabulary

landform
geography
fossil
mountain range
river basin

Key Places

Mississippi River
Ozark Mountains
Ouachita Mountains
Arkansas River

White River
Red River
Ouachita River
St. Francis River

 Read Aloud

I found the whole country a prairie, full of [thick] grass about knee high, in which we surprised herds of fleeting deer.

These words were written in 1819 by Thomas Nuttall when he saw the land of Arkansas for the first time. Nuttall's journey took him over hundreds of miles of mountains and rivers. How do you think you would describe the land of Arkansas if you were seeing it for the first time?

Read for Purpose

1. **WHAT YOU KNOW:** Why do you think people enjoy living in Arkansas?
2. **WHAT YOU WILL LEARN:** What is geography? What is the geography of Arkansas?

ARKANSAS'S LAND

When Thomas Nuttall came to Arkansas in 1819, he traveled by boat and on foot. Today we have other ways of seeing the land. Imagine that you are in an airplane flying high enough so that you can see the entire state of Arkansas below you. What is the state's shape? Which landforms can you see far below? A landform is a shape on the earth's surface, such as a valley or a mountain.

These are questions about Arkansas's geography (jē og' rə fē). Geography is the study of the earth and the way people live on it and use it.

A VIEW FROM ABOVE

As your plane passes over Arkansas, you might be surprised to see that the state looks almost like a square. Arkansas extends about 250 miles (402 km) from its eastern border, the Mississippi River, to its western border. The distance from the Missouri border on the north to the Louisiana border on the south is almost the same—240 miles (386 km).

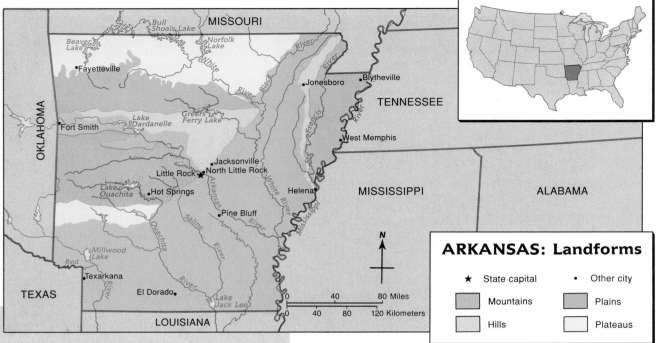

MISSOURI

Bull
Shoals Lake
Beaver
Lake
Norfolk
Lake
•Fayetteville
White
River
Black
River
•Jonesboro •Blytheville
TENNESSEE
OKLAHOMA
Lake
Dardanelle
Greers
Ferry Lake
St. Francis River
•Fort Smith
•West Memphis
•Jacksonville
Little Rock ★ •North Little Rock
Arkansas River
Lake
Ouachita •Hot Springs
Helena •
White River
MISSISSIPPI
ALABAMA
•Pine Bluff
Ouachita River
Saline River
Mississippi River
Millwood
Lake
Red River
•Texarkana
El Dorado•
Lake
Jack Lee
N
0   40   80 Miles
0 40 80 120 Kilometers
TEXAS
LOUISIANA

ARKANSAS: Landforms

★ State capital   • Other city

Mountains   Plains

Hills   Plateaus

MAP SKILL: In which parts of our state might you find **landforms** like those you see in the photo below?

If your airplane approaches Arkansas from the north, it will fly over the state of Missouri. From the west, it will cross either Oklahoma or Texas. And should your airplane approach Arkansas from the south, it would probably fly over the state of Louisiana. Use the map on this page to compare these different routes.

If your airplane approaches Arkansas from the east, it must fly over either Tennessee, Mississippi, or Missouri. Then it must cross the Mississippi River. Trace the route of this flight on the map above.

Whichever direction you come from, though, there's a great deal to see. Arkansas covers 53,850 square miles (139,472 sq km). In terms of size, this puts our state near the middle of the 50 states.

From the airplane you may also notice that the surface of the state is not level. Instead it slopes downward toward the southeast. The top of the slope is in the northern and western parts of the state. That is why people in Arkansas say they are going "down to" Pine Bluff or "up to" Fayetteville.

ANCIENT ARKANSAS

Have you ever been to the Gulf of Mexico? Today you would have to travel over 300 miles (483 km) south, through Louisiana, to get there. Millions of years ago, though, all the land of present-day Arkansas was covered with sea water. The place where your town is located once lay far beneath the Gulf of Mexico!

During that time many kinds of sea life lived in what would become the northern part of the state. When the tiny plants and animals in the warm water died, their skeletons sank to the floor of the sea. These skeletons piled up over thousands and thousands of years. Finally, they formed the limestone that is now found in the hills and mountains of Arkansas. If you look closely, you may find a skeleton in the rocks. This kind of trace or impression of a plant or animal that lived long ago is called a fossil (fos′ əl).

Over time, two mountain ranges (moun′ tən rānj′ əz) rose up above the sea. A mountain range is a series of mountains connected together. The Ozark Mountains rose above the sea in the northwestern part of our state. The Ouachita (wäsh′ ə tô) Mountains appeared in western Arkansas. You will learn more about these mountain ranges in the next chapter.

Although two mountain ranges had appeared, sea water still covered the southern and eastern parts of the land. But slowly the water began to recede, or move back. At some point around 2 million years ago, all of Arkansas's land was finally above sea level.

RIVERS AND LAKES

As you read before, the surface of Arkansas slopes downward from the northwest to the southeast. For this reason water tends to flow in a southeasterly or downhill direction. Streams carry water into small rivers which, in

Both the spectacular Blanchard Springs Cavern in Stone County and the delicate fossil of a shell once existed underwater.

turn, carry the same water into larger rivers. The area drained by a river and by all of the streams that flow into the river is called a river basin (riv′ ər bā′ sin). Arkansas's land is drained by five major river basins.

The largest is that of the Arkansas River. Almost 40 percent of the state's water flows through this basin. The White River basin is the next largest. The remaining three basins drain into the Red River, the Ouachita River, and the St. Francis River. All five of these basins empty, in turn, into the Mississippi River.

Oxbow lakes are formed when a river changes its course. These lakes are used for fishing, boating, and swimming.

Arkansas also has more than 30 major lakes, including Lake Ouachita, Bull Shoals Lake, and Greers Ferry Lake. Some of these, such as Lake Chicot, came into being when a river changed its course. Because of their shape, these lakes are called "oxbow lakes." Look at the picture on this page to see what an oxbow lake looks like. Other lakes, such as Lake Hamilton, have been created by people. Whether they were man-made or formed by nature, the lakes are used for making electricity, for fishing, and for swimming and boating.

A SPECIAL PLACE

You have just been given a view of Arkansas. You have seen the shape of the state and which other states are its neighbors. You have learned what the state was like long ago and what it is like today. In the next lesson you will read about some other things that make Arkansas a special place.

 Check Your Reading

1. What is geography?
2. Which states are neighbors of Arkansas?
3. What traces remain of the sea water that once covered the entire land of Arkansas?
4. GEOGRAPHY SKILL: Why do Arkansas's rivers flow to the southeast?
5. THINKING SKILL: Imagine and describe some ways in which the land of Arkansas might change in the future.

14

2 The Climate of Arkansas

READ TO LEARN

Key Vocabulary

climate	precipitation
weather	agriculture
temperature	

Read Aloud

Today, and indeed for more than a week past, the weather, except for being cloudy, has felt to me like May.

Do you remember Thomas Nuttall, whose first impression of Arkansas you read in the last lesson? He wrote the words above during the same journey through the land of our state. Nuttall was amazed to find such springlike weather in late January. Have you ever been surprised by Arkansas's weather?

Read for Purpose

1. **WHAT YOU KNOW:** How often does it rain in the part of Arkansas where you live? How often does it snow?
2. **WHAT YOU WILL LEARN:** What effect does climate have on life in our state?

WEATHER AND CLIMATE

Courtney Muir and Mandy Ross are two fourth-grade students in Conway. One day their teacher asked them to do a report on the climate and weather of Arkansas. At first they thought that the two words had the same meaning. But when they looked up the words in a dictionary, they found that *climate* and *weather* have two different meanings.

They found that weather is the condition of the air at a given time and place. From one day to another, the weather may be hot or cold, damp or dry, calm or windy. And weather can change very quickly, often in a matter of hours. Perhaps this is the reason that people often say, "If you don't like the weather in Arkansas, wait five minutes and it will change."

Climate is the weather that a place has over many years. When climate changes, it does so very slowly. While the weather affects how you live day to day, climate affects long-range plans, such as which crops to plant in a particular area.

One of the key parts that makes up climate is the temperature, which is a measure of the heat or cold in the air. Another key part is the amount of precipitation (pri sip i tā′ shən) an

15

GRAPH SKILL: (*above*) Huge windstorms called tornadoes are part of Arkansas's **climate**. According to the graph, what is the average high **temperature** in Little Rock during April?

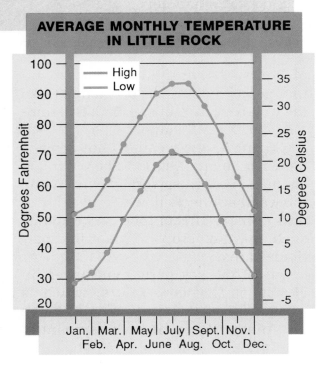

AVERAGE MONTHLY TEMPERATURE IN LITTLE ROCK

area receives. Precipitation is the moisture that falls to the earth as rain, snow, sleet, or hail.

Climate, then, is a pattern of temperature and precipitation over a period of years. It may rain a great deal on one particular day in your hometown. But that does not mean that your town has a wet climate. It may be that your town receives very little precipitation for most of the year.

TEMPERATURE IN ARKANSAS

As Thomas Nuttall noted during his travels, our state has a mild climate. In other words, our climate is usually a gentle one, without harsh extremes of temperature. Look at the graph on this page to study the average high and low temperatures in Little Rock. Which months are the hottest in that city?

There have been times, however, when the temperatures in Arkansas were not mild. In 1905 the temperature in Gravette, in Benton County, fell to −29°F. (−34°C). That is about 29 degrees colder than the inside of your refrigerator's freezer compartment! Arkansas can get hot, too. During August 1936 the people of the town of Ozark, in Franklin County, suffered through temperatures that reached 120°F. (49°C). This is about 30 degrees hotter than an average summer day in the Sahara Desert.

We are lucky that such temperatures are not normal for Arkansas. Our daytime temperatures average about 82°F. (28°C) in July. In January, they average about 40°F. (4°C).

PRECIPITATION IN ARKANSAS

The climate in Arkansas is fairly wet. Although areas in the northwest may get as much as 1 foot (0.3 m) of snow each year, most of the state's precipitation falls as rain. Average yearly precipitation ranges from 42 inches (107 cm) in the mountain areas to 60 inches (152 cm) in the southeastern part of the state.

Forty-two inches of rain may not sound like a lot when it's spread out over a whole year. But in the state of Nevada, for example, some areas average only 4 inches (10 cm) of rainfall each year.

Most of Arkansas's precipitation comes in winter and spring. Summer and fall are fairly dry in our state. Look at the map on this page to see the average precipitation in different parts of Arkansas. Which part of the state has the driest climate?

The climate of Arkansas has made our state a good place for agriculture (ag' ri kul chər), or farming. Many crops need a long growing season. A growing season is a period during which there is no frost or freezing weather that would kill the plants. Because our climate is so mild and damp, the growing season in Arkansas is long. It may last from 180 to 200 days in the northern part of the state. In the southern part of the state it lasts an average of 230 days. You will read more about farming in Arkansas in Chapter 10.

A GOOD PLACE TO LIVE

"These crisp fall mornings hold the promise of days to come, days when the air is clear as silver. . . ." Roy Reed, an Arkansas writer and farmer, used these words to describe what he likes about our climate. Other Arkansans may prefer spring, summer, or winter, but most will agree that our climate makes Arkansas a good place to live.

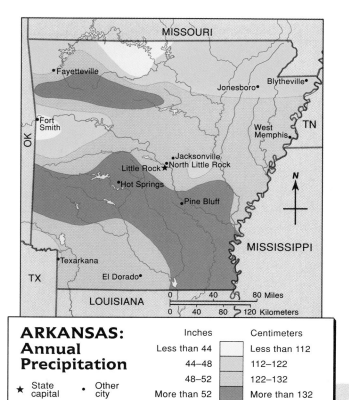

ARKANSAS: Annual Precipitation

★ State capital ・ Other city

Inches		Centimeters
Less than 44		Less than 112
44–48		112–122
48–52		122–132
More than 52		More than 132

MAP SKILL: Annual precipitation is the amount of moisture that falls to the earth in one year. What is the annual precipitation of Hot Springs?

Check Your Reading

1. What is the difference between weather and climate?
2. What do we mean when we say that Arkansas has a mild climate?
3. Why do you think the growing season is shorter in the northern part of Arkansas?
4. **GEOGRAPHY SKILL:** Look at the map on this page. Which town would you move to if you wanted to live in the driest part of the state?
5. **THINKING SKILL:** How do you think life in Arkansas would be different if our state had a very hot climate? A very cold one?

Understanding Latitude and Longitude

Key Vocabulary

grid
latitude
parallel
degree
hemisphere
longitude
meridian
prime meridian
global grid

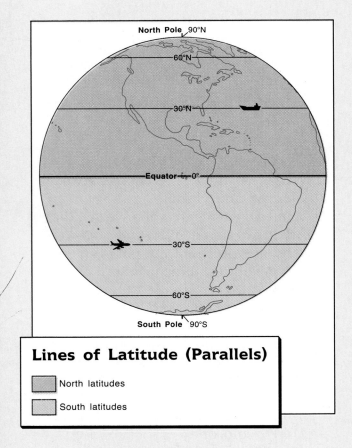

Lines of Latitude (Parallels)

North latitudes

South latitudes

You have just read about Arkansas's land and water. Suppose that you had to draw a map showing where a waterfall had been found in a large forest area of Arkansas. How would you describe the exact spot? To help us locate places on a map, mapmakers draw a pattern of criss-crossed lines called a grid. The lines are evenly spaced on the map. Using these imaginary lines, you can locate any place in the world.

Using Latitude

Look at the map on this page. It shows lines of latitude. Notice that these lines run east and west around the globe. Lines of latitude are also called parallels. This is because the lines are always parallel, or the same distance apart.

The starting point for reading latitude is the equator. Find the equator on the map. Notice that the equator is labeled 0°. We call this zero degrees. The symbol ° stands for degrees. Degrees are used to measure the distance between the imaginary lines of latitude.

The equator is an important reference point when you are using latitude. The equator lies midway between the North and South poles. As you can see, the lines of latitude north of the equator are labeled *N* for north. Parallels south of the equator are labeled *S* for south.

As you have read, lines of latitude run east and west, but they measure distance north and south of the equator. Latitude goes from 0° at the equator to 90° at the poles. At which latitude is the North Pole located? At which latitude is the South Pole located?

18

The equator divides the globe into two imaginary halves. These two halves are called hemispheres (hem′ is fẽrz). The part that is located north of the equator is called the Northern Hemisphere. The part that is located south of the equator is called the Southern Hemisphere.

Find the small ship on the map on page 18. In which hemisphere is it located? The ship is moving west. Along which parallel is it traveling? Now find the small airplane on the map. On which parallel is it traveling? Is the airplane moving east or west?

Using Longitude

Look at the map to the right that shows lines of longitude. Lines of longitude run north and south around the globe. These lines are also called meridians.

Find the meridian labeled prime meridian. Like the equator, the prime meridian is an important reference point. *Prime* means "first." The prime meridian is used as the starting point when we measure longitude.

Longitude measures distance east and west of the prime meridian. Notice that the prime meridian is labeled 0°. The meridians west of the prime meridian are labeled *W* for west. Meridians east of the prime meridian are labeled *E* for east.

Lines of longitude extend from 0° to 180°. The 180° line of longitude is on the other side of the globe, exactly opposite the 0° line of longitude. Since 180°E and 180°W are the same meridian, this line is marked neither *E* nor *W*.

These lines, 0° and 180°, divide the globe into two different imaginary halves.

These halves are called the Eastern Hemisphere and the Western Hemisphere. Look again at the map on this page. What color is the western hemisphere?

Look at the ship on the map on this page. The ship is moving south in the Western Hemisphere. Along which meridian is it traveling? Look at the airplane on the same map. It is flying over the continent of Africa in the Eastern Hemisphere. In which direction is the airplane on the map traveling?

Notice that meridians are not parallel. Instead, they meet at the North Pole and at the South Pole. Meridians are farthest apart at the equator.

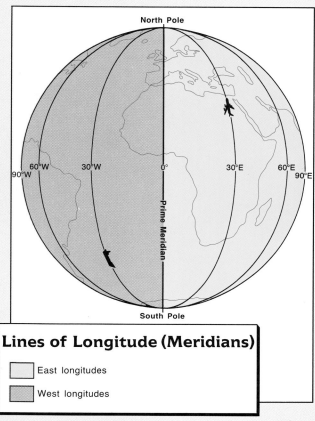

Lines of Longitude (Meridians)

▢ East longitudes

▨ West longitudes

Using the Global Grid

Mapmakers put lines of latitude and longitude together to form what is called a global grid. A global grid can be used to find the exact location of any place on the earth.

Look at the world map below. Find the equator and the other lines of latitude. At what intervals are the lines of latitude labeled? Next find the prime meridian and the other meridians east and west of the prime meridian. Through which continents does 90°W run?

Find the airplane on the global grid map. It is flying over the Pacific Ocean. Between which parallels of latitude is the airplane located? Between which lines of longitude is it located?

Locating Places on a Map

You can give the location of any place on earth by knowing its latitude and longitude. Always give the latitude first. Then give the longitude.

Look at the map of the United States on the next page. Notice that the city of New Orleans, Louisiana, lies where lines of latitude and longitude cross. It is located at 30°N latitude and 90°W longitude. Its location is shortened to 30°N, 90°W.

Most places do not lie exactly on the labeled lines of the grid. On the map on the next page, the lines of latitude and longitude are marked at 5° intervals. You can locate other places by imagining the lines in between. Little Rock, Arkansas, for example, lies at 34°N, 92°W.

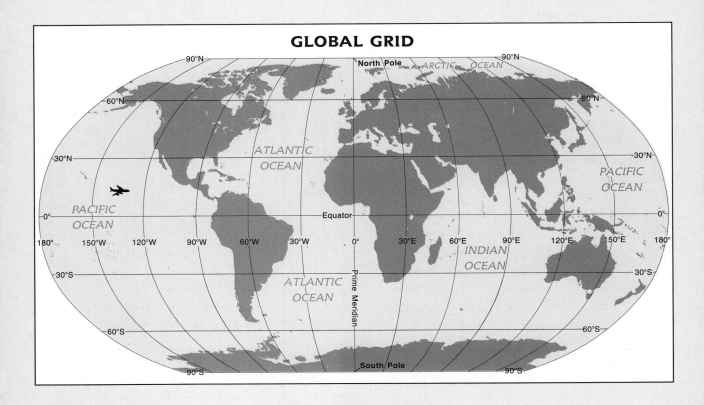

GLOBAL GRID

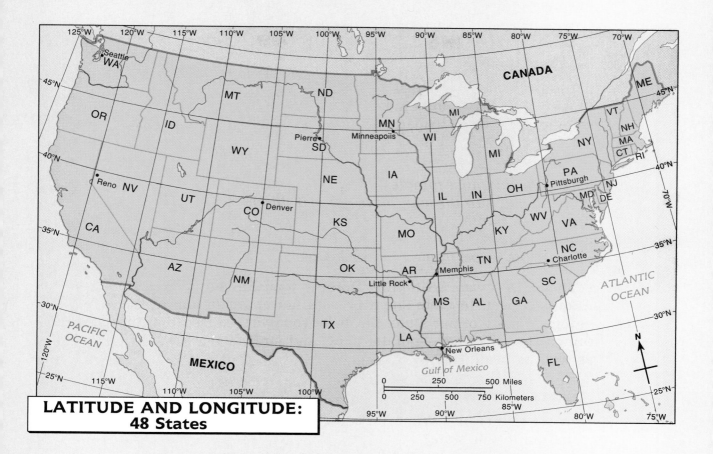

LATITUDE AND LONGITUDE:
48 States

Find Minneapolis, Minnesota, on the map. How would you describe its location using lines of latitude and longitude?

Suppose that you wanted to find out which state you would be in if you visited a city located at 35°N, 110°W. First, put your finger at the line of latitude labeled 35°N. Follow the line until it crosses 110°W. Which state are you in?

Lines of latitude and longitude are also useful as a way to measure the distance between places. How many degrees north of New Orleans is Denver located? How many degrees west of New Orleans is Denver located?

Reviewing the Skill

1. What are lines of latitude? What are lines of longitude?
2. Between which lines of latitude is Arkansas located? Between which lines of longitude is Arkansas located?
3. Describe the location of Reno, Nevada, using latitude and longitude.
4. Describe the location of Memphis, Tennessee using latitude and longitude.
5. If you were drilling for oil at 30°N, 100°W, in which state would you be working?
6. Why is it important to understand latitude and longitude?

21

3 Arkansas's Natural Resources

READ TO LEARN

Key Vocabulary

natural resource	fertile
timber	mineral
sediment	irrigation

Read Aloud

Early morning mist mingles
With filtered sun through leaves of ash, birch,
And green maple,
Falling in rays
Against the wood framed Flatrock Creek.

These lines were written by Dorothy Jones, a young Arkansas poet. In them she expresses her appreciation for the natural beauty of our state. But have you ever realized that the things she describes—plants, trees, and streams—are useful as well as beautiful?

Read for Purpose

1. **WHAT YOU KNOW:** What are some of the ways you can enjoy nature in our state?
2. **WHAT YOU WILL LEARN:** What are some of Arkansas's most important natural resources?

"THE NATURAL STATE"

In 1933 the people of our state created the first Arkansas State Parks. Since then Arkansans have set aside land in 44 different locations, from Withrow Springs to Moro Bay, from Lake Frierson to Devil's Den.

By setting aside land in this way, we recognize the value of our natural resources. A natural resource is something that is found in nature that is useful to people. In Arkansas we are lucky to have many such resources. For this reason Arkansas is sometimes called "The Natural State."

FORESTS AND PLANTS

"Their country is very beautiful, having abundance of peach, plum, and apple trees," wrote one early visitor to the land of Arkansas. In fact, the trees and forests of our state remain one of our great resources.

Timber, or trees that may be used for buildings or to make wood products, blankets more than 18 million acres (7 million ha) of Arkansas. This area equals more than half the entire state! The mountain slopes of the northwest are thick with hardwoods and pines. Cypresses, pines, and hardwoods grow in the southeast. Look at the Natural Resources map on this page to study the location of Arkansas's forests. Arkansas also has some 26,000 different kinds of plants.

SOIL AND MINERALS

In Lesson 1 you read that Arkansas was once covered with sea water. As the water receded, millions of years ago, it left behind sediment. Sediment is rock, sand, or mud left behind by moving water, wind, or ice.

This sediment still plays a part in the kind of soil we have. For example, in southwest Arkansas the sea left behind great amounts of sand and mud. For this reason the soil in that area remains sandy to this day. In the Ouachita Mountains, the soil is rich in two kinds of rock, called sandstone and shale. These rocks, too, were left behind long ago by the sea.

You may not think of the soil beneath your feet as a natural resource. But the eastern part of our state, along the Mississippi River, has some of the most fertile soil on earth. Soil that is fertile is good for growing crops.

The ground beneath your feet contains other treasures, too. Our state is very rich in minerals. A mineral is a substance found in the earth that is neither plant nor animal. Two such substances are oil and natural gas. These were discovered near El Dorado during the 1920s. Since that time, oil and gas production has become a big business in Arkansas.

MAP SKILL: (*above*) Lookout towers are used for spotting forest fires. (*below*) Which natural resources are found in the forested parts of our state?

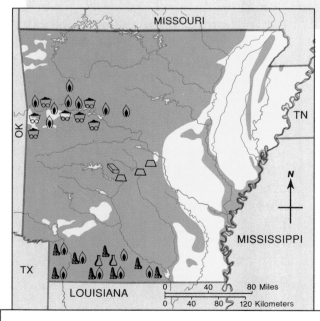

ARKANSAS: Natural Resources

△ Bauxite	◇ Novaculite	▧ Forests
⬱ Coal	▲ Oil	
◈ Natural gas	⏛ Bromine	

23

Farmers use **irrigation** to make sure their crops get enough water.

Rich deposits of coal are located beneath the soil of Sebastian and Crawford counties. Scientists have also located supplies of lignite coal throughout the state. Lignite is a less valuable kind of coal, but it offers hope as a future energy source.

Another mineral resource that has been important to our state is bauxite. There is even a town called Bauxite, in Saline County, which is located on the spot where the mineral was first mined. Other mineral resources include bromine, marble, and novaculite (nō vak′ yə līt), a very hard rock used for sharpening tools. In 1906 a Pike County farmer plowing his fields discovered diamonds! His mine, now Crater of Diamonds State Park, is the only diamond mine in the United States. Look at the Natural Resources map again to study the location of Arkansas's mineral resources.

WATER RESOURCES

As you read in Lesson 1, Arkansas has five major river basins, as well as many lakes and streams. Arkansans use these water resources in many ways. Farmers often irrigate their crops. Irrigation (ir i gā′ shən) is a method in which water is brought to dry fields by means of ditches. People in their homes use water for washing and cooking. Minnow farms, nuclear power plants, and wildlife preserves also use water.

Our water is useful in other ways, too. We can fish, swim, go boating, or simply enjoy the beauty of one of our most visible natural resources.

GUARDING OUR RICHES

As you have read, our state has a great wealth of natural resources. But these resources must be treated carefully. If we respect and protect our natural resources, Arkansas will always remain the "Natural State."

Check Your Reading

1. What is a natural resource?
2. Why is Arkansas's soil full of "hidden treasures"?
3. **GEOGRAPHY SKILL:** Which part of our state has some of the most fertile soil on earth?
4. **THINKING SKILL:** Which of our state's natural resources are found above ground? Which resources are found underground?

REVIEWING VOCABULARY

agriculture   natural resource
climate   precipitation
fertile   river basin
geography   timber
mineral   weather

Number a sheet of paper from 1 to 10. Beside each number write the word or term from the list above that best matches the definition.

1. The study of the earth and the way people live on it and use it
2. The area drained by a river and by all of the streams that flow into the river
3. The condition of the air at a given time and place
4. Something found in nature that is useful to people
5. The weather that a place has over many years
6. A substance found in the earth that is neither plant nor animal
7. Farming
8. Trees that may be used for buildings or to make wood products
9. The moisture that falls to earth as rain, snow, sleet, or hail
10. Good for growing crops

REVIEWING FACTS

1. Which states border Arkansas? In which direction would you have to travel from Arkansas to reach each of these states?
2. What was the land of Arkansas like millions of years ago?
3. What is a fossil? Where in Arkansas can fossils be found?
4. Name three river basins in Arkansas.
5. How are oxbow lakes formed?
6. Describe Arkansas's climate.
7. Give two reasons that Arkansas is a good place for agriculture.
8. What are three of the major natural resources found in Arkansas?
9. Why is there sediment in Arkansas's soil?
10. What is irrigation?

WRITING ABOUT MAIN IDEAS

1. **Writing a Paragraph:** In which part of Arkansas is your community located? Find the area on the maps on pages 12, 17, and 23. Use the information on the maps to write a paragraph about the area in which your community is located.
2. **Writing a Letter:** Imagine that you have a pen pal in another state. Write a letter to your pen pal telling how water (in rivers, lakes, and rainfall) affects life in Arkansas.

BUILDING SKILLS: UNDERSTANDING LATITUDE AND LONGITUDE

1. What is a global grid?
2. Use the map on page 21 to give the latitude and longitude of Denver, Colorado.
3. Which line of longitude runs through the state of Utah?
4. If you were mining for coal at 39°N, 80°W, in which state would you be working?

CHAPTER 2

THE SIX REGIONS OF ARKANSAS

FOCUS

Take only what is needed from the earth.
Remember to give thanks in all you do.
Pick up a stone and feel your own soul's worth.
Keep nothing that does not belong to you.

These are the words to a song about the Ozark Mountains. People from every part of Arkansas share this appreciation for the gifts our land has given us. This chapter will help you to understand what is special about each part of our state.

1 What Is A Region?

READ TO LEARN

Key Vocabulary

region
highland
lowland

Read Aloud

There are little corners of this earth put aside by nature to be discovered . . . and to bring joy. . . . The lands over which you look here, across this beautiful river, are such a corner. . . .

These words are on a sign overlooking the Buffalo River, in the Ozark Mountains. The "little corners" the author talks about can be found in every part of our state. In this lesson you will learn about the many parts of Arkansas.

Read for Purpose

1. **WHAT YOU KNOW:** How would you describe the part of Arkansas in which you live?
2. **WHAT YOU WILL LEARN:** What is a region? What are the names of the six regions of Arkansas?

ARKANSAS'S LAND

It was the first morning of school in Little Rock. In one fourth-grade classroom three of the students were more nervous than the others. John Qualls, Doris Mankins, and Craig Lee had each moved to Little Rock that summer. Each of them had lived in a different part of Arkansas.

Later in the morning, the teacher, Ms. Bearden, asked the students to describe Arkansas's geography. The first student she called on was Doris.

Doris had moved from Monticello, which is in southeastern Arkansas.

She said, "Arkansas's land is flat, with some low hills and sandy ridges."

Next it was Craig's turn. He had moved to Little Rock from Mena, in southwestern Arkansas. "Arkansas," Craig told the class, "has mountains and thick hardwood forests."

John, who was from Van Buren, in the northwestern part of Arkansas, gave yet a different description. He said, "The best way I can describe Arkansas is to say that it has many large rivers and streams."

The other students looked at Ms. Bearden and wondered who was right.

27

Which of the new students had described Arkansas correctly? When they asked the teacher this question, her answer surprised them.

"They all did," Ms. Bearden said. "Our state has so many different kinds of land that there's no 'correct' way to describe it."

WHAT IS A REGION?

Ms. Bearden was right. There is no one "correct" way to describe the geography of a state with so much variety. Each part of our state has its own special kind of land. For this reason Arkansas is divided into six different regions. A region is a large area with common features that set it apart from other areas.

HIGHLAND AND LOWLAND REGIONS

In the next two lessons you will read about each of Arkansas's six regions. First, however, you should know that these six regions are evenly divided between highland and lowland regions. What kinds of geography do these words describe?

As you read in Chapter 1, the state of Arkansas slopes upward toward the northwest. The three regions at the "top" of the slope, in northwest Arkansas, are called the highland regions. These regions are the Ozark Mountains, the Arkansas River Valley, and the Ouachita Mountains. Look at the map on page 29 to locate these regions. Which highland region is the farthest north?

Our state's other three regions, at the "bottom" of the slope, are called the lowland regions. These include the Mississippi Alluvial (ə lü′ vē əl) Plain, Crowley's Ridge, and the West Gulf

Rivers, plains, and mountains are just three of the features which give great variety to our state's geography.

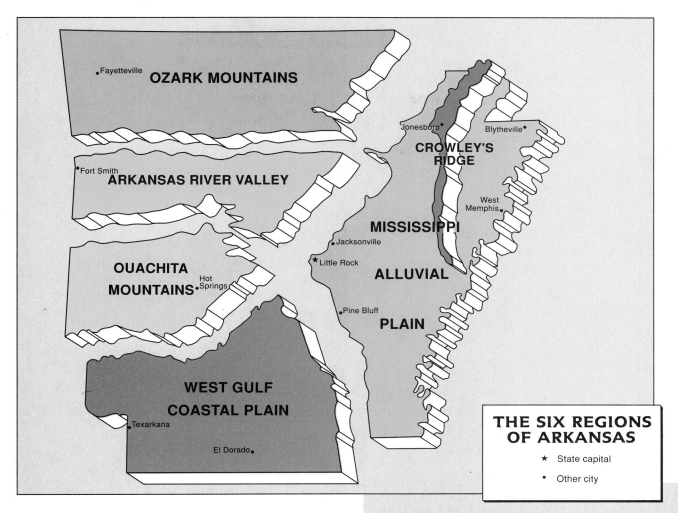

Fayetteville

OZARK MOUNTAINS

Jonesboro

Blytheville

CROWLEY'S RIDGE

Fort Smith

ARKANSAS RIVER VALLEY

West Memphis

MISSISSIPPI

OUACHITA MOUNTAINS

Hot Springs

Jacksonville

★ Little Rock

ALLUVIAL

Pine Bluff

PLAIN

WEST GULF COASTAL PLAIN

Texarkana

El Dorado

THE SIX REGIONS OF ARKANSAS

★ State capital

• Other city

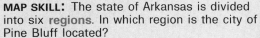

MAP SKILL: The state of Arkansas is divided into six **regions**. In which region is the city of Pine Bluff located?

Coastal Plain. Look at the map above to locate these three regions. Which one is actually contained within another region?

A STATE OF MANY FACES

In Chapter 1 you read about how Arkansas is a land rich in natural resources. It has fertile soil and mild weather for farming. It has forests, minerals, and water resources. Now you will read about each of Arkansas's six regions. You will see how we use all these riches to make our state a good place in which to work, live, and enjoy ourselves.

Check Your Reading

1. How did Doris describe the land of Arkansas? How did Craig? How did John?
2. What is a region?
3. **GEOGRAPHY SKILL:** Why is Arkansas divided into highland regions and lowland regions?
4. **THINKING SKILL:** How might your life be different if you lived in a different region of Arkansas?

Reading Elevation Maps and Profiles

Key Vocabulary

elevation   profile

If you planned to hike across Arkansas, which kind of map would you find most useful? Earlier in this book you looked at different kinds of maps, such as natural resource maps and climate maps. Another kind of map is an elevation map. Elevation is the height of land above sea level. An elevation map shows the changes in the earth's surface.

As you read in Lesson 1, Arkansas has six regions. The regions in the northwest are higher than those in the southeast. An elevation map shows these differences.

Landforms and Elevation

The earth's surface varies greatly. In Chapter 1 you read about different landforms in Arkansas. Changes in the earth's surface result in four kinds of landforms— plains, plateaus, hills, and mountains. A plain is a large area of flat or nearly flat land. A plateau is a large area of high, flat land. A hill is a raised part of the earth's surface that is often rounded and is smaller than a mountain. A mountain is a highland area that rises sharply from the surrounding land.

Each of these landforms has a different elevation, or height above sea level. We measure elevation in feet or meters. Elevation at sea level is 0 feet (0 m). A place that is close to sea level has a low elevation. A place that rises far above sea level has a high elevation.

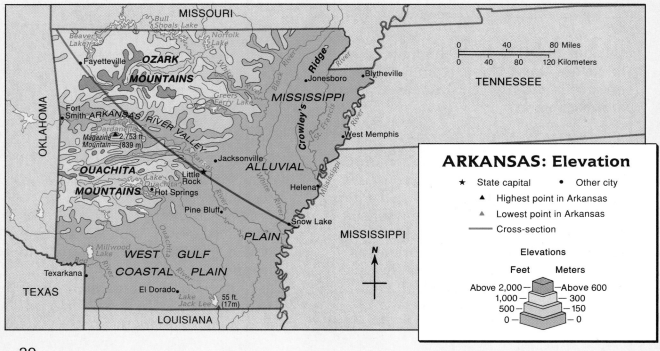

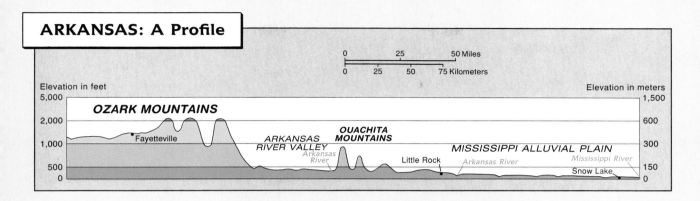

ARKANSAS: A Profile

0   25   50 Miles
0   25   50   75 Kilometers

Elevation in feet
Elevation in meters

OZARK MOUNTAINS

Fayetteville

OUACHITA MOUNTAINS

ARKANSAS RIVER VALLEY

Arkansas River

Little Rock

MISSISSIPPI ALLUVIAL PLAIN

Arkansas River

Mississippi River

Snow Lake

Using an Elevation Map

On page 30 is an elevation map of Arkansas. It shows the height above sea level of the entire state. Compare this map with the landform map of Arkansas on page 12. How do the two maps differ?

An elevation map uses different colors to show the height above sea level of each area or region. Each color shows a range of elevation, which is explained in the map key. An area that is all one color is nearly level, but it can be a highland or lowland area.

Notice that the different colors show the land changing from lowlands to highlands. Which color shows elevations between 500 feet (150 m) and 1,000 feet (300 m)? If an area is colored orange, what range of elevation does it have? Find the Ozark Mountains on the map. What is the elevation of that area?

Using a Profile

The information on an elevation map can be used to draw a profile. A profile is a side view of a part of the earth. Look at the diagram above. It shows a profile of Arkansas along a line from Fayetteville in the northwest through Little Rock to Snow Lake in the southeast. Find the red line on the elevation map to the left that shows the area covered by the profile.

The lines on the profile let you read the elevation. Study the profile. What is the elevation of the highest point shown on the profile? Compare the profile with the elevation map on the left. Use the profile to figure out the elevation of Little Rock. Then use the elevation map to answer the same question. Which one lets you read elevation more accurately?

Using a profile like this one, you could plan your hike across Arkansas. It would show exactly where you would have to climb up or down.

Reviewing the Skill

1. What is the most important purpose of an elevation map?
2. Which part of Arkansas has the highest elevations?
3. What is the highest elevation in Arkansas?
4. Suppose that you were building a road across Arkansas from east to west. If you wanted the road to pass through areas of low elevation, in which areas would you build it?

2 The Lowland Regions of Arkansas

READ TO LEARN

Key Vocabulary

alluvium
levee
loess
bayou

Key Places

Blytheville
Helena
El Dorado

Read Aloud

Although you can't see the river, you can get to it by taking the side roads, and you'll never fail to be impressed by its majestic sweep. Perhaps in the distance a tugboat thrashes behind a string of barges, so slowly that it seems to stand still.

This is how the Mississippi River looked to a writer traveling through eastern Arkansas almost 50 years ago. The river has always played an important role in this lowland region. In this lesson you will learn about the three lowland regions of our state.

Read for Purpose

1. **WHAT YOU KNOW:** Do you live in one of our state's lowland regions?
2. **WHAT YOU WILL LEARN:** In which ways are the three lowland regions different? In which ways are they similar?

THE MISSISSIPPI ALLUVIAL PLAIN

The largest of the state's six natural regions is the Mississippi Alluvial Plain. Find this region on the map on page 33. You will see that it makes up roughly the eastern third of Arkansas.

The Mississippi River, which gives the region its name, is the longest river in the United States. It flows all the way from northern Minnesota to the Gulf of Mexico. The Arkansas River and the White River also flow through the Mississippi Alluvial Plain.

But what exactly is an alluvial plain? *Alluvial* comes from the word alluvium. Alluvium is the mud, sand, or other material left behind by a flowing river. As the Mississippi River flows south along Arkansas's eastern boundary, it leaves alluvium in the surrounding soil. These deposits of mud and sand have made the soil amazingly fertile.

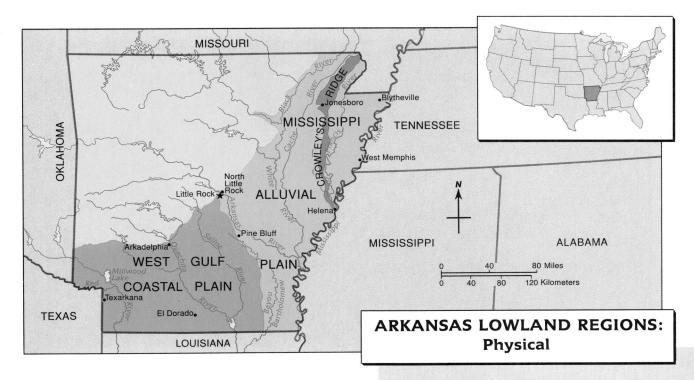

MISSOURI

Black River

RIDGE

Jonesboro

•Blytheville

MISSISSIPPI

TENNESSEE

Cache

CROWLEY'S

White River

•West Memphis

North Little Rock

Little Rock★

ALLUVIAL

Helena•

OKLAHOMA

Arkansas River

•Pine Bluff

Arkadelphia•

WEST GULF PLAIN

Millwood Lake

COASTAL PLAIN

Saline River

Ouachita River

Mississippi River

MISSISSIPPI

ALABAMA

N

0   40   80 Miles

0   40   80   120 Kilometers

•Texarkana

Red River

El Dorado•

Bayou Bartholomew

TEXAS

LOUISIANA

ARKANSAS LOWLAND REGIONS: Physical

MAP SKILL: (*below*) This prizewinning watermelon was grown in the fertile soil near the Red River. Through which lowland region does the Red River flow?

173 POUNDS
Grown by
IVAN + Lloyd Bright
HOPE, ARKANSAS

But the Mississippi River has often brought great destruction, too. Swelled by heavy spring rains and melting snow, it can rise and flood the surrounding country.

In April of 1927 the Mississippi flooded its banks and covered almost one quarter of the state with water at depths of up to 19 feet (5.8 m). "At noon," wrote the captain of one rescue boat, "the streets of Arkansas City were dry and dusty. By two o'clock mules were drowning in the main streets of that town faster than they could be unhitched from wagons."

For a long time, frequent flooding kept much of the region's land wet and swampy. In more recent years farmers living in this area have drained the land. They have built large earthen walls called levees (lev' ēz) along the banks of the river to prevent flooding.

Today the Mississippi Alluvial Plain is a center of world agriculture. Arkansans grow soybeans, rice, and cotton in the fertile soil. In 1989 the region produced 6.4 billion pounds (2.9 billion kg) of rice—more than one out of every three pounds grown in the United States.

The towns in this region often grew up around farms. Blytheville is still a center for cotton and soybeans. But factories in town also employ more

33

(*above*) Many people in the lowland regions earn their living from agriculture.
(*below*) Others work in factories that make products such as rocket parts.

than 4,000 men and women, who can foods and make computer supplies and many other products.

CROWLEY'S RIDGE

Crowley's Ridge is another natural region of the Arkansas lowlands. Although it is 200 miles (322 km) long, it is only a few miles wide. For this reason it is the smallest of our state's natural regions. Find Crowley's Ridge on the map on page 33. Which other lowland region completely surrounds the region of Crowley's Ridge?

Crowley's Ridge soars 550 feet (168 m) above the flat Mississippi Alluvial Plain. If you were traveling west across the alluvial plain, this sudden height would probably surprise you.

Long ago the area of Crowley's Ridge was simply a low hill. Over thousands of years, though, the winds blew soil up against the sides of this hill. Slowly the hill became taller. This sandy, windblown soil, called loess (les),

Crowley's Ridge rises suddenly from the Mississippi Alluvial Plain. It is the smallest of our state's six regions.

finally formed the rugged, scenic ridge we see today.

Many of the early settlers of northeastern Arkansas decided to live on Crowley's Ridge. Why do you think this happened? For one thing, the settlers wanted to avoid the muddy swamps and mosquitoes of the surrounding alluvial plain. The height of Crowley's Ridge also allowed them to escape the Mississippi River floods. In fact, this was the reason that one of Arkansas's earliest roads ran along the top of Crowley's Ridge. Today Arkansas State Highway 1 continues to follow this same route.

Most of the Arkansans who live on Crowley's Ridge are involved in the agriculture of the alluvial plain below. Helena is located at the southern tip of the region. It overlooks the Mississippi from a high spot that the writer Mark Twain called "one of the prettiest situations on the river." The people of Helena help to pack and ship soybeans, rice, and other crops.

THE WEST GULF COASTAL PLAIN

The third lowland region of Arkansas is the West Gulf Coastal Plain. Look at the map on page 33 to see where this region is located. With which states does this region share a boundary?

Much of the region is flat, with small rolling hills. But if you took a trip across the region from east to west, you would notice the change in the landscape. To the east the land looks much like the Mississippi Alluvial Plain. As you traveled west, the land would begin to look like the Texas prairies across the border.

To the south, the West Gulf Coastal Plain includes the area of Bartholomew Bayou. A bayou (bī' ü) is a sluggish inlet of water. In addition, two major rivers flow through the region, the Ouachita River and the Red River.

35

(*above*) Timber has long been an important resource in the West Gulf Coastal Plain. (*below*) Bromine, which is used to make plastics and medicines, is an important new resource.

Timber is an important natural resource in this part of Arkansas. A thick carpet of pines covers the rolling hills of the West Gulf Coastal Plain. Oak, hickory, beech, willow, and sweet gum also grow on the hillsides and bottomlands.

Other important natural resources are fuels, such as oil and natural gas. These fuels result from the fossils you read about in Chapter 1.

Oil was discovered near **El Dorado** in 1921. Almost overnight, people poured into town. A newspaper of the time described how the "roads loaded . . . with traffic got muddy, then boggy, and in some cases disappeared." El Dorado is still the oil center of Arkansas.

THE LOWLAND REGIONS

You have just learned about the three lowland regions of our state—the Mississippi Alluvial Plain, Crowley's Ridge, and the West Gulf Coastal Plain. Each region has its own kind of geography and natural resources. Each has its own contribution to make. In the next lesson you will learn about the three highland regions of Arkansas.

 Check Your Reading

1. Why is the soil of the Mississippi Alluvial Plain so fertile?
2. How was the landform of Crowley's Ridge originally formed?
3. Name two natural resources of the West Gulf Coastal Plain.
4. **GEOGRAPHY SKILL:** Which river is the longest in the United States?
5. **THINKING SKILL:** Choose two of the lowland regions, and list one way in which they are similar and one way in which they are different.

3 The Highland Regions of Arkansas

READ TO LEARN

Key Vocabulary

plateau
erosion
tributary
population

Key Places

Eureka Springs
Little Rock
Fort Smith
Hot Springs

Read Aloud

We came upon it suddenly. The sun
Shone brightly on the mountain ledge. Below,
Trapped in the valley where the river curled,
Spread the dawn fog. . . .

This description of a scene in the Ozark Mountains is by Rosa Marinoni, a well-known Arkansas poet. As are many Arkansans, she was proud of the natural beauty of this highland region. In this lesson you will read about all three of our state's highland regions.

Read for Purpose

1. **WHAT YOU KNOW:** Which two mountain ranges can be found in western Arkansas?
2. **WHAT YOU WILL LEARN:** In which ways are the three highland regions of Arkansas different? In which ways are they similar?

THE OZARK MOUNTAINS

The Ozark Mountains form one of the three highland regions of our state. These flat-topped mountains, which also extend into Oklahoma and Missouri, are located in the northwestern part of Arkansas. Many people just call these mountains the "Ozarks."

If you had seen the Ozarks long ago, you would not have seen a range of separate mountains. Instead, you would have seen one large area of land that was raised above its surroundings like a table. This kind of flat, raised land is called a plateau (pla tō').

Over many centuries, rivers and streams flowed over this plateau and carved deep valleys and canyons into it. This wearing away of the land by water or wind is called erosion. Thousands of years of erosion produced the jagged land of the present-day Ozarks.

37

Most of the Ozarks are covered with rocks and stones, and the soil is very shallow. For this reason many early settlers of the region lived in the valleys. The alluvium left there by the larger streams made farming a little easier. Still, these settlers often had to spend hours prying the stones out of their fields.

These difficulties caused the Ozarks to be settled more slowly than some of the other regions of our state. But the settlers who came were glad they did. The forests and mountains of the Ozarks include some of Arkansas's most beautiful scenery.

Much of the land in this region is owned and protected by our national government. One such area is the Ozark National Forest, which covers more than 800,000 acres (323,760 ha) of pine and hardwood trees. Many peo-ple from outside Arkansas come to enjoy these lands. Others come to live in this region after they have retired from jobs in other states. Look at the map below to locate the Ozark Mountain region. Which lowland region lies immediately to the east of the Ozarks?

Eureka Springs has attracted visitors since the 1880s. The town clings to the Ozark hillsides, with its lowest street more than 1,000 feet (305 m) below its highest street. In recent years Eureka Springs has also become a center for the arts and crafts of the Ozark region. Visitors can buy quilts, dolls, and other traditional handicrafts.

THE ARKANSAS RIVER VALLEY

The Arkansas River Valley is another highland region of our state. Find the Arkansas River, which you read about in Chapter 1, on the map below. Two tributaries of the Arkansas River, the

MAP SKILL: What are three lakes which are located in the Ouachita Mountains region?

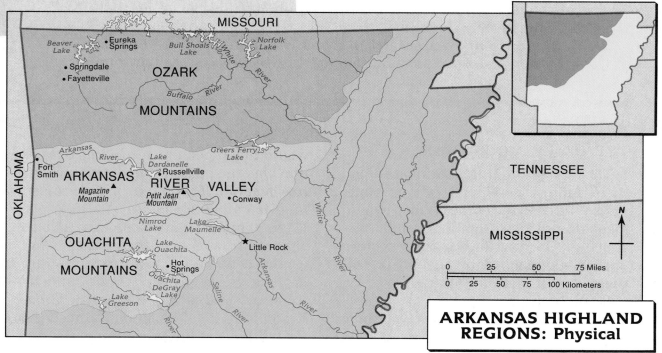

ARKANSAS HIGHLAND REGIONS: Physical

Visitors from all over the world come to Eureka Springs to see the local crafts.

Petit Jean River and the Maumelle River, flow through this region. A tributary is a river or stream that flows into a larger body of water.

The Arkansas River Valley is sometimes called an "in-between region." This is because it is located between two mountain ranges, the Ozarks to the north and the Ouachitas to the south.

At one time there probably was no "in-between." Scientists think that the two mountain ranges were once joined together. Over many centuries the Arkansas River carved out a deep ditch between the Ozarks and the Ouachitas. But two of the region's peaks, Magazine Mountain and Petit Jean Mountain, may be left over from the days when the two ranges were connected. Find these mountain peaks on the map on page 38.

The region is very rich in natural resources. The soil near the river is good for growing cotton, wheat, soybeans, and other crops.

An even more important resource is the river itself. For hundreds of years the Arkansas River has been an important transportation route. It connects the highland and lowland regions of our state. It allows people to ship goods from one area to another, or simply to travel.

The Arkansas River also helps to meet our state's energy needs. At Dardanelle a large electrical plant called Nuclear One uses water from the river to generate electricity.

These water and soil resources have made the region one of Arkansas's major population (pop yə lā' shən) centers. Population is the number of people living in a place. Little Rock, our largest city, is located on the southeastern edge of the Arkansas River Valley. A center for trade and shipping, Little Rock is our state capital. If you followed the Arkansas River upstream to the Oklahoma border, you would reach Fort Smith, our state's second-largest city.

HOW A RIVER LOCK WORKS

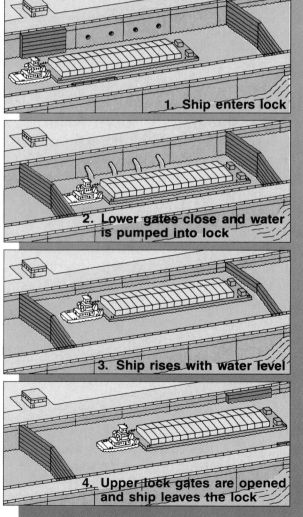

1. Ship enters lock

2. Lower gates close and water is pumped into lock

3. Ship rises with water level

4. Upper lock gates are opened and ship leaves the lock

Since 1971 a system of dams and locks on the Arkansas River has made travel even easier. Look at the diagram on this page to see how a system like this works. More than 10 million tons (9 million metric t) of sand, oil, chemicals, and gravel were shipped through the Arkansas River Navigation System in 1986 alone.

THE OUACHITA MOUNTAINS

The Ouachita Mountains are the third highland region of our state. This mountain range stretches across the west-central part of Arkansas, south of the Arkansas River Valley. Look again at the map on page 38. Which neighboring state shares a boundary with the Ouachita Mountains?

Although the Ouachitas and the Ozarks are both mountain ranges, there are some important differences between them. The Ouachitas are much less steep and rugged. Instead of jagged, erosion-carved peaks, they have long, narrow ridges. These ridges run from east to west. Today many of the roads and highways in the region

People travel from many states to go fishing in the beautiful lakes of the Ouachita Mountains region.

run in this same direction because it was easier to build them along the mountain ridges.

Valleys up to 20 miles (32 km) wide are located between these ridges. Since the soil in these valleys is often fertile, agriculture has always played an important part in the region. On larger farms Arkansans grow cotton and soybeans. On the smaller farms on the ridges, the crops include corn, potatoes, squash, and tomatoes. In addition to growing crops, the people of the Ouachita Mountains also produce timber and minerals. The region is particularly rich in novaculite, one of the minerals you read about in Chapter 1.

Hot Springs, the largest city in the region, is located in the central Ouachita Mountains. It was built on the site of a natural hot spring—a stream that emerges from beneath the ground at temperatures up to 143°F. (62°C). For centuries, people have believed that these springs are healthy to bathe in. Many people also come to the Ouachita Mountains to visit the region's lakes.

OUR STATE'S REGIONS

In this chapter you have read about all six natural regions of Arkansas. You have learned about the resources each region has to offer. In the next chapter you will read about the first people to live in the land of Arkansas.

 Check Your Reading

1. Why is farming difficult in the Ozarks?
2. How is transportation important to the Arkansas River Valley?
3. What are two differences between the Ouachita Mountains and the Ozark Mountains?
4. GEOGRAPHY SKILL: Why is the Arkansas River Valley sometimes called an "in-between" region?
5. THINKING SKILL: List one town and one landform in each of our state's six regions.

HELPING FAMILY FARMERS

In 1976 Calvin King, the son of a farmer from Lee County, earned a degree in business from Little Rock's Philander Smith College. Soon after, he received job offers from as far away as Florida. After thinking it over, however, King turned them all down.

Instead, he decided to return to the Delta—the cotton-growing area of the Mississippi Alluvial Plain. There were few jobs in the Delta, and much hardship. But King soon fixed his sights on a longstanding problem: the shrinking number of African-American farmers in our state.

In 1930, 1 out of every 3 Arkansas farmers was an African American—almost 80,000 altogether. Over the next 50 years, however, falling crop prices and many other problems had driven most of these African Americans off the land. By 1982 less than 1,500 remained. King worried that farming was becoming a vanishing

way of life in Lee County. He said, "If everyone leaves the area . . . it becomes basically a place of emptiness."

In 1980 King helped to start the Arkansas Land and Farm Development Corporation. He continues to work his family's farm near Marianna. But as director of the ALFDC, King works long hours with the family farmers of the Delta. He helps to arrange loan programs and trains farmers to plant crops such as peas and okra, which are better suited to small acreage. Today over 1,300 Delta farmers have joined King's fight to save an important part of Arkansas life.

The battle is far from over for these Delta farmers. But King sees his work as part of a long, slow process. "I'm definitely making a contribution," he said, "and it makes you feel good when you feel you're helping other people . . . that's what it's all about."

REVIEWING VOCABULARY

alluvium   loess
bayou   plateau
erosion   population
highland   region
levee   tributary

Number a sheet of paper from 1 to 10. Beside each number write the word from the list above that best completes the sentence.

1. Sandy, windblown soil, called ____, formed Crowley's Ridge.
2. Mountains are the main landform in some ____ regions.
3. Many people lived there; the ____ was large.
4. The ____ of the land caused deep canyons to form.
5. The flooding of the Mississippi River has left a great deal of ____ in the surrounding soil.
6. Each ____ of Arkansas has features that set it apart from other areas.
7. A ____ is a sluggish inlet of water.
8. A ____ is a landform shaped something like a table.
9. The people built a ____ along the river to prevent floods.
10. The smaller river was a ____ of the Mississippi.

REVIEWING FACTS

Number a sheet of paper from 1 to 10. Beside each number write the name of the region that relates to each item in the following list.

1. smallest region
2. Red River flows there
3. flat-topped mountains
4. largest region
5. Helena
6. "in-between region"
7. Hot Springs
8. Bartholomew Bayou
9. shallow soil
10. levees to prevent floods

WRITING ABOUT MAIN IDEAS

1. **Writing a Paragraph:** Look through this chapter and choose one picture. Describe what is shown in the picture. Tell how the scene is typical of the region shown.
2. **Writing an Opinion Paragraph:** Imagine you could choose a part of Arkansas in which to live. Which region would you choose? Write a paragraph explaining why you would choose that region.

BUILDING SKILLS: READING ELEVATION MAPS

1. What is an elevation map?
2. What is a profile?
3. Use the map and profile on pages 30 and 31 to answer these questions.
   a. Which range of elevation is shown by the color dark green?
   b. What is the elevation of Snow Lake?
4. Why is it helpful to be able to read an elevation map?

REVIEWING VOCABULARY

Number a sheet of paper from 1 to 15. Beside each number write **C** if the underlined word is used correctly. If it is not, write the word that would correctly complete the sentence.

1. The <u>weather</u> in Arkansas makes the state a good place for farming.
2. The impression of a plant or animal left in a rock is called a <u>timber</u>.
3. A river that flows into another, larger river is called a <u>river basin</u>.
4. A hill is an example of a <u>landform</u>.
5. Farmers use <u>alluvium</u> to bring water to their dry fields.
6. A <u>loess</u> has been built along the river to prevent floods.
7. The <u>precipitation</u> has been about 100°F. (38°C) every day this week. It is hot!
8. Arkansas can be divided into six sections, called <u>regions</u>.
9. A sluggish inlet of water is called a <u>plateau</u>.
10. When water wears away part of the land, this process is called <u>geography</u>.
11. A plain is an example of a <u>highland</u>.
12. Another word that we use to describe farming is <u>agriculture</u>.
13. When the soil is <u>fossilized</u>, crops will grow well.
14. Fertile soil and novaculite are examples of <u>landforms</u>.
15. As the river flowed by, it left behind a great deal of <u>timber</u>.

WRITING ABOUT THE UNIT

1. **Writing a Diary Entry:** Imagine that you are flying across Arkansas in a hot air balloon, moving from east to west. What would you see? Write a diary entry describing the trip.
2. **Writing a Paragraph:** Reread the words to the song on page 26. What do you think the song means? In your own words, explain the lesson taught by the song. Then think of one way in which the lesson could apply to your own life.

ACTIVITIES

1. **Making a Collage of Arkansas:** Gather pictures from newspapers or magazines showing landforms and other natural features of our state. Use the pictures to make a collage about Arkansas. Write a caption describing each picture in the completed collage.
2. **Making an Advertising Billboard:** Choose one site in Arkansas that people from elsewhere might like to visit. Design an advertising billboard about the place. The billboard should tell the main features of the place. It should also make people want to go there.
3. **Working Together in a Small Group Discussion:** With three or four of your classmates, discuss the following questions.
   a. How are our daily lives affected by the natural resources found in Arkansas?
   b. How have Arkansans changed the natural features and landforms of our state to help people?

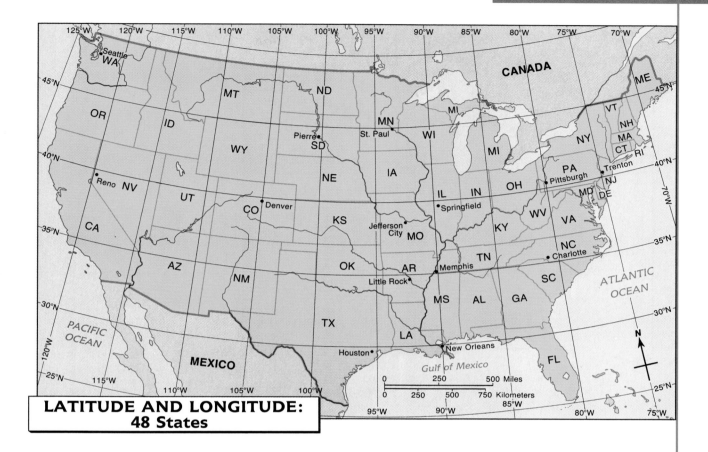

**LATITUDE AND LONGITUDE:
48 States**

BUILDING SKILLS: UNDERSTANDING LATITUDE AND LONGITUDE

Study the map above and answer the following questions.

1. Explain the meaning of each of these measurements: 30°N; 110°W.

2. Name another city located at about the same longitude as Little Rock.

3. If you were to travel to a place located at 40°N, 80°W, which state would you be in?

4. Give the location of Houston, Texas by using latitude and longitude.

LINKING PAST, PRESENT, AND FUTURE

Fossils are one way of learning about what a place was like in the past. What are some other sources that can teach us about the past? How will people of the future learn about the Arkansans of today?

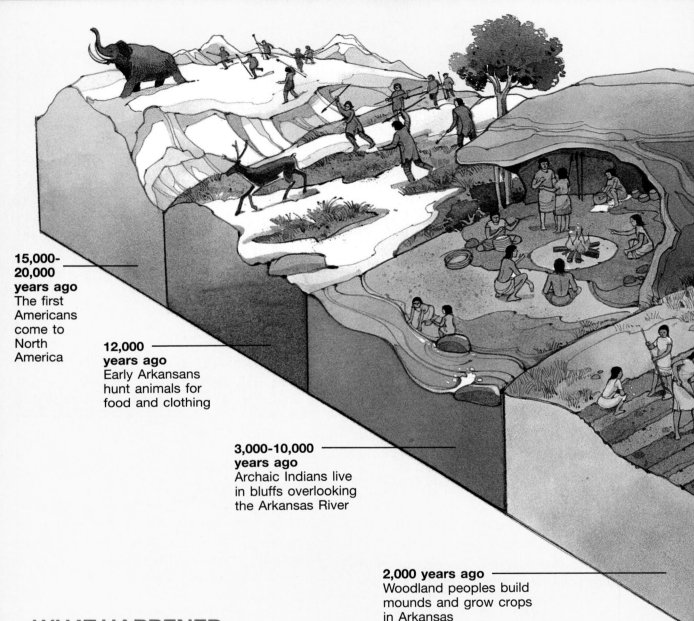

15,000-20,000 years ago
The first Americans come to North America

12,000 years ago
Early Arkansans hunt animals for food and clothing

3,000-10,000 years ago
Archaic Indians live in bluffs overlooking the Arkansas River

2,000 years ago
Woodland peoples build mounds and grow crops in Arkansas

150-400 years ago
The Quapaw live in Arkansas

WHAT HAPPENED

The story of our state reaches far back into the past and stretches far into the future. It begins with hunters who arrived in our state from lands far away. The story continues with farmers who settled in communities throughout the land of Arkansas. In this unit you will read about these first Arkansans.

UNIT

2

THE FIRST PEOPLE OF ARKANSAS

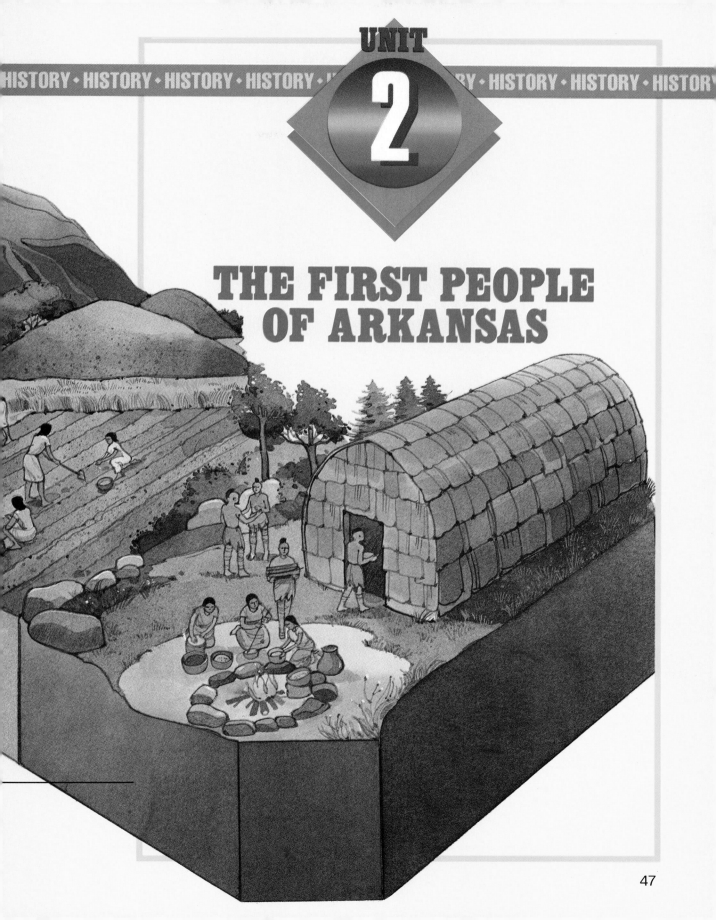

CHAPTER 3

THE FIRST ARKANSANS

FOCUS

In the beginning all the animals could talk, and but one language was used. All were at peace.

These lines come from a story called "The Creation of the Earth." It was told by one of the many Native American groups who lived in our state. By telling stories about their beginnings, they hoped to answer some questions we still ask today: Where did the first Arkansans come from? What were their lives like long ago? In this chapter you will learn some of the answers to these questions.

1 Hunters and Bluff Dwellers

READ TO LEARN

Key Vocabulary

history	land bridge
prehistory	Paleo
archaeologist	Archaic
artifact	
strait	

Key Places

Bering Strait
Beringia

Read Aloud

The ragged sides and roof of this cave, [along with] its great extent and deathlike stillness, inspire both wonder and awe. . . .

This is a description of one of the many rock shelters that the first Arkansans used for temporary homes. In this lesson you will read what we know about these ancient people.

Read for Purpose

1. **WHAT YOU KNOW:** What do you think are some of the ways we can learn about people who lived long ago?
2. **WHAT YOU WILL LEARN:** Who were the first people to live in our state? Where did they come from?

WHO LIVED HERE?

As Angie Reed and Carolyn Sabo waded across the small stream in northwestern Arkansas, they looked at the cliffs and bluffs on the other side. Most of the other students were already there, along with Mr. Gillum, the leader of their school's Nature Club.

The Nature Club had traveled to the Ozarks on a field trip. By the time Angie and Carolyn reached the group, Mr. Gillum was answering questions about the beautiful mountainous region they were exploring.

He reminded the students that they had already studied how the Ozarks had risen above the sea. "Now," he said, "we can study the first people to live in these mountains."

STUDYING THE PAST

If people want to learn about you sometime in the future, they might begin by looking at your birth certificate. Next they might read your school records, or look at letters you had written to your family and friends.

The first Arkansans, however, left behind no written records. Why? They lived thousands of years before writing was invented.

Archaeologists dig carefully in places where people lived long ago. The artifacts that they find, such as this stone weapon point, tell us about the way these people lived.

We use the word history to describe past events that are preserved in written records. To describe the period before writing was invented, we use the word prehistory. You can understand the difference between these two words by remembering that *pre* usually means "before."

Prehistoric people, then, are those who have left behind no written records. Learning about prehistoric people is the job of a special kind of scientist, called an archaeologist (är kē ol′ ə jist). Archaeologists dig up the remains of ancient cities, villages, and tombs or burial sites. They study the objects that people have left behind, such as tools, weapons, or pottery. These objects are called artifacts. For an archaeologist, each artifact is like a clue. By piecing together many of these clues, he or she can slowly solve part of the mystery of how people lived long ago.

THE FIRST AMERICANS

Archaeologists have studied the artifacts left by the earliest Americans. These objects tell us that those first people probably came here from Asia. But how did they reach the North American continent?

Look at the maps on pages 51 and 228–229 to answer this question. Notice that North America and Asia are separated by the Bering Strait. A strait is a narrow waterway that connects two larger bodies of water.

Between 12,000 and 20,000 years ago the area that is now the Bering Strait was dry land. It formed a wide, marshy land bridge between the two continents. This land bridge is called Beringia (ber′ ən gē ə). Archaeologists think that Asian hunters crossed this land bridge to North America in search of food. Follow the route of these hunters on the map on this page. Over the next several thousand years, these people moved farther south and east. Eventually they came to live all over North America and South America.

These first Americans later became known as Indians. Today we often call these people Native Americans. The word *native* means "one of the first people to live in a land."

THE PALEO-INDIANS IN ARKANSAS

The first Indians may have reached the land of Arkansas around 12,000 years ago. Archaeologists have a special name for this time period in history. They call it the Paleo (pā′ lē ō) period, after a Greek word meaning "ancient" or "far-off." For this reason these first Arkansans are sometimes called the Paleo-Indians.

As you have read, the Paleo-Indians lived long before the invention of writing. For this reason we do not know much about them. But the artifacts they left behind have taught us something about their lives.

These artifacts include stone weapon tips. These sharp stone points can still be found in the Ozarks. They are sometimes called arrowheads.

In fact, the Paleo-Indians did not have bows and arrows. The stone points were tied or fixed to wooden poles. The hunters hurled these spears at deer, rabbits, or squirrels. They also used a special spear-thrower called an atlatl (ăt′ lät əl). Look at the drawing on this page to see a hunter using an atlatl. The Paleo-Indians may have hunted along with their dogs, which they had tamed as pets.

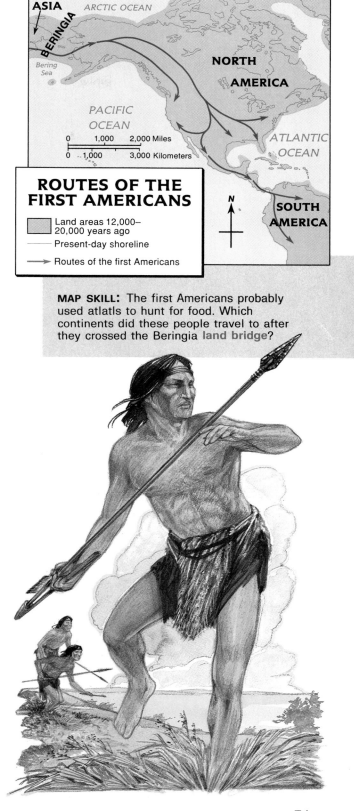

ROUTES OF THE FIRST AMERICANS

- Land areas 12,000–20,000 years ago
- Present-day shoreline
- Routes of the first Americans

MAP SKILL: The first Americans probably used atlatls to hunt for food. Which continents did these people travel to after they crossed the Beringia **land bridge**?

Indians of the **Archaic** period often lived in bluffs and caves like this one. What purpose might this tool have served?

Besides hunting, the Paleo-Indians gathered wild fruit, berries, and roots. They probably did not plant crops. This prevented them from staying in one place very long, since the supply of food would soon run out. Groups like the Paleo-Indians, who hunted and picked wild plants for their needs are called hunters and gatherers.

AN IMPORTANT DISCOVERY

About 10,000 years ago the lives of these first Arkansans began to change in some important ways. Archaeologists have a name for this time period, too, which lasted until around 3,000 years ago. They call it the **Archaic** (är kā′ ik) period. This name also comes from a Greek word, one meaning "beginning."

During this period the Indians made an important discovery. Nobody knows just how. Perhaps a Native American who was gathering roots and plants accidentally pushed some seeds into the ground. Imagine the surprise when the seeds later grew into new plants!

However it came about, this discovery changed the lives of the first Arkansans. They planted May grass and little barley, which were used to make bread and gruel. They no longer had to constantly search for food. They had become farmers.

Since they no longer needed to move from place to place, they began to live in more permanent shelters. In northwestern Arkansas the Native Americans often made their homes beneath overhanging bluffs. They also moved into caves. These bluff homes and cave homes protected the Indians from the rain, wind, and snow. Because these shelters were so dry, many of the artifacts left behind by these early Arkansans have been preserved.

Look at the photograph of the cave on this page. Archaeologists have found artifacts such as bowls, beads, and axes on these sites.

A NEW WAY OF LIFE

As you have read, the discovery of farming changed the lives of these early people of Arkansas. In the next lesson you will read about the ways in which their way of life continued to change and develop.

 Check Your Reading

1. How do archaeologists learn about the past?
2. Where do archaeologists think the first Native Americans came from?
3. What kinds of artifacts did the Paleo-Indians leave behind?
4. **GEOGRAPHY SKILL:** Why can we no longer take the same route that the first Americans took from Asia to North America?
5. **THINKING SKILL:** Compare and contrast the ways of life of the Indians of the Paleo and Archaic periods.

52

READ TO LEARN

Key Vocabulary

culture
ceremony

Key Places

Toltec Mounds State Park

Read Aloud

I thought I discovered a considerable [large] *hill, but it was, in fact, an enormous mound, not less than 40 feet high, situated towards the center of a circle of other lesser mounds. . . .*

Do you remember Thomas Nuttall, whose descriptions of our state you read in Chapter 1? He wrote the words above during the same journey. At the time, the mounds he described were great riddles. Who had built them? Why had they been built? In this lesson you will read some of the answers archaeologists have found for these riddles.

Read for Purpose

1. **WHAT YOU KNOW:** How did the first Asian nomads reach North America?
2. **WHAT YOU WILL LEARN:** Who were the mound builders, and what was their life like?

THE WOODLAND AND MISSISSIPPIAN CULTURES

About 3,000 years ago the Native Americans of Arkansas began to settle in permanent communities. They built most of their villages along the Mississippi River and in other lowland regions. The fertile soil helped them to raise such crops as beans, squash, sunflowers, and corn.

These Indian groups are considered part of the Woodland and Mississippian cultures. A culture is the way of life of a group of people. It includes the group's customs, beliefs, and arts.

The Woodland and Mississippian people were expert farmers and hunters. The artifacts they left behind tell us that they were also skilled craftspeople. On the sites where their villages were located, archaeologists have found jewelry, knives, and tobacco pipes. They have also uncovered many examples of their pottery. The Indians used these simple, undecorated pots for cooking and storing food. However, some groups liked to create pottery and pipes in the shapes of animals or people.

53

THE BUILDERS OF MOUNDS

Along with pottery, pipes, and other craft objects, these Indians left behind another type of artifact—great piles of earth called mounds. Hundreds of these mounds still exist in our state.

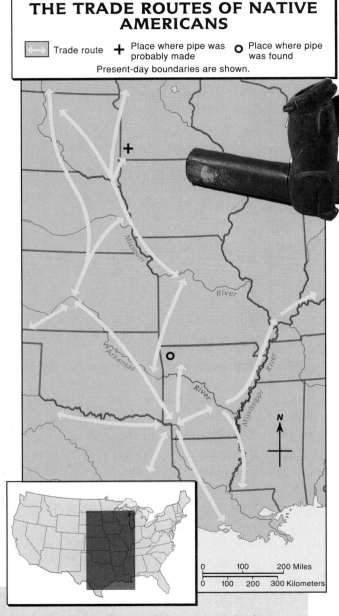

THE TRADE ROUTES OF NATIVE AMERICANS

Trade route
+ Place where pipe was probably made
o Place where pipe was found
Present-day boundaries are shown.

Missouri River
Arkansas River
Mississippi River

N

| 0 | 100 | 200 Miles |
| 0 | 100 | 200 | 300 Kilometers |

MAP SKILL: Along which routes might the Indian traders have carried this pipe?

One of them was measured by a visitor in 1882. He described the mound as being 100 feet (30 m) high, 165 feet (50 m) wide, and more than 200 feet (61 m) long. That is roughly half the size of our State Capitol in Little Rock!

When Thomas Nuttall discovered one of these mounds in 1819, he could only wonder about its purpose. Today we have learned more about why the early Arkansans built them.

Some of the mounds were used for burial. The Native Americans also buried pottery, statues, and beads alongside corpses in the mounds.

Around 1,000 years ago the Indians began to build mounds for other purposes. They were often the site of religious **ceremonies** (ser′ ə mō nēz). A ceremony is an act or a set of acts performed on a special occasion. On the tops of the mounds, the Indians would build temples, or places to worship.

Eventually large towns grew up around the mounds. Several thousand people lived in some of these towns. This is a population comparable to that of such present-day Arkansas towns as De Queen or Walnut Ridge.

The people of these towns traded tools and pottery with one another. They also traded with Indians who lived outside of present-day Arkansas. Look at the map on this page to see the routes that these traders traveled.

A NATIVE AMERICAN TOWN

What was life like in these towns? What were the houses like? What did the children do to amuse themselves? Imagine yourself stepping into a time machine. You fly backward in time. Finally the machine stops. You step out into a Native American town as it was 1,000 years ago.

This mound, located near present-day Scott, was once the site of a large community. What do these artifacts tell us about the community?

The first thing that you notice are hundreds of circular houses, packed tightly together. They are made of clay and branches, with thatched roofs. If you raise your eyes above the roofs, you can see the tops of the mounds in the town's center.

You can feel the excitement in the air. Today is the last day of the harvest festival. People from other towns have traveled as far as 200 miles (322 km) to join the celebrations. You stroll through the crowded streets toward the mounds. The open area in front of the mounds is large enough to hold all the visitors and townspeople. As you stand there, you see the boys and girls of the town sweeping the plaza clean.

You watch a special ceremony that is taking place on top of the largest mound. Afterwards the whole town sits down to a feast of bread, fruit, and fresh fish and meat. There is dancing and singing. You stand for a few minutes watching the girls and boys play stickball. You may even join the crowd as it claps and cheers.

Of course you cannot really travel back in time. But you can still visit the spots where these towns stood. And at Toltec Mounds State Park, you can still see some of the mounds themselves.

ARKANSAS INDIANS

For reasons nobody knows, the culture of the mound-building Indians began to disappear around 600 years ago. Several hundred years later these Indians were gone. But other Native American peoples had taken their place. You will read about these peoples in the next chapter.

Check Your Reading

1. Name three things that are included in the meaning of *culture*.
2. What kinds of artifacts did the Mississippian and Woodland people leave behind?
3. Why did the Mississippian and Woodland people build mounds?
4. GEOGRAPHY SKILL: In which area of present-day Arkansas did Native Americans build mounds?
5. THINKING SKILL: List the following things in the order in which they occurred: mound-building, crossing of Beringia land bridge, beginnings of agriculture.

Decision Making

Key Vocabulary

decision   alternative

Every day you make dozens of **decisions**, or choices. You decide what to wear, what to eat, and whether to play or study. Can you think of other decisions that you have made today?

Making decisions involves choosing from a number of **alternatives** to achieve a goal. An alternative is a choice between two or more things.

Some decisions are easy to make. Others are hard. When you make a decision, you have to live with the results. So you try to make the decision that is best for you. But how do you decide which alternative is the best one? In this lesson you will learn some steps to follow when making decisions.

Trying the Skill

In Lesson 2 you read about the mound builders. You also read that archaeologists have found artifacts that tell us about the culture of these people.

Let's imagine that Joan Fagan is a farmer who discovers a piece of prehistoric pottery while plowing her field. What should Joan Fagan do about her discovery? Read the paragraphs below and note how the farmer makes a decision.

Archaeologists have found many important artifacts in this area. There may be more artifacts near this one. I must decide whether to call in an archaeologist or to dig by myself.

If I call in an archaeologist, he or she will know how to dig properly. But it might take several days, and I won't be able to plant my crops. On the other hand, if I don't call in an archaeologist, I might destroy some important artifacts by mistake.

I think I will call in an archaeologist.

1. What decision did the farmer face?
2. Which alternatives does she identify?
3. What did she identify as the advantage of each decision?
4. Why was the decision difficult to make?

56

HELPING YOURSELF

The steps on the left will help you to make good decisions. The example on the right shows how Joan Fagan made her decision.

One Way to Make a Decision	Example
1. Define the goal that you want to achieve.	The farmer's goal is to find as many important artifacts as possible.
2. Identify the alternatives by which you can achieve your goal.	The farmer can dig up the artifacts herself, or she can call in an archaeologist.
3. Predict the likely results of each alternative.	The farmer predicts that if she calls in an archaeologist, she will be able to dig up the field properly. If she doesn't call in an archaeologist, she might destroy some valuable artifacts by mistake.
4. Judge each outcome by determining its advantages and disadvantages and whether it would help you and other people involved.	If the farmer calls in an archaeologist, no artifacts will be lost. If she does not call in an archaeologist, she will not achieve her goal of finding the most artifacts.
5. Choose the best alternative—the one that is most likely to help you reach your goal.	The best alternative is to call in an archaeologist.

Applying the Skill

Now apply what you have just read to improve your decision-making skills.

The Lesters want to buy a home. They cannot afford an expensive house in Little Rock. For this reason they must try to get the "most house" for the least amount of money. One choice is to build a house with the help of friends. Building a house alone would take too much time and effort.

Another choice is to buy an old house that is not expensive because it needs repairs. Houses were built well years ago, but an old house might still have many things wrong with it. A third choice is to build a new house outside Little Rock where the prices are lower.

1. What is the Lesters' goal?
   a. to buy their own home
   b. to move out of Little Rock
   c. to live in an old house

2. Which alternative do the Lesters *not* consider?
   a. renting a house
   b. buying an old house
   c. building a new house
3. What is an advantage of buying an old house?
   a. It would need a lot of repairs.
   b. It would be close to work.
   c. It would be well built.

Reviewing the Skill

1. What must you do when you make a decision?
2. What are some steps that you can follow in order to make a good decision?
3. Why should you consider all alternatives when you make a decision?
4. Think of a decision you have made recently. What were some of the alternatives you considered?

Teaching
ABOUT THE ENVIRONMENT

When the early Americans came to the land of Arkansas 12,000 years ago, they found open prairies, thick forests, and clear, rushing rivers. Today many of these natural resources are in danger of disappearing. Ellen Neaville is one Arkansan who is working hard to preserve these natural treasures for the future.

Neaville lives in Rogers in Benton County. When she was a little girl, she spent many happy hours exploring her grandfather's cypress swamp in the West Gulf Coastal Plain. It was there, among the ducks, herons, alligators, and other wildlife, that her interest in the environment first began.

Years later, Neaville became a high school biology teacher. She noticed that most schools lacked the time and equipment necessary to teach young Arkansans about their environment.

How could Neaville address this problem? She felt that the only way for students to really learn about nature was for them to go out and experience it.

With this thought in mind, she helped to start a summer camp for young people who were concerned about the environment. The camp was named Project Wet 'n' Wild. "It's the best long-term investment we can make in protecting the environment," said Neaville. The Arkansas Department of Education liked Ellen's idea and agreed to pay for this educational camp.

Each summer 30 talented high school students from every corner of our state travel to Huntsville in Madison County to spend two weeks at the camp. They study the environment of the Ozarks up close and think about ways to protect it.

These young "naturalists" study many different things—from owl calling to astronomy to finding their way through the backwoods. They even learn about the foods that black bears like to eat! In the evening everyone shares their experiences with nature by drawing pictures and writing poems.

Project Wet 'n' Wild is one way that Ellen Neaville—who is known as the "Bird Lady of Rogers"—tries to preserve Arkansas's environment. She said, "I know that the little I can do is a part of the whole, and the world needs *all* of us."

REVIEWING VOCABULARY

artifact
ceremony
history
prehistory
strait

Number a sheet of paper from 1 to 5. Beside each number write the word from the list above that best matches the definition.

1. A narrow waterway that connects two larger bodies of water
2. A man-made object that people leave behind after their death
3. An act or set of acts performed on a special occasion
4. Past events that we know about from written records
5. The time in the past before writing was invented

REVIEWING FACTS

Number a sheet of paper from 1 to 10. Beside each number write **T** if the sentence is true. If it is false, rewrite the sentence so that it will be true.

1. People have always been able to write down their ideas.
2. Beringia connected the present-day United States with Mexico.
3. Examples of artifacts include arrowheads, tools, and pottery.
4. Paleo-Indians were farmers.
5. Indians of the Archaic period were hunters and gatherers.
6. Archaeologists are not sure why early Native Americans built mounds.
7. Early Arkansas Native Americans lived only in small villages.
8. About 1,000 years ago, Indians in Arkansas lived in round houses with thatched roofs.
9. Some mound-building Indians still live in Arkansas today.
10. We know about the Indian mounds only through drawings that the people who built them left behind.

WRITING ABOUT MAIN IDEAS

1. **Writing a Descriptive Paragraph:** Look closely at the picture of the Toltec mound on page 55. Review the information about the mounds presented in the lesson. Then describe how the mound would look if you were to fly over it in an airplane.
2. **Writing a Paragraph:** Suppose an archaeologist is digging in an area of Arkansas where people lived thousands of years ago. The archaeologist finds the following artifacts: a clay bowl, some jewelry, a clay pipe, and some dried corn seed. What might these artifacts teach her about the people who once lived in this place? Write a paragraph stating the conclusions that you might draw from these artifacts.

BUILDING SKILLS: DECISION MAKING

1. Which steps should you follow in making a good decision?
2. Why is it important to be able to make decisions well?

CHAPTER 4

NATIVE AMERICANS OF ARKANSAS

FOCUS

I persuade myself [that] the beauty of the climate has a great influence on the character of the inhabitants, who are at the same time very gentle, and very brave.

This is how one traveler described the Native Americans of Arkansas. In this chapter you will read about three Native American groups who made the land of Arkansas their home.

1 The Caddo

READ TO LEARN

Key Vocabulary

migrate

Read Aloud

We saw several cottages. . . . In some of them are 15 or 20 families, each of which has its nook or corner, bed, and other utensils. . . . The cottages are round at the top, after the manner of a beehive.

A traveler used these words to describe a Caddo village on the Red River in 1687. How were the houses of the Caddo different from your own?

Read for Purpose

WHAT YOU KNOW: In which part of our state did the mound-building Native Americans live?

2. WHAT YOU WILL LEARN: Who were the Caddo, and what was their life like?

THE CADDO

Imagine that you are taking a drive with your family through southwestern Arkansas. As you near Arkadelphia, in Clark County, you pass the Caddo River. In town you notice a sign reading *Caddo Street*. When you glance at the road map, you notice the nearby towns of Caddo Gap and Caddo Valley. Did you ever think about how these places got their names?

The Caddo are the only Indians who did not migrate to Arkansas. To migrate means to move from one region to another in order to settle there. The Caddo culture developed from the mound-building cultures in the basins of the Ouachita River and Red River.

Some Caddo may have lived as far north as the Arkansas River Valley.

Of course, the Caddo were not the first people to live in the land of Arkansas. As you know, the mound builders had already lived here for centuries. The Caddo adapted to the life they found in their homeland. They built their farms on sites that had been occupied by earlier Indians. They rebuilt and used the mounds as places of worship and as burial grounds for their dead. They traded goods with other Native American groups nearby. By adapting these customs, the Caddo blended their culture with that of the mound builders.

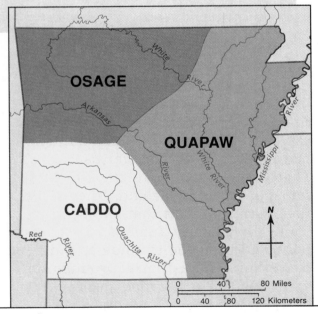

MAP SKILL: The Caddo traded salt that they found in springs near the Ouachita River. Which other river runs through the area where the Caddo lived?

OSAGE

QUAPAW

CADDO

Red River

Arkansas River

White River

White River

Mississippi River

Ouachita River

N

0   40   80 Miles

0   40   80   120 Kilometers

INDIANS OF ARKANSAS IN 1700

Present-day boundaries are shown.

Look at the map on this page to see where the Caddo lived. The map will also show you where the Quapaw and the Osage lived. You will read about these two other Native American groups later in this chapter.

CADDO FARMING

The Caddo relied on farming to feed themselves. Men and women worked together in the gardens and fields. Sometimes these skilled farmers would raise a crop, harvest it, and then raise a different crop in the same field—all in the same year. They grew pumpkins, beans, tobacco, and squash. But their main crop was corn, which grew easily in the sandy soil. From the corn they made bread and other foods.

Vegetables such as corn and beans contain little salt. For this reason, the Caddo had to find another source of salt for their diet. They found it in the salt springs that flow into the Ouachita River. First they would heat the salt water in clay pans. When the water had boiled away, a thick crust of salt would remain in the pan. The Caddo then used this salt to season their food. They also traded it for animal skins, feathers, tools, and pottery.

THE "ROUND-HEADED PEOPLE"

Visitors often commented on the round shape of the Caddo's heads. Why were their heads like this? The Caddo practiced the custom of "binding" the heads of children. Using leather cords, they tied a flat board to the front of a newborn baby's head. As a result, the child's forehead was flattened, and the top of the skull was raised into a round dome. The Caddo considered this shape very beautiful.

DAILY LIFE

As you have read, the houses of the Caddo were shaped like beehives. To build them the Caddo drove poles into the ground and then bent the poles together at the top. Next they mixed clay and straw together and filled the spaces between the poles with this mixture. Finally they covered this layer with straw and reeds.

Some of these houses were quite large—up to 50 feet (15 m) across. Several families would live in a house this size. The furniture was made of cane, and buffalo robes served as bedding. But as one traveler noted in 1687, the different families in the house shared only one thing.

> *They have nothing in common besides the fire, which is in the middle of the hut, and never goes out. . . .*

The fire was used for heating and cooking. The smoke escaped through a hole in the center of the roof.

Caddo women wore skirts made of woven grass or soft cloth. The men tattooed and painted colorful designs on their bodies. They also wore skirtlike clothing made of tanned deerskin and buffalo hide. Tanned hides are hides that have been treated with acid to make them last longer. The Caddo made this acid from bark and wood. Look at the photograph on page 62. How does the clothing of the Caddo differ from your own clothing?

WORKING TOGETHER

Does your community have any activities in which everybody plays a part? You have read that Caddo men and women worked together to raise crops. The Caddo also helped one another to build houses. Clearly these

People worked together to build the houses in a Caddo community. Several families lived in each of these houses.

people believed that some things could be done better if everybody worked together.

✓ Check Your Reading

1. In which part of present-day Arkansas did the Caddo live?
2. What was the Caddo's reaction to the mound-building culture that had existed in Arkansas?
3. Which activity did the Caddo men and women share?
4. **GEOGRAPHY SKILL:** How might Caddo life have been different if they had lived in the Ozarks?
5. **THINKING SKILL:** List three questions that you might have asked a Caddo to learn more about his or her way of life.

2 The Quapaw

Key Vocabulary   **Key Places**

settlement   Kappa

Read Aloud

In a council held with the Quapaws some years ago, a very old chieftain related that at a very remote period his nation had descended the Mississippi, and had there divided, one party continuing down the Mississippi. . . .

This is how one Quapaw described his people's journey to the land of Arkansas. In this lesson you will learn more about the Quapaw.

Read for Purpose

1. **WHAT YOU KNOW:** Has anyone in your family ever told you stories about the place where you live?
2. **WHAT YOU WILL LEARN:** Who were the Quapaw, and what was their life like?

THE "DOWNSTREAM PEOPLE"

At some time more than 300 years ago, a group of Sioux Indians left their home in the basins of the Ohio River and Wabash River. Nobody knows exactly why. They may have been pushed off their land by another group of Native Americans. They also may have left in search of animals to hunt. In any case they began moving westward, looking for a new home.

When they reached the Mississippi River, the Sioux first traveled downstream along the river. Then, at the point where the Missouri River enters the Mississippi, they divided into several smaller groups. Some went up the Missouri. Others continued farther downstream. The Indians of this second group came to be known as the Ugakhpah (ü gäk′ pô), which means the "downstream people." These people later came to be called the Quapaw (kwä′ pô). The Quapaw were also called the Arkansaw. Eventually this name came to be used for the land in which these people lived. Did you know that we owe the name of our state to the "downstream people"?

After traveling down the Mississippi, the Quapaw entered the land of Arkansas from the northeast. They built settlements along the Mississippi River, the White River, and the Arkansas River. A settlement is a village or group of houses in a new area. As the Quapaw spread throughout this area, they pushed out the members of a different Native American group, the Tunica. Only a small number of the Tunica lived in the land of Arkansas after that time.

Groups of Quapaw moved as far south as present-day Louisiana. Look at the map on page 62 to see where the Quapaw lived. In which direction would a Quapaw Indian have traveled to visit a Caddo village?

Some Quapaw villages grew to be quite large. The village of **Kappa** was home to almost 4,000 Quapaw. This village was located near the present-day town of Snow Lake, about 50 miles (80 km) south of Helena. In the 1600s life in Kappa might have been something like this. . . .

KAPPA

Even though it is early autumn in Kappa, the night is clear and cold. Eleven-year-old Kugee tosses and turns, unable to sleep. Finally he lies on his back and stares up at the roof. He can see some light from the moon and stars shining between the bark shingles.

Why can't Kugee sleep? Tomorrow will mark three years since the burial of his grandfather, Sig-Dah. Kugee's family will have a feast to honor the occasion. But now, as he lies awake in bed and stares into the darkness, Kugee remembers his grandfather.

Sig-Dah was a very special man. Like most Quapaw men, he was over 6 feet (2 m) tall. Handsome and friendly, he knew how to hunt, how to plant corn, and how to build a house. But the thing that Kugee remembers most about Sig-Dah is his stories. The old man loved to tell stories.

Kugee gazes up through the hole in the roof where the smoke from the fire escapes. Through the smoke he can see the night sky. He remembers the stories Sig-Dah told him about the sky. The old man called the Milky Way the "Road of the Ghosts." Sig-Dah said that the "Tannan," or Thunder People, lived up on the Road of Ghosts. When something strange or puzzling took place in the village, it was often the work of the Thunder People. But other spirits lived in the skies, too. Pointing to a circle of stars, Sig-Dah told Kugee that it was a group of dancing girls. Now, imagining the spirits in the night sky, Kugee finally falls asleep.

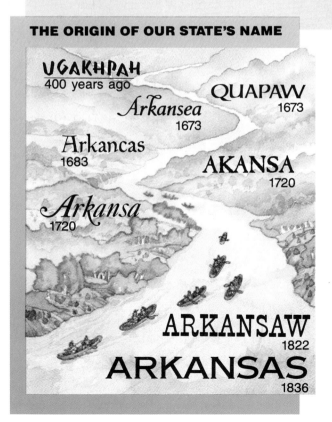

CHART SKILL: Our state's name comes from the word for the "downstream people." What was the land of Arkansas called in 1683?

THE ORIGIN OF OUR STATE'S NAME

UGAKHPAH
400 years ago

QUAPAW
1673

Arkansea
1673

Arkancas
1683

AKANSA
1720

Arkansa
1720

ARKANSAW
1822

ARKANSAS
1836

DAYTIME CHORES

At sunrise Kugee yawns, stretches, and rolls off of his sleeping platform. His older sister Mi-ji-tah is already busy at the fire, making cornmeal bread. The silver and beads in her hair glint in the firelight.

After eating breakfast with his mother and sister, Kugee leaves the house. First he feeds the chickens and turkeys outside the door. Then he walks through the village of Kappa, passing by groups of rectangular houses like his own.

Two houses are larger than the others. One is the council house, where the chief meets with the village elders. The other is the chief's own house. As Kugee watches, a group of Caddo from the Red River basin steps into the chief's house to talk with him. They carry pouches of salt, bows, and arrows. Last spring the Caddo had traded these goods for canoes. Maybe this time, Kugee thinks, they will trade them for pottery or animal hides.

Kugee moves on. Beyond the houses are neat rows of cornfields. Kugee waves to his friend Pah, who is guarding the fields against animals.

"Where are you going, Kugee?"

"Down to the river," Kugee replies. "This afternoon I will help my father pull in the fishnets."

Soon he reaches the edge of the fields. He walks beyond them. He can see other towns in the distance.

Finally he arrives at a small lake off the Mississippi River. His father

DIAGRAM SKILL: Why do you think the council house is bigger than the other houses in the village?

A QUAPAW VILLAGE

Fields

Council house

teaches him how to tug the heavy fish-nets up out of the water. Tonight, Kugee's father tells him, the family will eat fish, beans, roasted corn, dried plums, and watermelon.

"The earth has been good to us this year, Kugee. The earth has given our people its blessings."

THE VALUE OF SHARING

When Kugee's father spoke of the earth's blessings, he expressed a belief common to all the Quapaw. They spoke about the earth as if it were a mother who cared for her children.

The Quapaw felt that they should respect the earth in return. Nobody was supposed to take without giving, or to take more than he or she needed. The Quapaw also believed that nobody owned the earth—and that nobody could buy or sell it.

If nobody owned the earth, the Quapaw believed, then everybody did. For this reason they were happy to share what they had. Almost 200 years after Kugee's time, a Quapaw chief told Thomas Nuttall that his people still believed in sharing.

> But in his nation, he took a pride in assuring me, if I was found poor, I should be relieved to the best of their ability, and led to the shelter of their village, where the stranger was always welcome.

THE QUAPAW

As you read, the Quapaw arrived in the land of Arkansas more than 300 years ago. They built villages throughout the eastern part of our state. Although few Quapaw live in Arkansas today, the people of this Native American group continue to celebrate the heritage of the "downstream people."

Peter Clabber (left) and Tall Chief (right) were two important leaders of the Quapaw Indians.

Check Your Reading

1. How did the Quapaw arrive in the land of Arkansas?
2. Where did the Quapaw build villages in the land of Arkansas?
3. Why did the Quapaw believe that nobody could buy or sell the land?
4. **GEOGRAPHY SKILL:** Look at the map on pages 228–229 to locate the Ohio River basin. This was the original home of the Quapaw. In which direction did they travel in order to reach Arkansas?
5. **THINKING SKILL:** List three ways in which Kugee's life was different from your own.

Finding Directions

Key Vocabulary

North Star   Big Dipper   orient
Little Dipper   compass

Before roads and highways were built, how did people find their way around? When the Quapaw Indians followed buffalo herds as they hunted, how did they find their way home? They may have used the sun and other stars to find directions. Today we have other tools for finding directions.

Using the Sun

On a clear day you can use the sun to find directions. The sun rises in the east and sets in the west.

On a sunny morning stand with your back to the sun. You will see your shadow in front of you, and you will be facing west. If you live in the Northern Hemisphere and you face your shadow at noon, you will be facing north. If you face your shadow late in the afternoon, you will be facing east. Study the illustration below. Which times of the day are best for using the sun to find directions?

Using the North Star

People in the Northern Hemisphere can use the North Star to find directions on a clear night. The North Star is very bright. It seems to stand almost still in the sky, and the other stars seem to move around it. Because it lies in the direction of the North Pole, the North Star is also known as the Pole Star.

If you face this star, you will always be facing north. But how can you find the North Star? The North Star is part of a group of stars called the Little Dipper A dipper has a bowl and a bent handle. Look at the Little Dipper in the diagram below. It has seven stars. Four stars form the bowl, and three stars make up the handle. The North Star is the first star at the top of the handle of the Little Dipper.

If you need help finding the Little Dipper, you can start by looking for the Big Dipper. As you can see from the diagram, the Big Dipper is also a group of seven stars in the shape of a bowl and a bent handle. The two stars at the outside edge of the bowl are called pointer stars because they point toward the North Star.

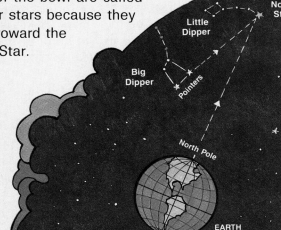

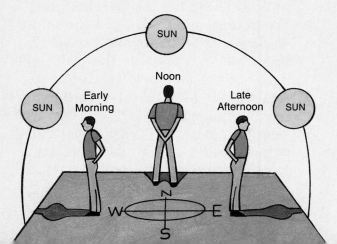

Using a Compass

Thousands of years ago the Chinese invented an instrument called the compass. A compass is an instrument with a magnetic needle that always points north when the compass is held level. A compass looks a bit like a watch, but instead of having 12 hours, it has 8 directions. It shows the four cardinal directions—*N* (north), *E* (east), *S* (south), and *W* (west). It also shows the four intermediate directions—*NE* (northeast), *SE* (southeast), *SW* (southwest), and *NW* (northwest).

To read a compass, hold the compass steady in the palm of your hand. Turn your body until the letter *N* lines up with the needle. You will then be facing north. To figure out the other directions, remember that south is directly opposite from north. If you face north, east is to your right, and west is to your left.

Using a Compass and a Map

If you have a map and a compass, you can easily find your way from one place to another. First turn the compass so that the needle and the letter *N* are lined up. Next find the direction arrow on the map. Then orient your map, or line it up with the compass. To do this, turn the map so that the north arrow points in the same direction as the compass needle. In the drawing above the girl has oriented herself and her map. In which direction should she go to find the treasure? Which obstacle stands in her path?

Reviewing the Skill

1. What are three possible ways of finding directions?
2. What are two methods that you might use on a sunny day to find which direction is north?
3. How does the Big Dipper help you to locate the North Star?
4. If you are holding a compass level, in which direction does the needle always face?
5. If you were heading north on the treasure hunt, which landmarks would you see to the east? To the west?

3 The Osage

READ TO LEARN

Key Vocabulary

treaty
ancestors

Read Aloud

We observed a pile of stones . . . which, I was informed, had been thrown up as a monument by the Osage when they were going to war, each warrior casting a stone upon the pile.

Thomas Nuttall, whom you have already read about, described this Osage "war monument" in 1819. In this lesson you will learn about this warlike Native American group.

Read for Purpose

1. **WHAT YOU KNOW:** Why were the Quapaw called the "downstream people"?
2. **WHAT YOU WILL LEARN:** Who were the Osage, and what was their life like?

THE OSAGE

In the last lesson you read that several Native American groups left their homes more than 300 years ago. When these groups reached the point where the Missouri River enters the Mississippi River, they headed in different directions. The Quapaw, "the downstream people," moved south down the Mississippi. Other groups moved upstream along the Missouri. Among these were the Osage (ō′ sāj).

For several hundred years the Osage did not actually live in the land of Arkansas. They settled in what is now southeastern Missouri. But the Osage made regular hunting trips throughout northwestern Arkansas. Look at the map on page 62 to see the part of our state that was considered Osage territory. The Osage marked the boundaries of their territory with painted wooden posts. Outsiders caught inside these boundaries were captured or killed.

A WARLIKE PEOPLE

Unlike the more peaceful Caddo and Quapaw, the Osage were warlike. Before going into battle, the Osage warriors would fast, or not eat, for several days. In a special ceremony, they raised a pipe full of tobacco toward the sky and asked the Great Spirit to help them fight. Then the warriors would sweep down from northern Arkansas to

The houses of the Osage were like upside-down bird nests. During the summer the Osage often lived in open-air houses.

raid Caddo and Quapaw settlements. One early traveler in our state received a warning about the Osage from a Caddo.

This chief warned me from trusting myself alone amongst the Osage, who, if they spared my life, would . . . leave me to perish for want.

Hunting and raiding, the Osage traveled as far south as the present-day state of Louisiana. On foot, they sometimes covered up to 60 miles (97 km) in one day!

DAILY LIFE

Although the Osage grew beans, corn, and squash, most of their food came from hunting. An entire Osage settlement would go on a hunting trip together. For weeks at a time, they hunted bear, bison, wildcat, and deer. Sometimes they stayed away from their villages for up to three months.

Each Osage village was arranged in a circle. The houses themselves were similar to those of the Quapaw. The Osage built them with poles and tree limbs, covering the branches with leaves, moss, and grass. One traveler described the buildings of an Osage village as being "perfectly tight and warm." He also said that the houses were shaped like "inverted [upside-down] bird nests."

The Osage believed in hard work. If any members of the community were lazy, they received less food. Often they had to eat the pieces of meat the others did not want.

Like the Caddo and the Quapaw, the Osage made much of their clothing out of leather. The women wore leather skirts and dresses, which they decorated with shells and fringe. The men wore leggings or breechcloths. Leggings are like leather stockings that lace up along the side. Breechcloths are short leather or cloth skirts.

71

The heritage of Native American groups such as the Quapaw (*above*) can still be seen in Arkansas.

The Osage men also painted their faces. They would cover even their eyelashes and ears with bright red paint. On sad occasions such as funerals, they would use black paint.

OUR NATIVE AMERICAN HERITAGE

During the 1800s the Caddo, the Quapaw, and the Osage all signed treaties (trē′ tēz) agreeing to give up their lands in Arkansas. A treaty is a formal agreement. You will learn more about these treaties in Chapter 6.

As a result of the treaties, these Native American groups were forced to leave our state forever. But their heritage and influence can still be seen in Arkansas today.

Thousands of modern Arkansans can claim Native Americans among their ancestors. An ancestor is a relative who lived long before you. In addition, many of our cities and towns take their names from Indian words. Some of these include Arkansas City, Bodcaw, Ouachita, Hiwassee, Chickasawbe, and Osage. Does your town's name come from an Indian word? Have you ever visited a town in Arkansas with an Indian name?

HONORING OUR PAST

No matter what your community is called, you live in a state named after the "downstream people." Every time you say the word *Arkansas*, you are remembering and honoring our state's Native Americans.

 Check Your Reading

1. Why were travelers in Arkansas afraid of the Osage?
2. How did the Osage get most of their food?
3. How did the Osage treat lazy members of their community?
4. **GEOGRAPHY SKILL:** Name three present-day states in which the Osage hunted and fought.
5. **THINKING SKILL:** Name two differences between the Osage and the other Native Americans who lived in Arkansas.

REVIEWING VOCABULARY

ancestors
migrate
settlement
treaty

Number a sheet of paper from 1 to 5. Beside each number from 1 to 4 write a sentence using one of the words listed above. In the fifth sentence use two of the words. The sentences should show that you understand the meaning of the words.

REVIEWING FACTS

Number a sheet of paper from 1 to 5. Beside each number write the letter of the phrase that best completes the sentence.

1. The Native American group that did not migrate to Arkansas was
   a. the Caddo.
   b. the Quapaw.
   c. the Osage.
   d. the Arkansas.
2. The Caddo
   a. got their food mainly by hunting.
   b. were known as the "Downstream People."
   c. lived in houses that were shaped like beehives.
   d. were nomads.
3. The Quapaw
   a. first lived to the south of the land of Arkansas.
   b. built large villages such as Kappa.
   c. were known as the "Round-Headed People."
   d. sometimes traded with the Osage.

4. The Quapaw believed that
   a. lazy people should not get as much food as hard workers.
   b. strangers should be feared.
   c. the land was for everyone to share.
   d. if you have good luck, the crops will grow well.
5. The Osage
   a. got their food mainly by farming.
   b. built square houses made of stone and branches.
   c. traded peacefully with the Caddo.
   d. migrated to Arkansas from the east.

WRITING ABOUT MAIN IDEAS

1. **Making an Outline:** Review the information in Lesson 1 and make an outline of the main ideas. Headings might include: "Where the Caddo Lived," "Daily Life," "Clothing," and "Food."
2. **Writing a Paragraph of Comparison:** Write a paragraph that compares the ways of life of the Quapaw and the Osage. Include such points of comparison as where the two groups lived, how they got their food, and the main beliefs held by each group.

BUILDING SKILLS: FINDING DIRECTIONS

1. Name three methods of finding which direction is north.
2. At 4:00 P.M. on a sunny day, where would your shadow be if you were facing west?
3. If you are facing the North Star at night, in which direction is east?

REVIEWING VOCABULARY

ancestors	history
archaeologist	migrate
artifact	Paleo
ceremony	settlement
culture	treaty

Number a sheet of paper from 1 to 10. Beside each number write the word from the list above that best completes the sentence.

1. The arrowhead is an _____ left behind by Indians who lived long ago.
2. When the group of Indians arrived, they lived in a _____.
3. Because the people cannot find any food, they will _____ to a new place.
4. The people performed a special _____ to give thanks for a good harvest.
5. The _____ is digging in a place where Paleo-Indians once lived.
6. The nations reached an agreement and signed a _____.
7. Your great-great-grandfather is one of your _____.
8. The first people of Arkansas lived during the _____ period.
9. Past events that took place after writing was invented are part of _____.
10. The Osage _____ involved different beliefs and ways of life than that of the Quapaw.

WRITING ABOUT THE UNIT

1. **Making a List:** Each Native American group discussed in this unit had a unique culture. Review the meaning of *culture*. Then list one aspect of the culture of each of these groups: Paleo-Indians, mound-building Indians, Caddo, Quapaw, and Osage.
2. **Writing a Paragraph of Comparison:** The Caddo had strict ideas about how a person should look. How did their ideas of beauty compare and contrast with ours today? Write a paragraph comparing their ideas of beauty with our own.

ACTIVITIES

1. **Researching a State Park:** Find out more facts about Toltec Mounds State Park. You might read a book from the library or write to the park for information. Then prepare a pamphlet about the park, describing what you would see if you were to visit it.
2. **Reading an Arkansas Map:** Find a map of Arkansas that shows many towns and natural features. Make a list of place names that sound as though they may have come from a Native American language. Then try to find out the origin of these names, what they mean, and which language they come from.

3. **Making a Diorama:** Choose a Native American group discussed in this unit. Make a model or diorama of a typical community belonging to that group. Then write labels to explain each feature of the diorama.

4. **Working Together to Review the Unit:** Help divide the class into two teams for a "baseball game." Each team makes up questions based on the information in this unit. Each "batter" must answer a question made up by the other team. Each correct answer is a "base hit." A wrong answer is an "out," and the two teams switch roles after three outs. Play two or three "innings."

BUILDING SKILLS: DECISION MAKING

Imagine that you are the leader of a group of Native Americans during the Archaic period. Your people have just learned how to plant seeds to grow maygrass and little barley. Some people want to settle in one place to grow crops for food. They argue that a steady food supply will allow the group to lead an easier life. Others want to keep to the old ways of hunting and gathering. They argue that the known ways are better. As the leader, you must decide what the group will do.

1. In order to make your decision, it is most important to
   a. talk to your husband or wife.
   b. state your goal.
   c. decide what is best for the whole group.
2. Your decision should help you to
   a. clothe your people.
   b. predict the weather.
   c. feed your people.
3. One reason to settle down is that
   a. you do not like being chief.
   b. other tribes have done it.
   c. your group will have a steadier supply of food.
4. Why is it important to know how to make good decisions?

LINKING PAST, PRESENT, AND FUTURE

The Caddo worked together to perform many chores. The men and women raised crops together. The whole group helped when a house needed to be built. Have there been times in which people in your family or community have worked together to accomplish something? How do these activities help the group? How do these activities help each individual? Think of a situation when, as an adult, you might become involved in a group project.

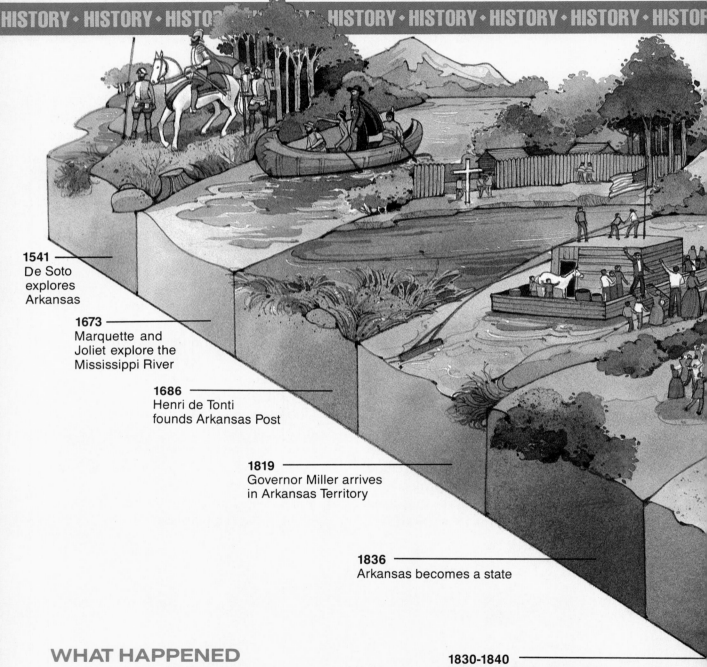

1541
De Soto explores Arkansas

1673
Marquette and Joliet explore the Mississippi River

1686
Henri de Tonti founds Arkansas Post

1819
Governor Miller arrives in Arkansas Territory

1836
Arkansas becomes a state

1830-1840
Native Americans travel the Trail of Tears

1840s
Pioneers settle in Arkansas

WHAT HAPPENED

You have already read about some of the first people to live in our state, but the whole story has not been told. In this unit you will read about the European people who explored the land of Arkansas. You will also read about the pioneers who built new lives here, and who worked to make Arkansas part of the United States.

UNIT 3

EXPLORERS AND PIONEERS

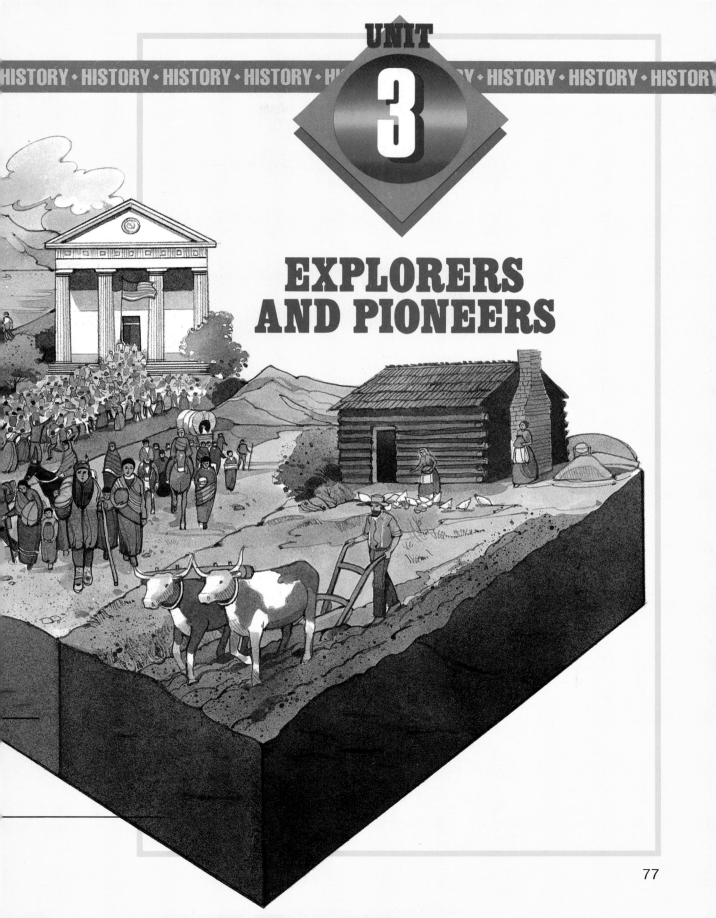

CHAPTER 5

THE EUROPEAN EXPLORERS

FOCUS

My first evening on arriving at this village has been to learn from the Quapaw Indians the course of the river and about the nations that live along it; they know the river only up to the Rock, which they estimate at 20 days journey. . . .

These words were written more than 200 years ago by a French visitor to the land of Arkansas. He was one of the first Europeans to explore the Arkansas River. After almost a month, he finally reached the "Rock"—the site of present-day Little Rock. In this chapter you will read about these first European explorers.

1 Hernando de Soto

Key Vocabulary   **Key People**

expedition   slavery   Hernando de Soto

Read Aloud

They say that gold, silver, and many pearls are there.

In the 1500s many people in Europe came to believe that North America was full of gold and jewels. Some set out to search for these treasures. One of these explorers, who wrote the words above, was led by his search to the land of Arkansas. You will read about him in this lesson.

Read for Purpose

1. **WHAT YOU KNOW:** What might make you want to explore a place?
2. **WHAT YOU WILL LEARN:** Who was Hernando de Soto, and which parts of the land of Arkansas did he explore?

THE SEARCH FOR GOLD

After Christopher Columbus reached America in 1492, rulers in Europe began sending explorers to these lands across the ocean. The explorers were eager to claim these regions for their own countries. They also hoped to find gold and silver. Such precious metals would make both their countries and themselves rich.

Spanish explorers discovered great amounts of these treasures in South America. Ship after ship returned to Spain loaded with riches. Encouraged by this success, the rulers of Spain sent expeditions (ek spi dish' ənz) into North America, too. An expedition is a journey made for a special purpose.

HERNANDO DE SOTO

One such expedition to North America was led by a Spanish explorer named **Hernando de Soto** (er nän' dō də sō' tō). De Soto had first crossed the Atlantic when he was 19. Over the next 15 years he helped the Spanish to conquer the lands that are modern-day Panama and Peru. After returning to Spain he was appointed "Governor of Florida" in 1538.

"Florida" was the name the Spanish rulers gave to the area that is today the southeastern United States. This area included the land of Arkansas.

In 1539 De Soto led 622 men into the area that he was supposed to govern. His expedition first landed in the present-day state of Florida. The search for gold had begun! But as they traveled north and west, the Spaniards found little in the way of riches.

For two years De Soto led his men through the southeastern United States. At least 200 of his soldiers were killed fighting the Indians or died of disease. The Spaniards also lost one third of their horses and most of their baggage. Finally, in May 1541, the frustrated members of the expedition reached the eastern banks of a wide, muddy river— the Mississippi. One of De Soto's men described his commander as the men peered across the river.

> *I saw De Soto with a jacket all broken at the sides. His flesh showed through. He had no hat; was barefoot and without breeches; [wore] a sword without a sheath; and thus he marched in all that frost and cold.*

The Spaniards still hoped to discover gold on the other side of the Mississippi. Over the next month they built four barges, or flat-bottomed boats. At the end of June 1541 they were ready to cross the river. On the other side lay the land of Arkansas.

DE SOTO IN ARKANSAS

De Soto's men landed south of what is now West Memphis. For over a year the Spaniards wandered through the land of our state. Historians do not agree on the exact route of De Soto's expedition. However, they have been able to piece together much of his journey. Look at the map on page 81 to see where De Soto's expedition traveled in Arkansas. Which of Arkansas's rivers did the expedition cross?

As soon as they landed, the Spaniards encountered groups of Native Americans. The Spaniards were impressed by the many Indian settlements they saw. The land was "full of great towns," one soldier wrote.

De Soto and his men traveled from village to village. Most of the Indians were friendly. However, the Spaniards

Hernando de Soto led an **expedition** in search of gold and silver through the land of Arkansas.

were more interested in gold and silver than friendship. They threatened the Native Americans, stole food and clothing from them, burned their villages, and forced many of them into slavery. Slavery is the practice of one person owning another.

Sometimes the Indians tried to fight back, but their weapons were no match for the Spanish guns. One member of the expedition remembered a battle with the Caddo Indians.

> They got up on the housetops, where they endeavoured to defend themselves with their bows and arrows. . . . Of the Indians 15 were slain, and 40 women and boys made prisoners. . . .

The expedition crisscrossed the land of Arkansas, marched into what is now Texas, and then returned to Arkansas. The Spaniards continued to die from diseases such as malaria, or from fighting battles. By the spring of 1542 nearly half the expedition was gone.

Tired and disappointed, the Spaniards made their way back east to the Mississippi River. After burying De Soto, who had died south of present-day Helena, the expedition left Arkansas. The surviving soldiers marched south to Mexico.

A FIRST ATTEMPT

De Soto's expedition was the first attempt by Europeans to explore the land of Arkansas. But because De Soto had not located any gold or silver, his expedition was considered a failure. For many years the rulers of Spain lost interest in the region.

It would be more than 130 years before the next Europeans traveled to Arkansas. You will read about these explorers in the next lesson.

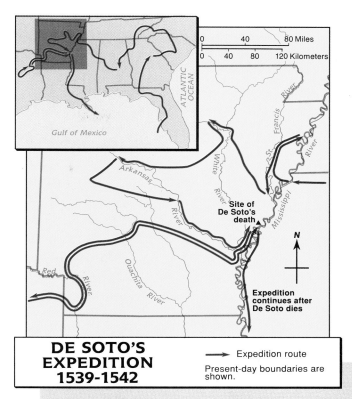

DE SOTO'S EXPEDITION 1539-1542

→ Expedition route

Present-day boundaries are shown.

MAP SKILL: De Soto and his men traveled slowly through present-day Arkansas. Which other states did De Soto explore?

 Check Your Reading

1. Why did European countries send explorers to America?

2. Which area did the Spanish rulers call "Florida"?

3. What did Hernando de Soto expect to find on his expedition through the land of Arkansas?

4. **GEOGRAPHY SKILL:** If you were De Soto, why might you lead your expedition through the southeastern part of our state rather than the northwestern part?

5. **THINKING SKILL:** How were the lives of Arkansas's Indians different from those of the European explorers? How were they similar?

2 The French Explorers

READ TO LEARN

Key Vocabulary

colony
mouth

Key People

Jacques Marquette
Louis Joliet
Robert La Salle

Key Places

New France

Read Aloud

In the fog, from the right bank, we heard Indian war cries and the beat of drums. . . . [We] did not doubt there was a village. We came upon it . . . and were well treated.

This was how a French explorer described an encounter with the Quapaw Indians. In this lesson you will read about the first French explorers to come to the land of Arkansas.

Read for Purpose

1. **WHAT YOU KNOW:** Why were people from Europe interested in exploring the land of Arkansas?
2. **WHAT YOU WILL LEARN:** Which parts of Arkansas did French explorers visit, and what did they accomplish?

A FRENCH COLONY

During the 1500s other European nations began to follow Spain's example in America. France, England, and Holland all sent expeditions in search of land and wealth.

French explorers soon claimed most of present-day Canada. In 1608 the French started a colony called New France in their new territory. A colony is a settlement that is ruled by another country. Today Quebec City is located on the site of this first colony. In 1673 a French expedition set out from New France and traveled down the Mississippi River.

MARQUETTE AND JOLIET

This expedition was led by Jacques Marquette (zhäk mär ket′), a priest, and Louis Joliet (lü′ ē jō′ lē et), a fur trapper. Unlike the Spanish explorer De Soto, the two Frenchmen chose to travel with a small group. Their expedition of seven people hoped to follow the river to its mouth—the part where a river empties into another body of water. They planned to claim all the surrounding land for France.

After paddling hundreds of miles down the Mississippi, the expedition saw the shore of present-day Arkansas to the west. They explored the area

82

where the Arkansas River empties into the Mississippi. At a point not far from the place where De Soto had died over 131 years earlier, the French were met by a group of Quapaw.

The French, however, treated the Indians better than the Spanish had. Both Marquette and Joliet had lived among the Indians in Canada. They understood their culture much better than De Soto had. For this reason the French explorers and the Quapaw immediately became friendly. Marquette even tried to learn the Quapaw language, although, as he wrote, "I never could pronounce a word of it."

The Quapaw invited the French to come to their village. Marquette described their visit in his journal.

They had prepared a kind of scaffold [platform] *to receive us, adorned with fine mats, upon which we sat down with the old men and warriors. . . . The Indians are very courteous, and give freely of what they have, but they are afraid to go hunting on account of their enemies.*

The Quapaw told Joliet and Marquette that the mouth of the Mississippi was not far away. Five days of travel south would bring them to the point where the river emptied into the Gulf of Mexico. But this journey would take them through dangerous country. The Quapaw's enemies might kill or capture the explorers.

The two leaders wondered what to do. As Marquette wrote in his journal, he and Joliet discussed at length "whether to proceed further, or return to Canada, content with the discoveries we had made."

Rather than face the Quapaw's enemies, the two decided to return home. Marquette and Joliet did not find the mouth of the Mississippi River. However, they accomplished something even more important—they established friendly relations with a number of Native American groups along the river. And within ten years, another expedition set off to reach the mouth of the Mississippi.

LA SALLE'S EXPEDITION

This expedition was led by Robert La Salle (räb′ ərt lə sal′). La Salle, who came from a wealthy family, had been a brilliant young professor of mathematics and science in France. When he was only 23, his eagerness for adventure brought him to America.

La Salle thought that France needed to strengthen its claims in North America. One way to do this would be to sail down the Mississippi to the river's mouth. Like Marquette and Joliet,

Marquette and Joliet explored the Mississippi River with only five other people. They carried their canoes over rocks and logs in the river.

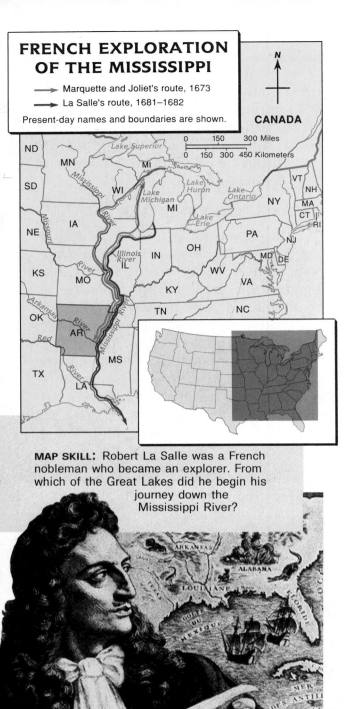

FRENCH EXPLORATION OF THE MISSISSIPPI

→ Marquette and Joliet's route, 1673
→ La Salle's route, 1681–1682

Present-day names and boundaries are shown.

CANADA

0   150   300 Miles
0 150 300 450 Kilometers

MAP SKILL: Robert La Salle was a French nobleman who became an explorer. From which of the Great Lakes did he begin his journey down the Mississippi River?

La Salle planned to claim all the surrounding land for France.

La Salle's expedition included more people than that of Joliet and Marquette. He took soldiers, Indians, and fur traders—54 people in all. In 1681 the group set off down the Mississippi.

On March 13, 1682, the expedition stopped at a place in Arkansas near the site of present-day Helena. La Salle, like Marquette and Joliet, received a warm welcome from the Quapaw. "They regaled [entertained] us with the best they had," wrote one member of the expedition.

La Salle and his companions traveled from one Quapaw village to the next. One man recorded his impressions of the Quapaw's land.

> *Their country is very beautiful. . . . Buffaloes, deer, stags, bears, [and] turkeys are very numerous. They have very little snow during the winter, and the ice is not thicker than a dollar.*

After leaving the land of Arkansas, La Salle continued down the Mississippi River. Look at the map on this page to trace his route down the river. On April 9, 1682, he reached the Gulf of Mexico. La Salle claimed the entire Mississippi Valley for France. He named the area "Louisiana" in honor of the French king Louis XIV.

LA SALLE'S LAST EXPEDITION

La Salle wanted to establish a colony close to the mouth of the river. To do this, he first needed Louis XIV's permission. He returned to France, where the king approved his idea.

But La Salle's dream was not to be fulfilled. In 1684 he sailed from France to Louisiana with an expedition of 400 colonists. Then, before he reached his

La Salle and his men traded beads and other goods with the Caddo Indians in exchange for weapons and clothing.

destination, disaster struck. His ships missed the mouth of the Mississippi and were wrecked off the coast of Texas.

La Salle and other members of the expedition managed to swim ashore. For almost two years they searched for the mouth of the Mississippi. Finally his companions, who blamed their leader for the failure of the expedition, killed La Salle.

A EUROPEAN SETTLEMENT

You have read about the first French explorers in the land of Arkansas. Throughout the 1670s and 1680s these explorers journeyed down the Mississippi River. They claimed the lands they explored for France. In the next lesson you will read about the first European settlement in our state.

Check Your Reading

1. How did Marquette and Joliet treat the Indians of Arkansas?
2. Who was La Salle, and what did he hope to achieve by sailing down to the mouth of the Mississippi River?
3. How did the area of Louisiana get its name?
4. **GEOGRAPHY SKILL:** Look at the map on page 84 to see which present-day states La Salle passed on his way down the Mississippi River.
5. **THINKING SKILL:** Compare and contrast the ways in which the Spanish and the French treated Arkansas's Native Americans.

Reading Time Lines

Key Vocabulary

time line
decade
century

You have read that Native Americans reached the land of Arkansas thousands of years ago. You have also read how, hundreds of years ago, Europeans explored the Mississippi River.

When you see phrases such as "500 years ago" or "in 1492," you are reading about events that took place in the past. Keeping track of dates and events can be difficult. A useful way to see how dates and events fit together is with a time line —a diagram that shows when events took place.

A time line also lets you see the order in which events took place. It shows you which event occurred first, second, third, and so on. Using a time line, you can also figure out how much time passed between one event and another.

Reading a Historical Time Line

The time line below includes some of the dates and events that you have read about in Lessons 1 and 2 of this chapter. Each date is marked with a red dot. The name of each event is written beneath the date on which it happened.

Notice that the time line covers a 200-year time period. The earliest date on the time line is on the left, and the latest date is on the right. Therefore you read a time line from left to right. Which is the earliest date on the time line? Which is the latest date?

A time line is divided into equal parts. Each part shows a time period such as 5, 10, or 500 years. How many years does each part include on the historical time line below?

Decades and Centuries

We often divide time into 10-year and 100-year periods. A 10-year period is called a decade. Have you ever heard people talk of the 1960s or the 1980s? Each of those time periods is a decade. Which decade are we living in now?

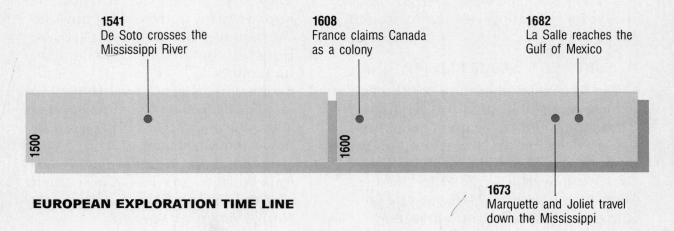

1541
De Soto crosses the Mississippi River

1608
France claims Canada as a colony

1682
La Salle reaches the Gulf of Mexico

1500

1600

EUROPEAN EXPLORATION TIME LINE

1673
Marquette and Joliet travel down the Mississippi

CENTURY TIME LINE

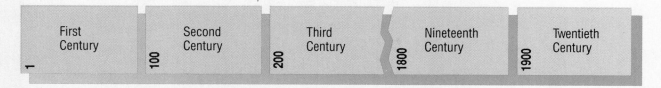

First Century	Second Century	Third Century	Nineteenth Century	Twentieth Century
1	100	200	1800	1900

CALENDAR TIME LINE

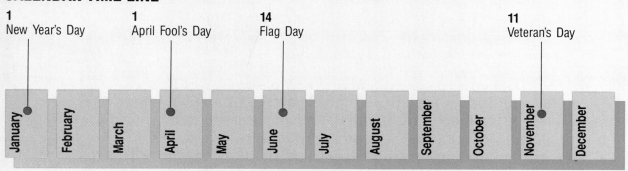

1
New Year's Day

1
April Fool's Day

14
Flag Day

11
Veteran's Day

January · February · March · April · May · June · July · August · September · October · November · December

A 100-year time period is called a **century**. Look at the Century Time Line above. Notice that the first century includes year 1 to year 99. The jagged line after the third century shows that a chunk of time has been left out.

Which is the last century shown on the Century Time Line? Which dates does it cover? Which years does the nineteenth century include?

Making a Time Line

Time lines can be divided into such time periods as an hour, a day, or a week. They can also be divided into time periods as long as 1,000 years. Make a time line of your own, using the calendar year. Place January, the earliest month, on the left, and December, the latest month, on the right. Mark off parts of equal size for each month of the year.

Next, include dates and events within each month. For example, within January you might write *January 1, New Year's Day*. Include other dates and events, such as the beginning of a school vacation, your birthday, or a national holiday. Try to include one event in each month.

Reviewing the Skill

1. Why is a time line useful?
2. Did De Soto reach the Mississippi River before or after La Salle? How can you tell from the time line?
3. How many years passed between the founding of France's colony in Canada and the voyage of Marquette and Joliet down the Mississippi River?

87

3 Under Two Flags

READU TO LEARN

Key Vocabulary

barter
religion
voyageurs
census

Key People

Henri de Tonti
John Law
Bernard de la Harpe

Key Places

Arkansas Post

Read Aloud

Coming to a river and looking over to the further side, we discovered a great cross, and at a small distance from it, a house, built after the French fashion. It is easy to imagine the inward joy we felt at this sight. . . .

The words above were written by a survivor of Robert La Salle's last expedition. After walking all the way from what is now Houston, Texas, this survivor came upon the first European settlement in the land of Arkansas. In this lesson you will read about this settlement and its founder. You will also read about an early exploration of the Arkansas River.

Read for Purpose

1. **WHAT YOU KNOW:** How did the French first claim the land of Arkansas?
2. **WHAT YOU WILL LEARN:** What early attempts did the French and Spanish make to settle the land of Arkansas?

HENRI DE TONTI

You have read about the Spanish and French explorers of the land of Arkansas. These Europeans came to search for gold, or to claim lands for their own countries. None of them stayed for more than a few months.

However, when La Salle first passed through Arkansas in 1682, one member of his expedition liked what he saw. This person was Henri de Tonti (än′ rī də ton′ tī), an Italian who was La Salle's second-in-command. In 1686 De Tonti returned to the land of Arkansas. He planned to claim some land that had been promised to him by the French king. Near the place where the Arkansas River meets the White River, De Tonti founded Arkansas Post. This was our state's first permanent European settlement. For this reason De Tonti is sometimes called the "Father of Modern Arkansas."

Henri de Tonti founded Arkansas Post in 1686 as a place to trade with the Quapaw and other Indian groups.

ARKANSAS POST

In the beginning, only six people lived at Arkansas Post. But it gave French traders traveling from Canada to the Gulf of Mexico a place to stop and rest.

The tiny settlement also helped the French settlers to grow more friendly with the Quapaw. De Tonti, who wore an artificial hand to replace the one he had lost in a battle, was called "Iron Hand" by the Quapaw.

Most importantly, Arkansas Post gave the French control over the nearby Mississippi River. In their hands this waterway became an important trade route. The French settlers would barter (bär′ tər) beads, blankets, and muskets with the Indians in exchange for furs and hides. To barter means to trade goods for other goods. The French shipped these goods upriver to Canada, and then to France.

As Arkansas Post grew, the French decided to teach the Indians the Christian religion. A religion is the way people worship the God or gods they believe in. The French sent a missionary (mish′ ə når ē) to Arkansas Post in

1689. A missionary is a person who teaches his or her religion to others who hold different beliefs.

THE "MISSISSIPPI BUBBLE"

Although the population of Arkansas Post slowly grew beyond six settlers, it always existed mainly as a trading post. In 1717, however, a man from Scotland named John Law decided to found a colony in the land of Arkansas. Law had never visited Arkansas, but he sketched out plans for a large city. He spoke of building factories and recruiting an army to protect the city. To accomplish all this, Law started a company called the Mississippi Company.

In 1717 the French government granted Law about 120 square miles (311 sq km) of land. This area lay just north of the Arkansas River. Law immediately made plans to send almost 10,000 settlers to the territory.

Law planned to sell his idea the same way we do today—by advertising. Although he knew little about

89

Arkansas, he advertised it as "a land of promise." A number of French people responded by investing money in the Mississippi Company. Law persuaded about 700 German settlers to move to the "land of promise." He also sent 300 enslaved Africans to the new colony. These were the first people to be forced to come to Arkansas. You will learn more about enslaved Africans in Arkansas in Chapter 7.

When the German settlers reached their new home they were disappointed. Life in the North American wilderness was much more difficult than Law had promised. By 1723 the discouraged settlers had left. Many of them went south to the coastal region of present-day Louisiana. Today this area is still called the "German Coast."

John Law's dream of a great city along the Arkansas River had grown larger and larger—and then had burst as suddenly as a bubble. For this reason his attempt at settlement is usually called the "Mississippi Bubble."

LA HARPE'S EXPEDITION

Although they founded no large settlements, the French continued to explore the land of Arkansas. One of these explorers was **Bernard de la Harpe** (ber' när də lä härp'). In 1721 La Harpe gathered together an expedition at Arkansas Post. He loaded his supplies—"13 barrels of corn, 3 of beans, and 1 of rice"—into several

SETTLEMENT AND EXPLORATION AROUND 1700

La Harpe's Route, 1721-1722

• Major Native American settlement
■ European settlement

Present-day boundaries are shown.

MAP SKILL: John Law started a community like the one below in 1721. What other European settlement was located near John Law's Colony?

Bernard de la Harpe traveled up the Arkansas River in this type of boat. He found the "little rock" that later became the site of our state's capital, the city of Little Rock.

small boats. Then his group of 22 explorers began paddling up the Arkansas River.

La Harpe planned to trade with the Indians, and may have been looking for gold and silver. He had also heard rumors from the Indians about a giant emerald embedded in a rock farther upstream. La Harpe hoped to find this emerald during his exploration.

After about a month of traveling upstream, La Harpe found the famous rock. Although it had a greenish color, it was not made of emerald, but of sandstone. The disappointed La Harpe called it the "little rock." This became the site of the city of Little Rock.

La Harpe continued up the river. About 2.5 miles (4 km) north of the "little rock," his expedition ran into difficulty.

> Our small boat, which had taken the lead, was dashed upon a log by the violence of the current, so that it turned over. The men hung to the log, but all that was in the boat was lost....

Look at the map on page 90 to trace the route of La Harpe's trip. If these explorers had continued up the Arkansas River, which present-day state would they have reached?

Other French hunters and trappers called **voyageurs** (voi ə zhərz′) also explored the land of Arkansas. A voyageur would often trade or transport goods for a fur company. These traders continued to have friendly relations with the Native Americans of Arkansas. They also left behind a scattering of place-names in our state, such as Petit Jean (pe tē′ jēn) and Des Arc (dez′ ärk). But French rule in Arkansas would soon end.

SPANISH RULE IN ARKANSAS

In 1762 France signed a treaty with Spain. In this treaty the French gave up their claim to the Mississippi Valley. Three years later the Spanish appointed a governor to rule the vast area of Louisiana. As you have read, this area included the land of Arkansas.

Now the Spanish flag flew over the rough settlement near the Arkansas River. The new rulers gave Arkansas Post a new name—Fort Carlos III. Otherwise, little changed. The French soldiers who had served under the French flag now served under the Spanish one. Settlement of the area may have actually slowed during this time, because Spanish law did not

Fur trappers, also known as **voyageurs**, journeyed through the land of Arkansas in search of beavers, rabbits, and other animals.

The non-Indian population of Arkansas continued to grow very slowly under Spanish rule. In 1785 a **census** (sen' səs) showed only 196 Europeans in the area. A census is a count of the population in a certain area. Other settlements founded during this period included Helena, Hot Springs, and West Memphis.

In 1800 the land of Arkansas changed hands once more. In a secret treaty Spain gave Louisiana back to France. The people in Arkansas, however, knew nothing of this change. As far as they could tell, they were still under Spanish rule.

THE RULES OF FRANCE AND SPAIN

During the years after the founding of Arkansas Post, France and Spain traded Arkansas back and forth. Neither nation paid much attention to their faraway land. But soon a third flag would fly over Arkansas Post. In the next chapter you will read about how our land became part of the United States of America.

allow anyone to travel more than 20 miles (32 km) without permission.

In 1783 the American Revolution briefly touched this sleepy outpost. A British officer named James Colbert led an army of 100 Europeans and 14 Chickasaw Indians against the fort. The Spanish commander later described how he and his soldiers had defended the fort.

> With the four Quapaw who were fortunately in this post, this gave me 14 men in all. I gave the orders to yell as the Indians do when they attack. Our enemy, upon hearing the shouts and at the same time a volley, retired quickly to the place where they had the camp. . . .

Check Your Reading

1. What was the first permanent European settlement in the land of Arkansas, and who was its founder?
2. List three reasons for La Harpe's journey up the Arkansas River.
3. **GEOGRAPHY SKILL:** How far north did La Harpe explore?
4. **THINKING SKILL:** Imagine that you are a businessperson like John Law and that you are trying to persuade settlers to come to the land of Arkansas. List five points you might include in your "advertisement."

REVIEWING VOCABULARY

Number a sheet of paper from 1 to 5. Beside each number write the letter of the definition that best matches the word.

1. *barter*
   a. To trap animals for their furs
   b. To teach your religion to another person with different beliefs
   c. To trade goods for other goods
2. *census*
   a. A count of the population
   b. A general agreement
   c. The place where a river empties into another body of water
3. *colony*
   a. A group of people
   b. A country that sends out expeditions to explore new lands
   c. A settlement ruled by another country
4. *expedition*
   a. The number of people in a place
   b. A journey made for a special purpose
   c. A type of fur trapping
5. *missionary*
   a. A French hunter or trapper
   b. A person who teaches his or her religion to others who have different beliefs
   c. An explorer

REVIEWING FACTS

Number a sheet of paper from 1 to 5. Beside each number write the letter of the description that matches the person.

1. Hernando de Soto
2. Jacques Marquette
3. Henri de Tonti
4. Bernard de la Harpe
5. Quapaw
   a. Founded Arkansas Post
   b. Native Americans who welcomed French explorers
   c. Explorer who found the "little rock"
   d. Spanish explorer who searched for gold
   e. French priest who searched for the mouth of the Mississippi River

WRITING ABOUT MAIN IDEAS

1. **Writing a Paragraph:** Why did so much time pass between De Soto's expedition and the expedition of Marquette and Joliet? Write a paragraph explaining the reasons.
2. **Writing an Opinion Paragraph:** Review the careers of Henri de Tonti, John Law, and Bernard de la Harpe. Which man do you think did the most to help Arkansas? Write a paragraph telling which man you chose, and explain why.

BUILDING SKILLS: READING TIME LINES

Use the time line on page 86 to answer these questions.

1. What do time lines show?
2. Which came first—the expedition of Marquette and Joliet or that of De Soto? How can you tell?
3. In 1686 Henri de Tonti founded Arkansas Post. Where would you put this event on the time line?
4. Why is it useful to know how to read a time line?

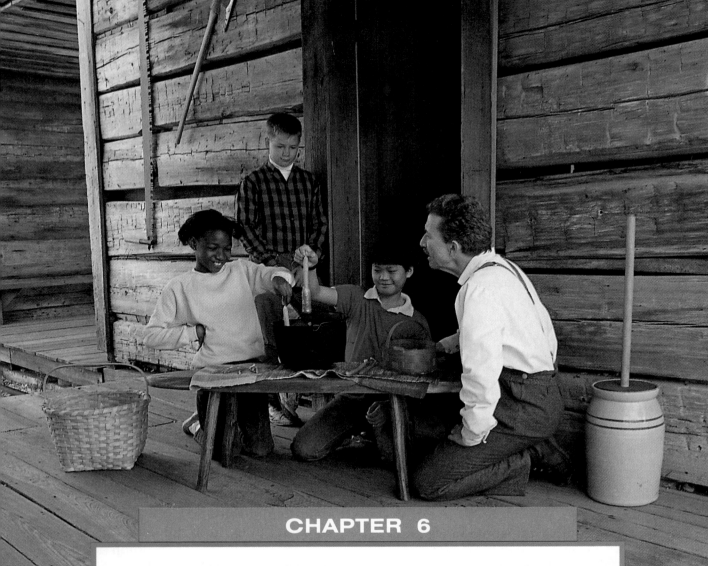

FROM TERRITORY TO STATE

FOCUS

*I was born in a Kingdom/Raised in an Empire/
[Reached] Manhood in a Territory/Am now citizen of a State/
And have never been 100 miles from where I live.*

These words were written by John Patterson, the first European American to be born in what is now Arkansas. As he said, he was born in the "Kingdom" of Spain, raised in the French "Empire," and lived the rest of his life in the "Territory" and "State" of Arkansas. In this chapter you will read about some of these periods in our state's history.

READ TO LEARN

Key Vocabulary

Louisiana Purchase
New Madrid Earthquake
speculators

Key People

Thomas Jefferson
James Miller
Robert Crittenden

Key Places

Orleans Territory
Louisiana Territory
Arkansas Territory

Read Aloud

My father, with two other families, moved from Middle Tennessee. . . . That was in 1814. We came to Arkansas Post in a flatboat. . . . Then we moved to Big Mulberry and lived there two years in all the luxuries of life that a new country could afford, such as buffalo, bear, deer, and elk and fish and honey. . . .

These are the words of John Billingsley, whose family settled in the land of Arkansas soon after it became part of the United States. You will read about the arrival of settlers like John Billingsley in this lesson.

Read for Purpose

1. **WHAT YOU KNOW:** Have you ever made a good bargain?
2. **WHAT YOU WILL LEARN:** How did Arkansas grow when it became part of the United States?

THE LOUISIANA PURCHASE

In the last chapter you read that the land of Arkansas was first claimed by France and then by Spain. In 1800 it became French land once again. But this time, it soon was to become part of a third nation—the United States of America.

In 1800 the people of the United States had elected a new President, Thomas Jefferson. When Jefferson learned that France had regained control of the Mississippi Valley, he grew worried. What if the French closed the Mississippi River to Americans? How would American traders and settlers travel through the area?

Jefferson offered to buy a small piece of land near the mouth of the Mississippi from the French. Imagine Jefferson's surprise when Napoleon, the French ruler, offered to sell him all of Louisiana! At that time this area included the entire western half of the Mississippi Valley, from New Orleans up to Canada. It also included the land of Arkansas.

95

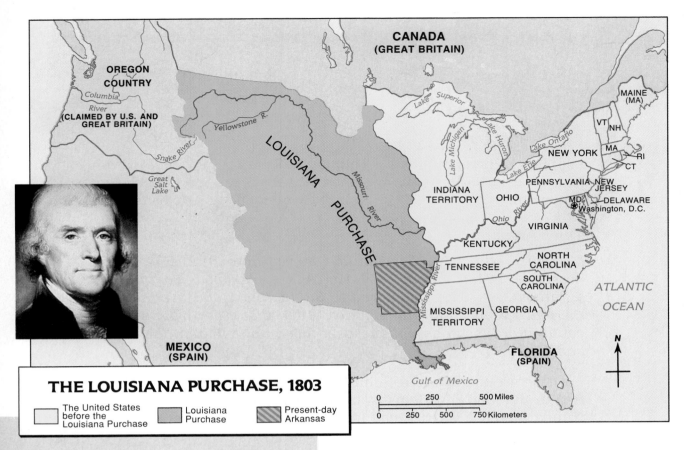

THE LOUISIANA PURCHASE, 1803

- The United States before the Louisiana Purchase
- Louisiana Purchase
- Present-day Arkansas

MAP SKILL: Thomas Jefferson's treaty with France, the Louisiana Purchase, doubled the size of the United States. What was the eastern boundary of this area?

THE LOUISIANA TERRITORY

Jefferson accepted Napoleon's offer. In 1803 the two nations signed a treaty called the Louisiana Purchase. The United States paid the French $15 million for 850,000 square miles (2,201,500 sq km) of land. At less than three cents per acre, the price was a great bargain. One French leader told the Americans: "You have made a noble bargain for yourselves, and I suppose you will make the best of it."

In 1804 the United States Congress divided this new land into two parts. The Orleans Territory covered most of what is today the state of Louisiana.

The Louisiana Territory included the rest of the western Mississippi Valley. The land of Arkansas was part of the Louisiana Territory. Find Arkansas on the map on this page.

NEW SETTLERS

Few people settled in the land of Arkansas during its early days as part of the Louisiana Territory. Settlers coming from the East wanted to avoid the swamps of the Mississippi Alluvial Plain. For this reason many people chose to start farms farther north, in the present-day state of Missouri.

New settlers had other problems besides swamps. On December 16, 1811, a large area of northeastern Arkansas was rocked by the New Madrid Earthquake. This was the most violent earthquake ever recorded in

North America. The ground rumbled and shook, causing church bells to ring hundreds of miles away. Some observers claimed that the Mississippi River ran upstream during the quake.

However, the War of 1812, which the United States fought against Great Britain, brought new settlers to Arkansas. In order to get people to join the army, our government had offered each soldier 160 acres (65 ha) of land. Much of this land was in Arkansas. If the soldiers didn't want to settle in Arkansas, they could sell their land to other people who did.

THE ARKANSAS TERRITORY

By 1818 the population of Arkansas had risen to 14,000. The area had been divided into five counties. The people of these counties began to think about whether Arkansas should become a separate territory.

Why would the settlers want Arkansas to become a separate territory? For one thing, the Arkansas Territory would have its own court system. This would help Arkansans to preserve law and order. In addition, the national government would help to build roads and levees throughout the territory. Speculators, or people who make money selling land, also welcomed the idea of the Arkansas Territory, since it would attract more settlers.

In 1819 Congress voted to establish the Arkansas Territory. The territory included all the land that is now Arkansas, along with much of present-day Oklahoma. President James Monroe appointed James Miller of New Hampshire to be the first territorial governor. He also appointed Robert Crittenden of Kentucky as the first territorial secretary.

Robert Crittenden (*left*) and James Miller (*right*) were appointed to lead the government of the Arkansas Territory. President Monroe signed the paper appointing Crittenden.

A GROWING TERRITORY

You have just read about how Arkansas became part of the United States. After years of slow growth, this rough land finally began to attract settlers. In the next lesson you will read more about the Arkansas Territory and how it became our nation's twenty-fifth state.

Check Your Reading

1. How did the land of Arkansas become part of the United States?
2. Why did Arkansas's population grow so slowly before 1812?
3. Why did settlers want Arkansas to become a separate territory?
4. GEOGRAPHY SKILL: Name three of our present-day states that were part of the Louisiana Purchase.
5. THINKING SKILL: What were two immediate effects of the New Madrid Earthquake?

Recognizing Point of View

Key Vocabulary
point of view

Two thirsty people were each given a glass of water. "Great, it's half full," said one. "Oh no, it's half empty," remarked the other. Each received the same amount of water, but each had a different response. Their responses showed different **points of view**.

Point of view is the way a person looks at or feels about something. The person who saw the glass as half full probably had a positive outlook on life. The other person was more likely to have a gloomy view of life.

When you read a story, it is important to be able to identify the writer's point of view. Recognizing how a person feels about a subject lets you judge how true a picture you are getting.

Trying the Skill
Below are two reports on the Louisiana Purchase of 1803. Read both reports. Then look for clues to the point of view of the writer of **Report A**.

Report A
We Americans can celebrate our good fortune. Our diplomats in Paris have won a great victory. With the stroke of a pen, we have more than doubled our territory. The future growth of our young nation is certain.

Report B
We have made a poor bargain. The French have trapped us into buying millions of acres of worthless land. We cannot afford $15 million, and we will never be able to absorb so much land into our young nation.

1. What is the point of view of the writer of **Report A**?
2. How do you know?

The steps on the left will help you to recognize a writer's point of view. The example on the right shows one way that you can apply these steps to **Report A**.

One Way to Recognize Point of View	Example
1. Identify the subject or topic.	The subject of **Report A** is the Louisiana Purchase.
2. Identify statements of fact.	To identify statements of fact, you can read about where and how the Louisiana Purchase was negotiated and how much land was involved.
3. Identify statements of opinion.	Calling the Louisiana Purchase a "great victory" and claiming that the "future growth of our young nation is certain" are both statements of opinion.
4. Identify words or phrases that suggest what the writer feels or believes about the subject.	Phrases such as "good fortune" and "great victory" suggest strong approval.
5. Identify parts of the subject that the writer does not talk about but probably could have.	The writer does not mention any problems that might be connected with the Louisiana Purchase.
6. Summarize the view or position expressed by the writer.	The writer's point of view is strongly in favor of the Louisiana Purchase.

Applying the Skill

Reread **Report B** on page 98.

1. Which of the following sentences is a statement of fact?
   a. The Louisiana Purchase was a poor bargain.
   b. The Louisiana Purchase involved millions of acres of land.
   c. The French trapped the Americans into buying millions of acres of worthless land.

2. Which fact did the writer leave out in order to make a more convincing report?
   a. The United States gained millions of acres and doubled its territory at less than three cents an acre.
   b. The French approved of the Louisiana Purchase.
   c. No one knew exactly which lands were included in the Louisiana Purchase.

3. What is the point of view of the writer of **Report B**?

Reviewing the Skill

1. What is a person's point of view?
2. What are some of the ways in which you can identify a person's point of view?
3. Why is it important to recognize a person's point of view when you read or hear a story?

2 Growth and Statehood

READ TO LEARN

Key Vocabulary

legislature   constitution
statehood   plantation

Key People

William Woodruff
Ambrose Sevier

Read Aloud

This is a fine healthy state, when you get back from the Mississippi. There are many [growing] towns in it and it is settling fast. I expect to settle in some healthy little town on the Arkansas River, bye and bye, and have a share in a store.

This is how one settler described Arkansas in 1851. In this chapter you will read about how Arkansas grew from a territory to a "fine healthy state."

Read for Purpose

1. **WHAT YOU KNOW:** How did Arkansas become part of the United States?
2. **WHAT YOU WILL LEARN:** How did Arkansas grow during its early years as a territory and as a state?

A GROWING TERRITORY

The early years of the Arkansas Territory were years of change and growth. As you have read, settlers began to pour into the new territory. But other important events also took place.

One was the founding of Arkansas's first newspaper. In 1819, the same year that Congress created the Arkansas Territory, a young man from New York named William Woodruff arrived in the territorial capital, Arkansas Post. Woodruff had brought a printing press with him. The first issue of his newspaper, the *Arkansas Gazette*, appeared on November 20, 1819. It reported that Governor Miller would soon reach the capital: "He is probably now on his way, and may be expected here as soon as the water rises." The *Arkansas Gazette*, the oldest newspaper west of the Mississippi, is still printed today.

Another important event was the change in the location of the territorial capital. Our legislature (lej' is lā chər) first met in Arkansas Post in 1819. A legislature is a group of people who have the power to make laws.

At their very first meeting the members of the territorial legislature decided to move the capital. The area around Arkansas Post was swampy and full of mosquitoes. Also, Arkansas

Post was located at the eastern edge of the Arkansas Territory. The members of the legislature thought that the capital should be located closer to the center of Arkansas.

They chose a site farther up the Arkansas River for the new location. There was no town or village there. However, the site chosen by the legislature was alongside a well-known landmark—the "little rock" that Bernard de la Harpe had discovered nearly 100 years earlier.

This landmark gave the capital its name. Little Rock grew quickly. Eight years later a settler named Hiram Whittington wrote this description of the town.

It is situated on the south bank of the Arkansas, [and] contains about 60 buildings, 6 brick, 8 frame, the balance log cabins. . . . The trees are not cut down in the town yet; instead of streets we walk in cow trails from one house to another.

You can see some of these buildings at the Arkansas Territorial Restoration in Little Rock. You can also visit the Old State House, which was built between 1833 and 1840 as a meeting place for Arkansas's legislature.

AN ARKANSAS CONSTITUTION

Throughout the territorial period, more and more settlers arrived from eastern states. Although most of these newcomers lived in frontier areas, small towns like Little Rock and Helena became centers for trade.

Some Arkansans believed that Arkansas was ready for statehood. In other words, they thought that Arkansas Territory should become a state. In 1833 Ambrose Sevier (am' brōz sə vîr') was

William Woodruff (*left*) started the *Arkansas Gazette*, the first newspaper west of the Mississippi. His friend, Ambrose Sevier (*right*), represented Arkansas Territory in Congress.

Arkansas's delegate to Congress. He asked Congress to allow Arkansas to become a state.

As a first step toward statehood, every territory needed to write its own constitution (kon sti tü' shən). A constitution is a plan of government. Arkansans from all 30 counties arrived in Little Rock to work out this plan. By January 1836 the first Arkansas constitution had been written and was sent to Congress for approval.

THE QUESTION OF SLAVERY

Once the members of Congress received Arkansas's constitution, they argued for a long time about whether Arkansas should become a state. One thing they argued about was slavery.

As you read in Chapter 5, slavery is the practice of one person owning

Many enslaved people in Arkansas lived in small houses. They worked in the cotton fields of large **plantations**.

another. When Hernando de Soto's expedition came to Arkansas in 1539, the Spaniards forced a number of Native Americans into slavery. However, most of the enslaved people in our nation's history have been from Africa.

As early as the 1600s, Africans were brought to North America. At first they worked on farms and in towns all over the continent. Over the years, however, slavery became less common in the northern states. At the same time more and more slaves were forced to work on the **plantations** and small farms of the southern states. A plantation is a very large farm that usually grows only a single crop.

By the time of the Louisiana Purchase, when Arkansas became part of the United States, the northern states had passed laws against slavery. In Arkansas, however, slavery was still allowed. In 1820, one year after the creation of the Arkansas Territory, Arkansans held 1,617 slaves. Ten years later, the number had climbed to 4,576. You will read more about slavery in Arkansas in Chapter 7.

The constitution that Arkansas sent to Congress in 1836 allowed slavery to continue. For this reason some members of Congress opposed the idea of statehood for Arkansas. They believed that if the United States admitted another state in which slavery was legal, the balance between slave states and free states would be upset.

STATEHOOD

Congress finally resolved this difficult issue by admitting Michigan, a free state, on the same day that it admitted Arkansas, a slave state. On June 15, 1836, an excited Ambrose

Sevier sent a letter to William Woodruff, editor of the *Arkansas Gazette.*

> *This day the President signed the bill for admission of the States of Arkansas and Michigan into the Union. . . . They will be approved today or tomorrow.*

On that same day Arkansas became the twenty-fifth state to join the United States of America. But as you will read in Chapter 7, this compromise was only a temporary answer to the question of slavery.

NEW LANDS, NEW SETTLERS

In the years after Arkansas became a state, the stream of new settlers turned into a great flood. Look at the graph on this page. It shows the number of people living in Arkansas during several time periods. How many people lived in Arkansas in 1820? As you can see, the population had reached 30,000 by the year 1830.

People from the nearby states of Kentucky and Tennessee were eager to buy our fertile land, which the national government was selling for as little as $1 per acre. As new settlers poured across the Mississippi, one Arkansan compared "the banks of that majestic river to the streets of a great city, with steamboats always in sight. . . . "

Arkansas had also become a stopping place for people on their way to Texas, which was opened for settlement in the 1840s. Others stopped here on their way to Mexico, against which the United States fought a war from 1846 to 1847. Thousands of eager settlers passed through our state, liked what they saw, and stayed. By 1860 the population of the state of Arkansas would reach 435,000.

GRAPH SKILL: The Old State House, where our state's **legislature** first met, was completed in 1840. What was the population of Arkansas in that year?

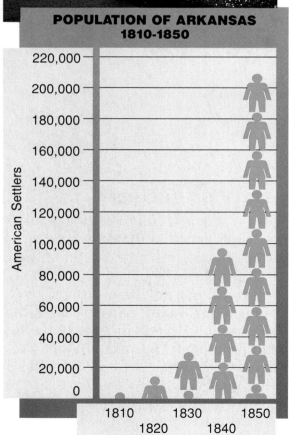

POPULATION OF ARKANSAS 1810-1850

American Settlers

220,000
200,000
180,000
160,000
140,000
120,000
100,000
80,000
60,000
40,000
20,000
0

1810   1830   1850
   1820   1840

Settlers arrived in wagons packed with all of their belongings. Tools such as (*from left to right*) the drawing knife, froe, and broadaxe were needed to survive in their new homes.

A STATE ON THE RISE

You have just read how Arkansas grew rapidly during its days as a territory and as a state. Thousands of new settlers flocked to this fertile land. They built farms and towns, and founded our state capital at Little Rock. Along with this growth, however, came problems. One was slavery. Another was the treatment of Arkansas's Native Americans. In the next lesson you will read about how these Native Americans lost their lands in Arkansas during the 1800s.

Check Your Reading

1. Who was William Woodruff, and why was he important?
2. Identify two reasons that Arkansas's first territorial legislature moved our capital to Little Rock.
3. How did the issue of slavery affect the discussion of statehood for Arkansas?
4. **GEOGRAPHY SKILL:** How did Little Rock's location make it a good choice for the territorial capital?
5. **THINKING SKILL:** Read the Read Aloud section on page 100. Which parts of this statement are fact? Which parts are opinion?

READ TO LEARN

Key Vocabulary

Trail of Tears

Key People

Sequoyah
Sarasen

Key Places

Indian Territory

Read Aloud

The land we now live on belonged to our forefathers. If we leave it, where shall we go to? All of my nation, friends and relatives are there buried. [I] myself am old, and in the same place I wish to deposit my bones.

These words were spoken by a Quapaw chief when he was told to leave Arkansas. His statement reflected the feelings of many Native Americans who were forced to move from their homeland. In this lesson you will read about the Indian groups who lost their lands in Arkansas.

Read for Purpose

1. **WHAT YOU KNOW:** How would you feel if you were forced to leave your home?
2. **WHAT YOU WILL LEARN:** What happened to the Native American groups living in Arkansas when the settlers arrived?

CHANGING WAYS OF LIFE

In Chapter 4 you read that the first European explorers found three major Indian groups living in the land of Arkansas. These groups were the Caddo, the Quapaw, and the Osage. As more and more American settlers came to Arkansas, these groups were affected in different ways.

THE QUAPAW AND THE CADDO

The lives of the Quapaw were soon changed by such diseases as smallpox, measles, and cholera. These diseases were brought to the land of Arkansas by European settlers. Because the Quapaw had never been exposed to these diseases before, they became ill much more easily than the Europeans. Many of them died. In 1682 there may have been up to 15,000 Quapaw. By the early 1800s, only 575 men, women, and children remained.

The Caddo, too, suffered from smallpox and measles. A report issued in 1805 described how diseases had reduced "the whole number of what they call warriors of the ancient Caddo nation . . . to about 100."

Fort Smith was built along the Arkansas River to keep peace among the Cherokee and Osage.

THE OSAGE AND OTHER GROUPS

The story of the Osage is different. Because they were constantly on the move, they had less contact with the settlers. This helped them to avoid the diseases that swept through the Quapaw and Caddo villages.

However, the Osage soon encountered a different problem. During the years after 1812, several new Native American groups had arrived in Arkansas. The Cherokee were one such group. As the United States government pushed them off their lands in Tennessee and Georgia, thousands of Cherokee flooded into Arkansas. Sequoyah (si kwoi' ə), a Cherokee who lived in northwest Arkansas during this period, is known for having invented the Cherokee alphabet.

Most of the Cherokee built villages in the Ozark Mountains and the Arkansas River Valley. These lands were the traditional hunting grounds of the Osage. Relations between the two groups quickly became tense.

By 1817 these tensions led the national government to establish Fort Smith at Belle Point. The 70 soldiers at the fort were given the task of keeping peace in northwestern Arkansas.

LOST LANDS

As you have read, the Cherokee and other Indian groups came to live in Arkansas because they had been pushed off their homelands farther east. By 1818 the national government decided that Arkansas, too, should be reserved for white settlers.

The Quapaw were the first to leave. In 1818 they agreed to give up their lands along the Mississippi River and Arkansas River. Six years later they were forced to join the few remaining Caddo who lived along the Red River.

The Quapaw disliked their new home. A Quapaw chief named Sarasen (sar' ə sin) led many of his people back to the lands they had lost. In 1833, however, the Quapaw were forced out of Arkansas altogether. The national government relocated most of them to the Indian Territory. This was a large area of land west of Arkansas. It later became the state of Oklahoma. Look at the map on this page to see the lands given up by the Quapaw.

The Osage and the Caddo met similar fates. By 1835 Arkansas's Native Americans had lost their lands forever.

THE TRAIL OF TEARS

The Quapaw, the Caddo, and the Osage were gone. However, Indians from other states continued to pass through Arkansas on their way to the Indian Territory. Along with the Cherokee, these groups included the Chickasaw, the Choctaw, the Creek, and the Seminole. The route the Cherokee traveled between 1838 and 1839 came to be called the Trail of Tears.

When a huge group of Cherokee marched through our state on their sad journey west, one observer in Little Rock described the Cherokee's misery.

Thousands of them are entirely [without] shoes or cover of any kind for their feet. . . . Many of them die and are thrown by the side of the road.

Of the 17,000 Indians who were forced to leave their homes, perhaps 4,000 died from starvation and disease.

Arkansans today are not proud of the way in which Native Americans were treated. Now we know that it is not right to force people to leave their homes. As Arkansas grew, its people would learn from their mistakes.

A VANISHED PEOPLE

By the mid-1830s the land of Arkansas was emptied of the Indians who had called it home. Many Native Amer-

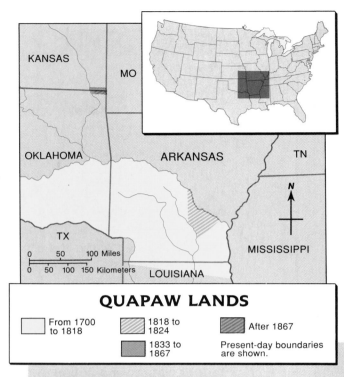

QUAPAW LANDS

From 1700 to 1818	1818 to 1824	After 1867
	1833 to 1867	Present-day boundaries are shown.

MAP SKILL: From 1824 to 1833 the Quapaw lived with the Caddo near the Red River. When did the Quapaw live in the area that is present-day Oklahoma?

icans had died of disease or ill treatment. Those who remained were forced to move west to the Indian Territory.

But for every Native American who left our state, dozens of new settlers arrived from the East. In the next lesson you will read about these settlers.

 Check Your Reading

1. What effect did disease have on Arkansas's Native Americans?
2. Why were there tensions between the Cherokee and the Osage?
3. What was the Trail of Tears?
4. **THINKING SKILL:** Compare and contrast the ways in which Arkansas's Indian groups were affected by the arrival of white settlers.

Should the Native Americans Be Removed?

When the first European explorers reached the land of Arkansas during the 1500s and 1600s, they probably seemed an odd sight to the Native Americans who lived here. These light-skinned strangers spoke an unknown language. They rode on four-legged beasts of a kind that the Indians had never seen before. Nonetheless, the Indians usually treated the Europeans as welcomed guests.

Later, when this land became part of the United States, the friendly relationship started to crumble. More and more American settlers arrived in Arkansas. Many of these newcomers claimed lands on which the Quapaw, the Caddo, and the Osage had lived for hundreds of years. As you have read, the United States government eventually decided that the Indians should be "removed" farther west to the Indian Territory.

Arkansas's Native Americans insisted that they belonged on their lands here. So did groups such as the Cherokee and Chickasaw, who had arrived in Arkansas more recently. Who had the right to live in the land of Arkansas?

The Granger Collection

Two DIFFERENT Viewpoints

The Native American View

Who should have the right to live in Arkansas? Heckaton, a great Quapaw chief during the 1800s, expressed his opposition to the "removal" of the Quapaw to the Indian Territory.

Since you have expressed a desire for us to remove, the tears have flowed freely from my aged eyes. To leave my home soil, and go among other men who are aliens to our race, is throwing us like outcasts upon the world. . . . Have mercy—send us not there.

The Cherokee, too, protested when they were forced to sell their treaty lands in northern Arkansas. One leader wrote this message to the government.

We do not wish to sell any of our land. We have but little and were promised it should be given to us here, and if we do not get it all, then our treaty . . . would be broken.

- According to the Cherokee leader, what had been promised to his people by treaty?

The Government's View

Andrew Jackson, who was elected President of the United States in 1828, believed that the Native Americans could not live peacefully with the white settlers. He made the following statement to a group of Cherokee.

Most of your people are uneducated, and are [certain] to be brought into collision at all times with your white neighbors. . . . How, under these circumstances, can you continue to live in the country you now occupy? Your condition must become worse and worse, and you will ultimately disappear, as so many tribes have done before you. . . .
You have but one remedy within your reach. And that is to remove to the West and join your countrymen, who are already established there.

- What did Andrew Jackson predict would happen to the Cherokee if they refused to move to the Indian Territory?

BUILDING CITIZENSHIP

1. Heckaton argues that Arkansas is his homeland. Do you think that his point is true? Explain your answer.
2. Why do you think the settlers and the Native Americans clashed?
3. Suppose you were a leader in the United States government at that time. What solution would you propose to the problem of who had the right to live on the land in Arkansas?

4 Pioneer Arkansas

READ TO LEARN

Key Vocabulary

pioneer   husking bee
frontier

Read Aloud

If I could rest anywhere it would be in Arkansas. . . .

These words were spoken in 1834 by Davy Crockett, a famous hunter and explorer. Crockett admired the courage, energy, and determination of Arkansas's early settlers. In this lesson you will read about what life was like for these settlers.

Read for Purpose

1. WHAT YOU KNOW: Has your family ever moved to a new place?
2. WHAT YOU WILL LEARN: How did Arkansans work together to build new lives on the frontier?

MOVING TO ARKANSAS

You have already read that more and more settlers moved to Arkansas during the early 1800s. Pioneers (pī ə nîrz') traveled to our state to make new lives for themselves. Pioneer is a term European Americans used for the first settlers of a region.

Where did these pioneer families come from? How did they live? The life of a typical pioneer family might have been something like this. . . .

THE SMITH FAMILY

Until she was ten years old, Hannah Smith had lived in Tennessee. In 1825 her father bought 160 acres (65 ha) of land near what is now Camden, Arkansas. Find Camden on the map on page 111. Which of Arkansas's six natural regions had the Smiths chosen for their new home?

Hannah's father said their new home was on the Arkansas frontier (frun tîr'). A frontier is the land lying along the border of a settled area. The land was not a frontier to the Native Americans who had lived there a long time, but for Hannah's family, it was. There would be few neighbors and no stores nearby. The Smith family would have to bring along nearly everything they would need.

"Would you help your mother and me think of what we need to take with us?" Mr. Smith asked Hannah. "Then, we can start packing everything into those barrels and boxes."

you can give me a hand packing everything into those barrels and boxes."

For just a moment, imagine yourself in Hannah Smith's place. What would you have taken with you to Arkansas?

The Smiths loaded up their small wagon one morning in April 1825. They took bundles of clothing and blankets, an ax and a rifle, tin pots, and an iron pan. Mrs. Smith carefully wrapped the family's Bible in a piece of cloth. Hannah helped her father fasten down his plow and hoe to the side of the wagon. Mr. Smith also tied a small table and chair to the back.

Hannah, her mother, and her sister Sarah climbed up into the wagon. Mr. Smith shook the horses' reins—and the trip west had begun.

MOVING WEST

The Smiths' wagon crept slowly toward the Mississippi. On a good day they traveled about 10 miles (16 km). Finally, after about three weeks, they reached the broad, muddy river.

"How will we get across?" Hannah asked her father.

Mr. Smith pointed to the middle of the river. A wide flatboat, loaded with wagons and settlers, was heading for the Arkansas shore. Hannah watched the shallow, squared-off boat dock on the other side of the river. When the flatboat returned, Mr. Smith drove the family's wagon aboard.

Soon the Smiths were traveling westward across the Mississippi Alluvial Plain. Although the land was flat, there were no roads. They moved slowly. After two weeks of travel, Mr. Smith halted the wagon near the bend of a rushing river.

"This is the Ouachita River," he said. "We've reached our new home."

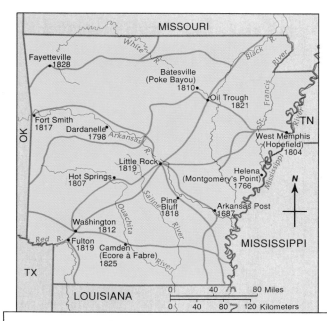

ARKANSAS TERRITORY, 1828

| •Fulton 1819 | Name and date of settlement | —— Trail or road | Present-day boundaries are shown. |

MAP SKILL: The Bowie knife, known as the "Arkansas toothpick," was invented by a blacksmith in Washington. In which year was Washington founded?

CLEARING THE LAND

Now that the Smith family had reached Arkansas, they had to start a new life. There were many things to do. They needed to build a cabin and to plant crops.

The first job, though, was to clear the land. Hundreds of trees still covered the land that Mr. Smith had purchased. Some of the trees were extremely thick—up to 6 feet (2 m) across. And once the trees were cut down, they had to be moved or burned.

Mr. Smith went to work. The steady thunk of his ax on wood echoed through the forest. Although he chopped down some of the trees, he cut many others only halfway, allowing them to die while standing. The rest of the family also worked. Mrs. Smith piled branches and brushwood for kindling. Hannah and Sarah pried stones and rocks from the ground.

BUILDING A CABIN

Once the Smiths had cleared a patch of land, their next job was to build a log cabin. Stacking the heavy logs on top of each other was a difficult task. However, pioneers on the Arkansas frontier believed in helping one another with such tough jobs. Several families in the area offered to lend a hand at the Smiths' "cabin-raising."

The neighbors arrived early in the morning. The men first cut the felled trees into logs that were about 15 feet (5 m) long. At the end of each log they made notches, or cuts. These notches would hold the heavy logs together when they were piled up to form a wall. Look at the diagram on this page to see how these notches work.

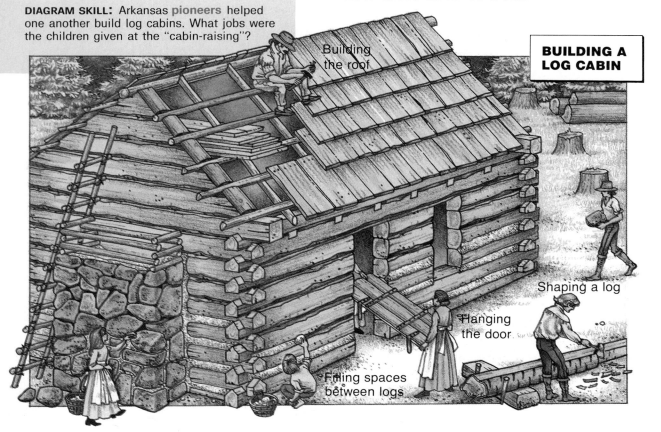

DIAGRAM SKILL: Arkansas pioneers helped one another build log cabins. What jobs were the children given at the "cabin-raising"?

Building the roof

BUILDING A LOG CABIN

Shaping a log

Hanging the door

Filling spaces between logs

Now the men began piling the logs on top of each other. The effort was great, but the men encouraged one another with jokes and laughter. Meanwhile, the women and children began to fill in the spaces between the logs with clay and mud.

Shortly before sunset, the men fastened the last thin board onto the log cabin's roof. The crowd let out a cheer— now it was time to celebrate! The women set out dishes of food. One settler brought out a fiddle, and the dancing began.

DAILY LIFE

The cabin that the neighbors had helped the Smiths to build was much smaller than today's houses. In fact, the whole cabin was about the size of one room in a modern house. The Smiths lived, ate, and slept in this small room.

Their life was a busy one. As soon as the cabin was finished, the whole family began to plant crops. Mr. Smith plowed the land between the stumps and dying trees. Then the family planted seeds for corn, beans, cabbages, and squash.

On a typical day Hannah woke up at sunrise. She folded up her mattress, a large cloth sack filled with straw. Then she and Sarah went outside to gather firewood for cooking. This was one of her favorite chores. The sticks had to be just the right size to fit in the cabin's fireplace.

Inside, her mother had started to cook corn bread and pork for breakfast. Coffee, made of coffee beans, cornmeal, and ground acorns, simmered in a pot over the fire.

On some days both girls would walk farther upstream to a one-room log

This log cabin was built in the 1830s. It was one of the first pioneer buildings put up in Washington County.

cabin to attend school. Today, though, they stayed home to help with the chores. Hannah and Sarah helped their mother to salt the meat of a deer Mr. Smith had shot. Salt would keep the meat from spoiling.

Hannah milked the family's cow, and then took turns with Sarah at the butter churn. In the afternoon Hannah collected ashes to help her mother make lye soap. This soap was used to wash the family's clothing.

Hannah's life was filled with hard work. But the Arkansas pioneers found ways to make hard work enjoyable. Today, for example, the whole family had to husk the corn, or remove its outer layer. Husking corn could be a dull, slow chore. Late in the afternoon, though, several neighbors came to the Smiths' cabin for a husking bee. This was a party that combined working, visiting, and enjoyment. Sometimes

Horseshoeing, spinning, and quilting were some of the skills used by pioneers in Arkansas. These skills are still practiced by Arkansans today.

there would be a contest to see who could husk the most ears of corn.

Other kinds of entertainment were rare for pioneer families like the Smiths. Hannah and Sarah's games were usually very simple, such as chase and hide-and-seek. Most of their toys were handmade by either their mother or their father.

HELPING ONE ANOTHER

Early Arkansas pioneers, such as the Smiths, worked hard and long to build new lives for themselves. But they also learned the value of helping one another. Whether they were working, having fun, or combining work with play, our state's pioneers depended on their neighbors and families. They helped one another to live on the Arkansas frontier.

Check Your Reading

1. What is a pioneer?
2. Describe how cabins were built on the Arkansas frontier.
3. How was cooperation important to Hannah Smith's family?
4. **GEOGRAPHY SKILL:** Why do you think that pioneer families traveled so slowly?
5. **THINKING SKILL:** What might have been the consequences of unusually cold weather during the Smiths' first months in Arkansas?

REVIEWING VOCABULARY

frontier
legislature
pioneer
plantation
Trail of Tears

Number a sheet of paper from 1 to 5. Beside each number write the word or term from the list above that best matches the definition.

1. One of the first people to move into a region
2. A large farm that usually grows only a single crop
3. A group of people who make laws
4. The route traveled by eastern Indians on their way to the Indian Territory
5. The land located along the border of a settled area

REVIEWING FACTS

1. How did Arkansas become a territory of the United States?
2. Where was the first capital of Arkansas located? To where was the capital moved?
3. What did the Arkansas constitution say about slavery? How did that affect Arkansas's effort to become a state?
4. Why did the Quapaw and Caddo populations become smaller after white people came? Why were the Osage less affected?
5. How did the presence of many trees help a pioneer family? How did it make work hard for the family?

WRITING ABOUT MAIN IDEAS

1. **Writing a News Story:** Imagine that you are a writer for the *Arkansas Gazette* in 1836. The United States has just accepted Arkansas as the twenty-fifth state. Write a news story about this event, telling the main facts.
2. **Writing a Speech:** Imagine that you are Sarasen, the Quapaw chief. You have just brought your people back to their old homes. Write a speech telling why your people should be allowed to stay in their old homes.

BUILDING SKILLS: RECOGNIZING POINT OF VIEW

Below is part of a letter written by John Pope, governor of Arkansas, to the United States government in the early 1830s. In this part of the letter Pope discusses the Quapaw Indians. Read the letter and then answer the questions that follow.

They are a kind of inoffensive [harmless] people and aid the whites in picking out their cotton and furnishing them with game. I have heard but one sentiment [belief] expressed in this territory with regard to this tribe, that of kindness and a desire that they should be permitted to live among us. I would be particularly gratified [thankful] to . . . assign them a township on the [Arkansas] river.

1. Which steps should you take to identify a person's point of view?
2. Name one statement of fact from the letter. Name one statement of opinion.
3. What is the governor's point of view?

115

REVIEWING VOCABULARY

barter   legislature
colony   missionary
constitution   pioneer
expedition   plantation
frontier   speculators

Number a sheet of paper from 1 to 10. Beside each number write the word from the list above that best completes the sentence.

1. The ____ tried to teach the Native Americans about his religion, which was different from theirs.
2. France ruled a ____ in America.
3. The family planned to move beyond most of the other settlements until it came to the ____.
4. That huge farm was a cotton ____.
5. The ____ sold the land, hoping to make a lot of money.
6. The ____ explored the river until it came to the mouth.
7. The ____ was the first settler to live in this new area.
8. The ____ passed a law that made slavery illegal.
9. The Indians would ____ animal skins for other goods that they needed.
10. The new ____ set up a plan of government for the territory.

WRITING ABOUT THE UNIT

1. **Writing a Letter:** Write a letter to Bernard de la Harpe telling him what has happened on the location of the "little rock" since he traveled there in 1721.
2. **Writing About Points of View:** Write one or two sentences telling how each of these people would have felt about Arkansas statehood: Robert La Salle, Henri de Tonti, Sarasen, a pioneer such as Hannah Smith.
3. **Planning a Historical Museum:** Plan a museum about the history of Arkansas up to the year 1840. Decide which exhibits you would include. What would each exhibit look like? Write a short description of each one.

ACTIVITIES

1. **Researching an Important Person:** Choose one of the Key People discussed in Unit 3. Find out more about the person. Prepare a written or oral report about the person that you have chosen.
2. **Making a Time Line:** Prepare a time line of the key events discussed in Unit 3. Review the Reading a Time Line lesson on pages 86–87 to help you get started.
3. **Working Together to Put On a Skit:** Working with a group of classmates, prepare a skit about the treatment of Indians in Arkansas between 1530 and 1830. Your skit might cover all major events or concentrate on one particular time period or event. Present your skit to the class.

BUILDING SKILLS:
RECOGNIZING POINT OF VIEW

Below is part of a speech that might have been given in Congress on the subject of Arkansas statehood. Read the speech and then answer the questions that follow.

> *We do not need another slave state. Today there are 12 free states and 12 slave states. It would greatly hurt the country to let Arkansas enter the union with its present constitution. Let us keep Arkansas a territory. We do not want the government power to tip in favor of the the slaveholders.*

1. What is point of view?
2. Identify at least one statement of fact in the speech. Identify at least one statement of opinion.
3. Which words suggest how the speaker felt about Arkansas statehood?
4. Which part of the subject does the speaker not talk about?
5. What is the speaker's point of view?
6. What might happen if you could not recognize this speaker's point of view?

LINKING PAST, PRESENT, AND FUTURE

In the days when pioneers first settled in Arkansas, children attended school for only a small portion of the time. If there were important chores to be done at home, the children did not go to school at all. What are the rules about attending school today? Why do we have those rules? Some people think that children should attend school even more—longer hours each day and more days each year. What might be some good results of this plan? What might be some bad results?

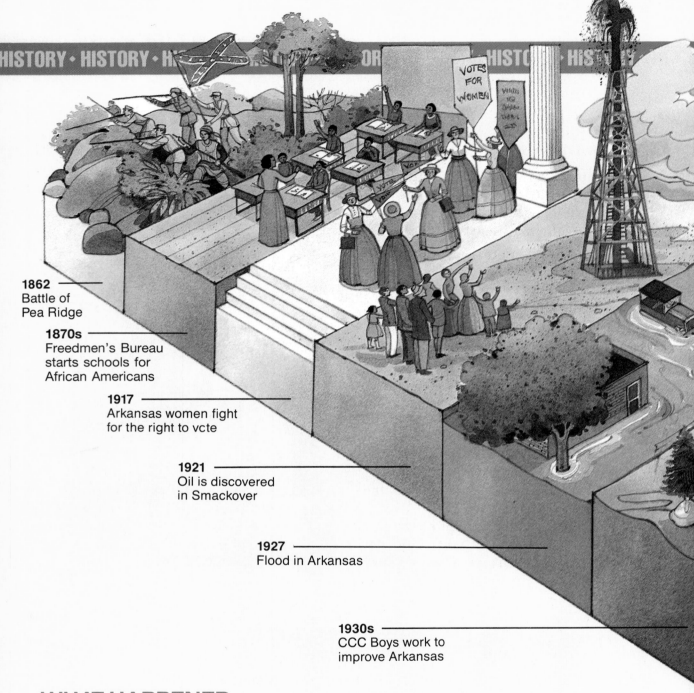

1862
Battle of
Pea Ridge

1870s
Freedmen's Bureau
starts schools for
African Americans

1917
Arkansas women fight
for the right to vote

1921
Oil is discovered
in Smackover

1927
Flood in Arkansas

1930s
CCC Boys work to
improve Arkansas

WHAT HAPPENED

In the years after Arkansas
had become a state, there were many
problems still to be solved. A terrible
war tore apart the people of our state and
nation. In this unit you will read about that war.
You will also read about how Arkansans moved on
to rebuild a stronger state after the war.

1960s
Arkansans march for
civil rights

1986
Arkansas celebrates
150 years of statehood

118

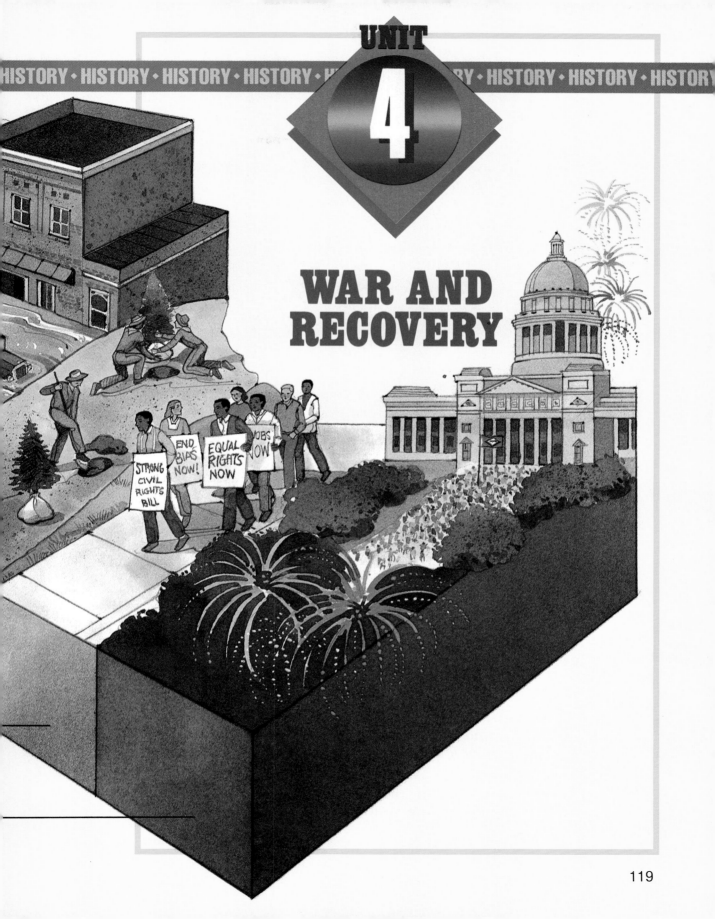

UNIT
4

WAR AND RECOVERY

STRONG CIVIL RIGHTS BILL

END BIAS NOW!

EQUAL RIGHTS NOW

JOBS NOW

CHAPTER 7

THE CIVIL WAR

FOCUS

A soldier's life is a hard one. I live on dried beef, flour, and grease . . . once in a while a little sugar and molasses. Worse still, my family is at home with no comforts. . . .

This is how one young Arkansas soldier described his life during the Civil War. In this chapter you will read about how this war began, and how it affected the people of our state.

1 Slave States and Free States

Key Vocabulary

abolitionist
secede
Union
Confederacy
Civil War

Key People

Abraham Lincoln
Henry Rector
Isaac Murphy

Key Places

Fort Sumter

Read Aloud

They'd put you up on the block and sell you. That is just what they'd do—sell you.

These were the words of Campbell Armstrong, who had been an enslaved person in Arkansas during the 1850s. In this lesson you will read about how the issue of slavery divided our country and our state.

Read for Purpose

1. WHAT YOU KNOW: Why is slavery wrong?
2. WHAT YOU WILL LEARN: Why did Arkansas decide to fight on the side of the Southern states in the Civil War?

SLAVERY IN ARKANSAS

In Chapter 5 you read about how the first African captives were brought to Arkansas by John Law. When Law's "Mississippi Bubble" failed in 1723, most of these captives probably were taken to Louisiana by their owners.

Few captives were brought to Arkansas over the next 100 years. But when the state began to fill with American settlers after 1836, the number of enslaved people rose again.

PLANTATIONS IN ARKANSAS

Why did the number of enslaved people in Arkansas grow? Starting in the 1820s cotton planters began buying land in our state. Some settled in the West Gulf Coastal Plain and in the Arkansas River Valley. Others built large plantations along the Mississippi Alluvial Plain. As you have read, this region was swampy and often flooded. However, if levees were built to drain the swamps, cotton would grow easily in the alluvial soil.

Cotton was an enormously profitable crop. However, it required a great deal of labor. Planters brought thousands of slaves to Arkansas to clear land, plant seeds, and pick the cotton bolls.

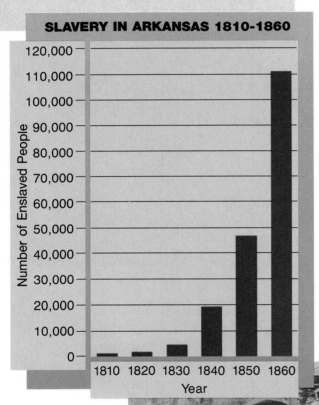

SLAVERY IN ARKANSAS 1810-1860

As cotton became Arkansas's biggest crop, slavery became part of our state's way of life. It was accepted by most Arkansans. Even the small farmers of the highland regions, who held few enslaved people, usually supported slavery as an important part of Arkansas's economy.

Look at the graph on this page. It shows that the number of enslaved people in Arkansas climbed from 136 in 1810 to 111,115 in 1860. During which ten-year period did their number increase the most?

PLANTATION LIFE

For an enslaved person on an Arkansas plantation, life was full of hard, unrewarding work. Columbus Williams was enslaved in Ouachita County. In 1937, when he was 96 years old, he recalled his days in slavery.

The very first work I did was to [take care of] babies. After that when I got a little bigger they carried me to the field—choppin' cotton. Then I went to picking cotton. . . . I believe that is about all I did. . . . You worked from before sunrise till after dark.

Some slaves worked as blacksmiths, carpenters, or servants. Women cooked and sewed for their owners' families.

122

But most slaves worked in the cotton fields, six or seven days a week.

Enslaved people who refused to work could be punished harshly by the owner or by an assistant called the overseer.

Even harsher punishments awaited those who tried to run away and were caught. If caught, runaways could then be branded, whipped, and put in chains. In spite of these punishments, many enslaved people still tried to escape.

Some owners treated their slaves more kindly. But even in these cases enslaved people were considered to be pieces of property. They had no rights under the law. It was illegal for a slave to learn to read and write. An owner could break up an enslaved family by selling its members, or even by giving members away as gifts.

A DIVIDED COUNTRY

Throughout the 1840s and 1850s the United States became more and more divided over the issue of slavery. Many people, most of them from the Northern states, opposed the spread of slavery. They wanted to make it illegal in the newer territories and states of the far West. Some people, called abolitionists (ab ə lish' ə nists), thought that slavery should be ended entirely. They argued that it was wrong for one person to "own" another person.

However, many people in the South disagreed with the abolitionists. Not all of these people actually held slaves. In fact, out of the 9 million people living in the South in 1860, only about 375,000 held slaves. But even most of the Southerners who didn't have slaves supported the idea of slavery. Some may have seen nothing

Abraham Lincoln was elected President of the United States in 1860. In 1861 the Confederate states seceded from the Union.

wrong with it. Others pointed out its importance to the South's economy. Some Southerners argued that whether slavery was right or wrong, decisions about it should be made by each state, not by the national government.

The arguments between the North and the South grew angrier in 1860. The United States was about to elect a new President. One of the candidates for this office was Abraham Lincoln, who spoke out against the spread of slavery. Many Southerners worried that if Lincoln were elected, slavery would be ended entirely.

After a bitter campaign Lincoln was elected President in November 1860. The next month the state of South Carolina decided to secede (si sēd'), or break away, from the United States. Mississippi, Florida, Alabama, Georgia, and Louisiana soon followed. The leaders of these Southern states claimed that their states were no longer part of the Union—that is, the group of states that made up the United States. Instead they decided to form a new country, the Confederate States of America, or the Confederacy.

123

A DIVIDED STATE

Should Arkansas join the Confederacy, or stay in the Union? Just as it had divided the country, the issue of slavery divided our state.

In the lowland regions, planters had built vast cotton plantations. Cotton had made them wealthy and powerful. They felt that slavery was necessary to continue growing this profitable crop.

Arkansans living in the northwestern highlands felt differently. High in the Ozarks or in the Ouachita Mountains, the soil was too thin for growing cotton. People in these areas had small farms, and few held enslaved people. Whatever they thought of slavery, many opposed leaving the Union in order to defend slavery.

On March 4, 1861, a group of Arkansans from all over the state met in Little Rock. Their job was to decide whether Arkansas should stay in the Union. Governor Henry Rector urged the group to vote for secession. Although most of the delegates wanted to stay in the Union, the debate was bitter. One delegate described how "the galleries and lobbies [of the State House] were always crowded, and it was feared violence would occur."

MAP SKILL: Arkansas joined the Confederacy in 1861. With which Union state did Arkansas share a border?

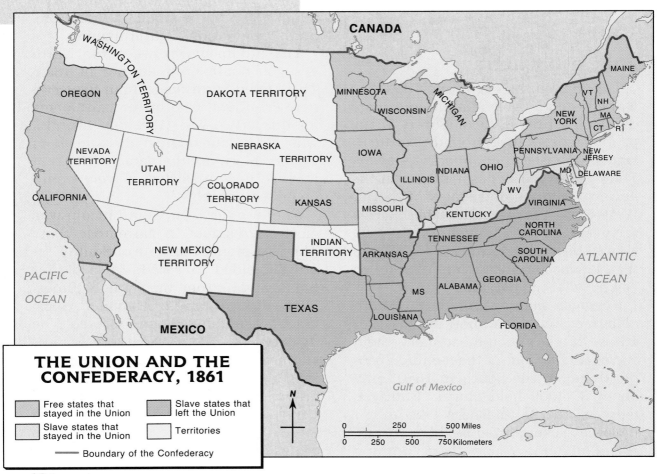

THE UNION AND THE CONFEDERACY, 1861

- Free states that stayed in the Union
- Slave states that stayed in the Union
- Slave states that left the Union
- Territories
- —— Boundary of the Confederacy

Isaac Murphy (*below*) and Henry Rector (*below, right*) disagreed about whether Arkansas should secede. The Confederate attack on Fort Sumter, however, thrust Arkansas into the Civil War.

Granger Collection

The delegates left Little Rock without making a decision. They had agreed to allow the people of the state to vote on secession.

WAR AND SECESSION

This vote never took place. On April 15, 1861, Confederate soldiers fired cannons at Fort Sumter, a Union fort off the coast of South Carolina. The Civil War had begun. Sometimes this war is also called the "War Between the States," because the Southern states fought against the Northern states.

Once the Civil War began, opinion in Arkansas shifted. Many people who had opposed secession changed their minds. One citizen of Little Rock wrote that Arkansans "could not be asked to fight our southern brethren [brothers]."

A second convention met in Little Rock. On May 6, 1861, the delegates voted once again. This time the delegates agreed to join the Confederacy. Look at the map on page 124 to see which states joined the Confederacy. Only one delegate, Isaac Murphy of Huntsville, voted against secession.

A FATEFUL DECISION

As you have read, the issue of slavery divided our nation throughout the 1800s. In 1860, when Abraham Lincoln became President, this argument split the United States into two warring sides. Once the war began, Arkansas decided to fight with the Confederacy. In the next lesson you will read about the Civil War in our state.

Check Your Reading

1. Where did cotton planters buy land in Arkansas? Why?
2. Who were the abolitionists?
3. How did the Southern states respond to the election of Abraham Lincoln?
4. GEOGRAPHY SKILL: How did the geography of Arkansas affect Arkansans' views about slavery?
5. THINKING SKILL: What were some arguments for and against each alternative open to Arkansas when the Civil War began?

The Union or the Confederacy?

As you have read, the issue of slavery divided the people of our state. Some Arkansans argued that slavery was a necessary part of life in Arkansas and throughout the South. Others believed that loyalty to the Union was more important than the defense of slavery.

In 1860, when Abraham Lincoln was elected President, South Carolina responded by seceding from the Union. Several other Southern states soon followed. The people of Arkansas had to decide whether their state should stay in the Union or join the Confederacy.

126

Two DIFFERENT Viewpoints

Arkansas Should Join the Confederacy

Not long after Lincoln's election, Governor Henry Rector delivered this speech to our state's House of Representatives. He argued that Arkansas's only course was to join the Confederacy.

I am convinced that the Union of these States . . . is practically severed [cut apart] and gone forever. . . . That we must seek an alliance, as a necessity, with a Confederacy of Southern States is as plain to my mind as the sun at noonday.

[Nothing] will stay the arm of Mr. Lincoln, elected and led on by the aggressive and vile . . . North.

I am not for war, but I am in favor of preparing for war in time of peace, and recommend to you who have authority to provide the means necessary for the defense of our citizens.

- Why did Governor Rector believe that Arkansans had to arm themselves against the North?

Arkansas Should Stay in the Union

Some citizens of our state hoped that Lincoln would find a way to lessen tensions between the North and the South. In the following letter, Arkansan David Walker wrote of his doubts about leaving the Union.

When I look at the blessings the Union has conferred upon us, I feel like it would be almost sacrilege to even think of seeing it dissolved. . . . I am afraid that having once divided it will be easy to get up new divisions, until we will be like the little republics of South America. I shall wait with much impatience and anxiety [for] the inaugural address of Lincoln. . . . It is to be hoped that every person in the government will realize that [Lincoln] is responsible . . . for the way in which the ship of state, and the glorious old Union, are to be conducted in the future.

- According to David Walker, had being part of the Union been good or bad for the people of Arkansas?

BUILDING CITIZENSHIP

1. Does Henry Rector believe that slavery is necessary in Arkansas?
2. David Walker argues that if one division is allowed, then it would be easier to allow other divisions until there were just many separate little countries instead of a United States. Is the Union more important to David Walker or is slavery more important?
3. Based on what is important to you and what you think is good for Arkansas, if you had lived at that time, would you have voted to stay in the Union or to join the Confederacy? Explain your answer.

Reading Historical Maps

Key Vocabulary

historical map

In earlier chapters you have read how the land of Arkansas was settled—first by Native Americans, and then by Europeans. You have seen a number of maps showing events that took place in Arkansas from earliest times until the 1800s. These maps are called historical maps because they show information about the past, such as the locations at which past events have taken place. For example, the map on page 124 is a historical map because it shows the Union and Confederate states at the beginning of the Civil War.

Identifying the Parts of a Map

In order to read a historical map you need to identify what it shows. First look at the map title. The title gives the subject of the map. What is the title of the map below?

Next study the map key. The map key tells the meaning of each color or symbol on the map. On this map, for example, free states are shaded orange. Which areas are shaded yellow?

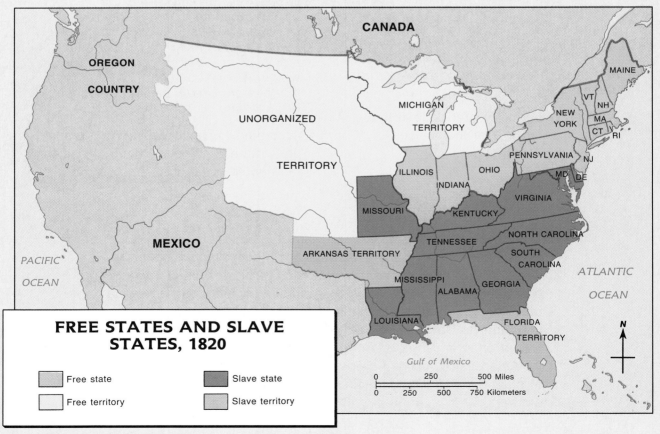

FREE STATES AND SLAVE STATES, 1820

Free state
Free territory
Slave state
Slave territory

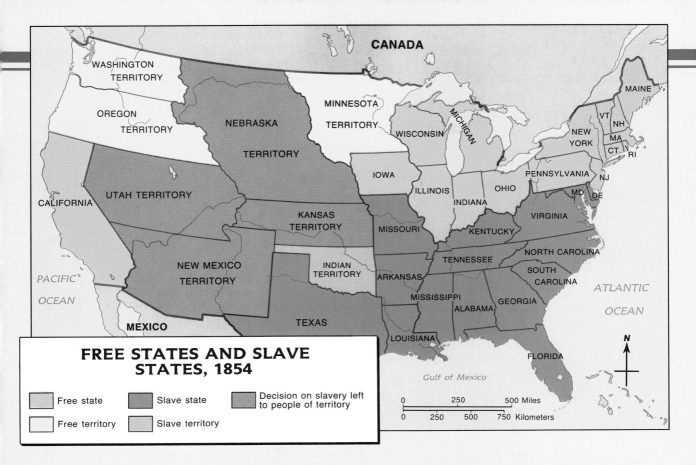

FREE STATES AND SLAVE STATES, 1854

- Free state
- Slave state
- Decision on slavery left to people of territory
- Free territory
- Slave territory

Which color on the same map shows the slave states? Which color is the Arkansas Territory?

Comparing Historical Maps

As you learn about historical events, you will see many maps of Arkansas. Sometimes you can learn important things about our state's past by comparing historical maps. Comparing historical maps lets you see how certain events unfolded, or how boundaries and places changed over time.

To compare maps, look at what each map shows. Then ask yourself, "How is the information on the two maps similar or different?"

What is the title of the map above? By reading the titles of this map and the map on page 128, what do you learn about the difference between the two maps?

Look at the map key for the map above. Then compare it to the map key for the map on page 128. How are the two map keys different?

Finally compare the maps themselves. What do the two maps tell you about the land of Arkansas?

Reviewing the Skill

1. What is a historical map?
2. How many free states were there in 1820? How many slave states were there?
3. How many free states were there in 1854? How many slave states were there?
4. Why are some areas on the map above shaded brown?
5. List three differences between the two maps.
6. Why are historical maps useful?

2 Arkansas and the Civil War

READ TO LEARN

Key Vocabulary
jayhawker
bushwhacker
Emancipation
   Proclamation

Key People
Harris Flanagin
Patrick Cleburne
David O. Dodd

Key Places
Pea Ridge
Washington

Read Aloud

The war spirit does not seem to [lessen]. . . . There is a company of cavalry in Desha County to start to Little Rock in a day or two and from [there] to the frontier.

An Arkansan wrote these words in May 1861, as our state prepared to go to war. The Civil War divided families, destroyed homes, and left thousands of Arkansans dead.

Read for Purpose

1. **WHAT YOU KNOW:** How had slavery divided our nation and our state?
2. **WHAT YOU WILL LEARN:** How did the Civil War change the lives of the people of Arkansas?

ARKANSAS AT WAR

When the Confederate cannonballs crashed down on Fort Sumter in April 1861, few Arkansans suspected that a long, bloody war would follow. Like most other Southerners, they expected a short clash.

Thousands of Arkansans enlisted to fight. Many arrived with nothing more than the clothes on their backs and "squirrel guns" in their hands. Boys as young as 13 years old joined up.

THE BATTLE OF PEA RIDGE

In the spring of 1862 this Arkansas army had its first major battle. A Union force of 11,000 men had moved across Arkansas's northern border. Almost 17,000 Confederate troops, including many Cherokee Indians, marched north to meet them. They hoped to drive the Union force out of Arkansas and back into Missouri.

On March 7 the two armies met at Pea Ridge, north of Rogers in Benton County. Find the site of the Battle of Pea Ridge on the map on page 131.

For two days and nights the armies were locked in battle, with neither side scoring a clear victory. At least 2,500 soldiers from both sides were killed.

Eventually the exhausted Confederate troops began to run low on ammunition. They slowly retreated south toward Fayetteville.

LIFE IN WARTIME ARKANSAS

After the Battle of Pea Ridge, Union forces continued their advance south into Arkansas. They captured Little Rock in 1863. The Confederate state government, which was led by Governor Harris Flanagin, fled to the town of Washington in Hempstead County.

For the next two years Arkansas had two state governments. One was set up by the Union army, with its capital in Little Rock. Isaac Murphy, about whom you read in the last lesson, was appointed governor. The other government, with its capital in Washington, remained loyal to the Confederacy.

As the war spread across the state, soldiers from both sides raided people's homes for supplies. Meanwhile, bands of thieves used the war as an excuse to rob and to destroy property. When these thieves favored the Union side, they were called jayhawkers. Those favoring the Confederate side were called bushwhackers. For example, Myra Cash of Clark was left with only "a one-eyed ox with which to make crops and to carry the corn and wheat to the Harrison Grist Mill."

NEW FREEDOM

For Arkansas's enslaved people, the war was a source of hope and confusion. Early in 1863 President Lincoln had issued the Emancipation Proclamation. This document freed all the slaves in the southern states, including Arkansas. As the Union army moved south, African Americans flocked to the Union army camps.

MAP SKILL: The Confederate army made a surprise attack on the Union forces at Pea Ridge. Which other major Civil War battle occurred in northwestern Arkansas?

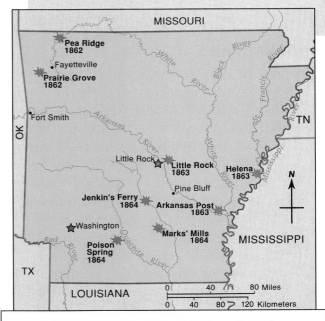

ARKANSAS: Civil War Battles

⚹ Battle • Town ☆ Union capital 1863–1865 ⚝ Confederate capital 1863–1865

David O. Dodd (*left*) was hanged for refusing to betray a friend who had given him information about Union troops in Little Rock (*right*).

Soon the Northern government began to allow former slaves to join the army. The First Arkansas Infantry, African Descent, was organized on May 1, 1863. Other units were formed soon after. Altogether, 5,526 former Arkansas slaves fought against the South.

ARKANSAS'S HEROES

About 60,000 Arkansans served in the Confederate army during the Civil War. Along with the African Americans you have just read about, some 9,000 whites also fought for the Union.

Soldiers on both sides of the war showed great courage. Patrick Cleburne (klē′ bərn) of Helena rose from private to major general in the Confederate army. He saved many lives in battle until he was killed in 1864.

Another Arkansas hero didn't actually serve in either army. In 1863 David O. Dodd was traveling from Union territory to his new home in Confederate Texas. Still a teenager, Dodd carried secret information about Union troops

in his boot. At the edge of Little Rock, he was searched by Union troops. They discovered the hidden papers. Because Dodd refused to say who had given him the information, he was hanged.

THE WAR ENDS

By the end of 1864 the Confederacy had begun to collapse. The Union had more people, more factories, and more money. No matter how bravely they fought, the Confederate armies were overwhelmed. In April 1865 Confederate general, Robert E. Lee, surrendered to Union general, Ulysses S. Grant, at Appomattox, Virginia. After four long years the Civil War was over.

 Check Your Reading

1. What was the result of the Battle of Pea Ridge?
2. Why is David O. Dodd a famous Arkansas hero?
3. What was accomplished by the Emancipation Proclamation?
4. **THINKING SKILL:** What facts helped to shape the way that plantation owners viewed slavery?

REVIEWING VOCABULARY

abolitionist   secede
Civil War   Union
Confederacy

Number a sheet of paper from 1 to 5. Beside each number write the word or term from the list above that best matches the definition.

1. The name of the country formed by Southern states just before the Civil War began
2. The group of states that remained part of the United States during the Civil War
3. A person who wanted to end slavery
4. The war fought between the Union and the Confederacy in the 1860s
5. To break away

REVIEWING FACTS

1. Why did the slave population increase in Arkansas in the 1800s?
2. Write three facts about slaves' lives in Arkansas.
3. Why did some Southern states secede in 1860 and 1861?
4. Why did some Arkansans favor joining the Confederacy? Why did some oppose it?
5. Describe the Battle of Pea Ridge.
6. Why did Arkansas have two state governments during the Civil War?
7. What were jayhawkers and bushwhackers?
8. What was the effect of the Emancipation Proclamation?
9. How did Patrick Cleburne help the Confederate cause? How did David O. Dodd try to help?
10. What were some of the reasons that the North was able to win the Civil War against the South?

WRITING ABOUT MAIN IDEAS

1. **Making a Time Line:** Make a time line of events leading to Arkansas's decision to join the Confederacy. Then list two examples in which one event caused or led to another event.
2. **Writing an Eyewitness Account:** Imagine that you are a Confederate or Union soldier who took part in the Battle of Pea Ridge. Write a paragraph describing the battle from your point of view.
3. **Writing Questions:** Suppose you could have interviewed Columbus Williams, the former slave mentioned on page 122. What would you have asked him? Write five questions that you would have asked.

BUILDING SKILLS: READING HISTORICAL MAPS

1. What is a historical map?
2. Study the map on page 129. Name three states that were slave states in 1854.
3. What does the color yellow stand for on the map on page 128?
4. Use the maps on pages 124, 128, and 129 to answer these questions.
   a. Which slave states were not part of the Confederacy?
   b. Which new states were added to the Union between 1820 and 1854?

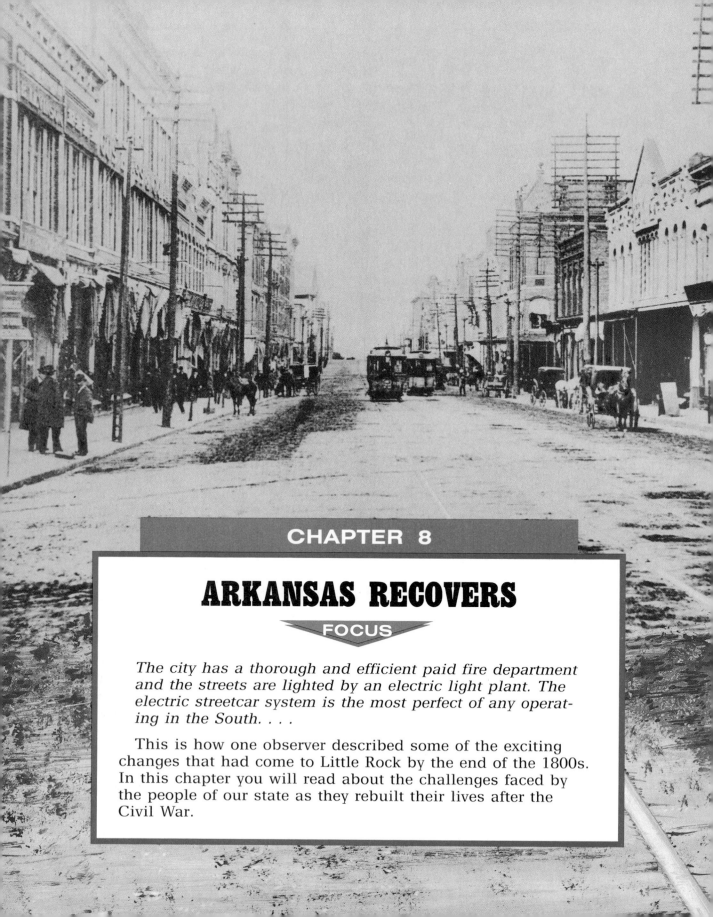

CHAPTER 8

ARKANSAS RECOVERS

FOCUS

The city has a thorough and efficient paid fire department and the streets are lighted by an electric light plant. The electric streetcar system is the most perfect of any operating in the South. . . .

This is how one observer described some of the exciting changes that had come to Little Rock by the end of the 1800s. In this chapter you will read about the challenges faced by the people of our state as they rebuilt their lives after the Civil War.

1 Reconstruction

Key Vocabulary

Reconstruction	Freedmen's Bureau	
carpetbagger	sharecropping	
scalawag	Ku Klux Klan	

Key People

Andrew Johnson
Powell Clayton
William H. Grey

Read Aloud

Grandma Nancy Hill was 59 when the war ended but she was an old woman. . . . Most of her beautiful linens had been torn up and rolled for bandages; blankets had been sent to the army; what horses and mules that could be spared from farming had gone too. Her home and her country were in ruins.

These words describe the damage that the Civil War brought to one Arkansan's life. In this lesson you will read about how the people of our state recovered from the war's destruction and loss.

Read for Purpose

1. **WHAT YOU KNOW:** How did the Civil War affect the people in Arkansas?
2. **WHAT YOU WILL LEARN:** What was Reconstruction, and what took place in Arkansas during this period?

A DAMAGED STATE

As you read in Chapter 7, the Civil War ended in April 1865. During the spring of that year thousands of Arkansas soldiers returned to their homes. So did many refugees, or people who had fled during the war.

One refugee wrote this description of her journey home.

[We saw] half-starved women and children; gaunt, ragged men, stumbling along the road . . . trying to find their families and friends. . . . We found our home burned to the ground.

In northwest Arkansas many farms had been destroyed. Livestock and farming equipment had been lost or stolen. In some areas whole towns lay in ruins. The southern part of the state was not as badly damaged. But without slaves to work the land, the vast plantations remained idle.

The human cost of the war had been even greater. About 15,000 Arkansas soldiers had died in battle. Many civilians had also died of disease or had been left homeless.

President Lincoln was killed before his plan for **Reconstruction** could be put into action. Powell Clayton (*below*) was Arkansas's governor during much of Reconstruction.

Governor Isaac Murphy urged his fellow Arkansans to put the anger and violence of the war behind them. But as they worked to repair their damaged state, Arkansans faced another problem. In 1861 they had decided to leave the Union. Now how would Arkansas once again become part of the United States of America?

"WITH CHARITY FOR ALL"

If you had been President of the United States at the end of the Civil War, what would you have done to bring the nation together? Abraham Lincoln, who had been reelected President in 1864, thought long and hard about **Reconstruction**. We use this word to describe the process of returning the former Confederate states to the Union after the Civil War.

In 1865, shortly after his reelection, Lincoln spoke about his plans for Reconstruction. He promised to restore the Union "with malice toward none . . . and charity for all." Lincoln wanted to bring about Reconstruction as quickly and as smoothly as possible. He opposed punishing the Southern states for leaving the Union in 1861. Instead he called on all Americans to help "bind up the nation's wounds."

However, before Lincoln could put his plans into action, tragedy struck. On April 14, 1865, Lincoln was shot in a theater in Washington, D.C.

The new President, Andrew Johnson, tried to carry out Lincoln's plans. However, many members of Congress felt differently about Reconstruction. They believed that the South should be harshly punished. They also worried about the treatment that the newly freed enslaved people might receive.

President Johnson and the Congress fought for nearly two years. In 1867 Johnson finally lost the fight. Congress passed a much tougher plan for Reconstruction. This plan began by placing the Southern states, including Arkansas, under military rule.

RECONSTRUCTION IN ARKANSAS

Congress appointed General Edward Ord as military ruler of Arkansas. One of Ord's first tasks was to organize a new state government. In 1868 he called for new elections.

However, Congress had decided that no Southerner could vote unless he swore loyalty to the United States. Congress also refused to allow anyone to vote who had volunteered to serve in the Confederate army, or who had held an office in the Confederacy. As a result most voters were either those who had been enslaved or people who had supported the Union.

Many Arkansans complained about these elections, which they felt represented the views of only a small part of the population. Still, a new state constitution was approved in 1868, and Arkansas was soon readmitted to the Union. Powell Clayton, who had come to Arkansas as a Union cavalry officer, was elected governor.

CARPETBAGGERS AND SCALAWAGS

Northerners like Clayton, who had settled in the South after the war, were unpopular with many Arkansans. They were called carpetbaggers—a reference to the inexpensive suitcases made of carpeting that they sometimes carried. Like Southerners in other states, Arkansans accused these new arrivals of using the situation in the South for their own private gain. Sometimes this was true. In many other cases, the carpetbaggers genuinely felt that the South needed their help to rebuild after the war.

Equally unpopular were those Arkansans who decided to work with

Although many Arkansans viewed Northerners as carpetbaggers (*above*), the Reconstruction government was responsible for founding the University of Arkansas (*below*).

the carpetbagger government. These people were often called scalawags.

Despite its unpopularity, Clayton's government accomplished some important things during Reconstruction. The government built roads, levees, and public schools and founded the University of Arkansas in Fayetteville.

NEW FREEDOMS

For Arkansas's African Americans the Reconstruction years were both hopeful and uncertain. The Emancipation Proclamation had freed over 100,000 enslaved people in our state. But many of them were unsure of how to make lives for themselves in postwar Arkansas. Few had money to pay for food or shelter. Most freed African Americans lacked skills for any jobs except farm work.

In 1865 Congress established the Freedmen's Bureau. The purpose of this organization was to help the formerly enslaved people adjust to their new lives. The bureau established hospitals and orphanages, and distributed clothes and food to many people throughout the South. In Arkansas members of the bureau ran 27 schools. They also worked to register African Americans to vote.

Arkansas's African Americans made great gains during this period. Many were elected to public office. One was William H. Grey of Helena, who served in the state senate. By the end of Reconstruction, about 160 of our state's judges were African Americans. African Americans also served as sheriffs and military officers.

In other ways, though, life remained hard for them. Very few owned any land. For this reason many returned to working for their former "owners". In exchange for being allowed to farm the land, they agreed to give up a large share of their crops to the owner. This system, which is called sharecropping, usually prevented the freed African Americans from making any profit. As a result, most of them remained extremely poor.

During Reconstruction the **Freedmen's Bureau** established schools like the one below. William H. Grey became one of the first African Americans to serve in the Arkansas state senate.

138

Joseph Brooks (*left*) and Elisha Baxter (*right*) ran for governor in 1872. They organized armies that clashed in the Brooks-Baxter War.

They also suffered harassment and violence from some white Arkansans. The **Ku Klux Klan**, a group that sought to bully and intimidate African Americans, appeared in Arkansas and many other Southern states during Reconstruction.

THE BROOKS-BAXTER WAR

By the early 1870s many Americans, including Arkansans, wanted to put the war behind them. In our state, however, Reconstruction reached a strange climax with the Brooks-Baxter War.

This "war" first began when Joseph Brooks and Elisha Baxter both ran for governor in 1872. Baxter was elected. However, Brooks claimed that he had actually won. Over the next two years Brooks and Baxter continued to quarrel, and the two men eventually organized armed groups of supporters. As many as 200 people were killed as the two "armies" clashed. The dispute was finally settled by President Ulysses S. Grant, who decided that Baxter was the rightful governor.

RECONSTRUCTION ENDS

As you have read, Reconstruction was a period of confusion, disagreement, and hardship for many Arkansans. By 1874 Reconstruction had come to an end in our state. However, other challenges lay ahead for the people of Arkansas.

Check Your Reading

1. What kinds of damage needed to be repaired in Arkansas after the Civil War?
2. Who was Powell Clayton?
3. What problems faced freed African Americans in Arkansas during the years of Reconstruction?
4. What was the Freedmen's Bureau?
5. **THINKING SKILL:** Compare and contrast the ways in which Abraham Lincoln and the Congress wanted to handle Reconstruction.

Drawing Conclusions

Key Vocabulary

conclusion

Imagine that you have planted some tomato seeds in a garden. Every week you water, fertilize, and weed the garden. Later you put in stakes to support the growing tomato plants. In time the plants produce delicious tomatoes. You might conclude that your work helped the plants to grow.

Drawing a conclusion means pulling together pieces of information so that they mean something. A conclusion is an end point of a process. It is a statement about information that has been presented, but it does not repeat any of that information.

You draw conclusions from several facts. You look outside and see that it is cloudy, cold, and damp. You might then conclude that the weather is not good for camping. In drawing that conclusion you use the facts that you have learned, and you give meaning to them.

Trying the Skill

In this book you have read many facts about Arkansas at different times in the past. As you read the facts about a particular time or event, try to draw conclusions about what you are reading.

Read each of the following statements. Then draw a conclusion about Reconstruction in Arkansas.

- After the Civil War many Arkansans were hungry or homeless.

HELPING YOURSELF

The steps on the left will help you to draw conclusions. The example on the right shows you one way to apply these steps to the statements on page 140.

One Way to Draw Conclusions	Example
1. Identify the subject of all the information that is given.	The subject is Reconstruction in Arkansas.
2. Skim, or quickly read through, the information.	Read through the information quickly to get the general picture that the facts create.
3. Look for common features in the information that is given.	The statements all concern some difficulty that Arkansans faced during Reconstruction. For example, many Arkansans had lost their homes and were unable to vote for their own leaders.
4. Write a sentence that tells about the common features and how they are connected to the subject.	Put the ideas in each statement together, so you can get an overall sense of the subject. One conclusion that you might draw from the information is that life was difficult for many Arkansans during Reconstruction.

- From 1865 to 1868 Arkansans lived under military rule.
- Many Arkansans were not allowed to vote in elections because they had supported the Confederacy.

1. What conclusion did you draw?
2. What did you do to draw your conclusion?

Applying the Skill

Now apply what you have learned by drawing a conclusion from the following statements.

- From 1875 to 1896 Isaac C. Parker was a federal judge who helped to keep order in western Arkansas.
- Judge Parker heard more than 13,000 cases, and in more than 9,000 cases the defendants were convicted.
- Judge Parker worked from dawn to dusk throughout the year.

1. What is the subject of all the information given?
   a. Judge Isaac C. Parker
   b. law and order in western Arkansas
   c. the federal court system
2. Which common feature do all the statements share?
   a. the lack of justice in Judge Parker's court
   b. the harsh punishments handed out by Judge Parker
   c. Judge Parker's hard work
3. Write a sentence that draws a conclusion from the information that is given.

Reviewing the Skill

1. What is drawing a conclusion?
2. Name four steps that you can take in order to draw conclusions.
3. Why is it important to draw conclusions about the information you read?

2 New Challenges

READ TO LEARN

Key Vocabulary

manufacturing
New South
industry
Progressive Era

Key People

Charlotte Stephens
Joe T. Robinson

Read Aloud

Our best farmers work hard year after year supporting their families in the most economical manner, [and yet] they have nothing left at the end of the year. . . .

This is how one Arkansas farmer described his frustrations during the 1880s. In this lesson you will read about the hardships faced by our state's farmers during those years. You will also read about the economic changes in Arkansas.

Read for Purpose

1. **WHAT YOU KNOW:** How can forming an organization help people to get things done?
2. **WHAT YOU WILL LEARN:** What were some of the challenges faced by Arkansans during the years after Reconstruction?

RAILROADS AND INDUSTRIES

After the Civil War many Southerners felt that the South should shift much of its economy from agriculture to manufacturing. *Manufacturing* means "making products by machinery." These Southerners imagined a New South in which factories would replace farms.

In Arkansas one of the most important signs of the New South was the growth of railroads. In 1861 less than 50 miles (80 km) of railroad track had been built throughout our entire state. Arkansans were forced to travel on foot, by boat, or on horseback.

During Reconstruction, companies finally began to build railroads in Arkansas. Both the national and state governments encouraged such companies by offering them loans and land. By 1900 about 3,400 miles (5,471 km) of track crisscrossed our state—a distance greater than the width of the United States! Look at the map on page 143 to see how the railroads in Arkansas grew between 1860 and 1915.

This growing transportation system helped other industries to develop. An industry is a company or group of companies that makes a certain product or provides a certain service.

The timber industry, for example, saw an opportunity to make enormous profits in Arkansas. During the years after the Civil War many companies set up large steam-driven sawmills along the West Gulf Coastal Plain.

Other companies tried to develop Arkansas's mineral resources. Coal, manganese, lead, and zinc were all mined in our state during the years after the Civil War.

FARMERS BAND TOGETHER

While industry slowly took root in Arkansas, life grew harder for our state's farmers. Prices for farm products were falling. Look at the graph on this page to see how cotton prices changed over a period of 50 years. What was the price of cotton in 1900?

As profits fell, however, the farmers' costs rose. Also, most banks refused to lend money to farmers for fear that they would be unable to repay the loans. Caught in a trap, many farmers lost their land.

In an effort to solve some of these problems, farmers across the state began to band together in organizations. In 1882, seven Des Arc farmers gathered in an old log schoolhouse to found what was to become one of the most important organizations, The Agricultural Wheel. Another organization, The Sons of the Agricultural Star, was founded by African American farmers. The farmers demanded laws that would regulate industry and the railroads. They also pushed for more public schools and for government aid to farmers. Eventually, many of these ideas were taken up by a new national political party called the Populists.

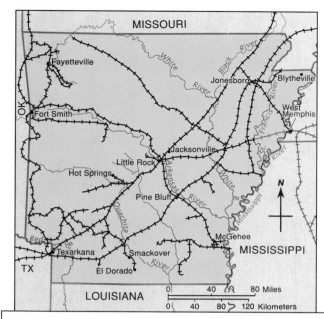

RAILROADS IN ARKANSAS, 1915

+++ Railroads before 1860   +++ Railroads 1860–1915

MAP SKILL: With which other state did the first railroad connect Arkansas?

GRAPH SKILL: In which year were cotton prices highest?

COTTON PRICES 1860-1910

Cents per pound (y-axis: 8 to 18)

Year (x-axis): 1860, 1870, 1880, 1890, 1900, 1910

143

During the **Progressive Era** Arkansas women gathered on the steps of the state capitol to demand the right to vote. Charlotte Stephens began her career in the Little Rock public schools during this same period.

THE PROGRESSIVE ERA

In 1901 Theodore Roosevelt was elected President, and he pushed for many of the farmers' demands. The **Progressive Era** had begun. During this period, which lasted until about 1920, many leaders strove for changes in our state and in our nation.

Arkansas's state government built many new schools during the Progressive Era. The first school buses—flatbed trucks with benches on the back—began to roll over the rural roads. **Charlotte Stephens** became the first African American to teach in a Little Rock public school. Stephens spent her whole life working to improve our state's educational system.

Joe T. Robinson, who was elected governor in 1912, fought to make the workplace safer for Arkansans. He also pushed for laws to limit the number of work hours in the day.

WOMEN'S RIGHTS

Another important part of the Progressive Era was the women's rights movement. Until this time women in the United States lacked the right to vote. Arkansas's women formed organizations that worked to gain the vote. These groups also worked to increase women's rights in the courts. One Arkansas woman wrote of this struggle: "No one is so well calculated [qualified] to think for womankind as woman herself."

DAYS OF CHANGE

The years following Reconstruction brought many changes to our state. Railroads and industry grew. Farmers' and women's organizations fought for a better life. As our state entered a new century, however, even greater changes lay just ahead.

 Check Your Reading

1. Explain the term *New South*.
2. What were two signs of the New South in Arkansas?
3. How did Arkansas's farmers react to the difficulties of the 1870s and the 1880s?
4. **THINKING SKILL:** In what ways did farmers' and women's organizations contribute to the gains of the Progressive Era?

REVIEWING VOCABULARY

carpetbagger   scalawag
industry   sharecropping
manufacturing

Number a sheet of paper from 1 to 5. Beside each number write the word from the list above that best completes the sentence.

1. The _____ came to Arkansas from the North after the Civil War.
2. Most Arkansans did not like the _____ because he helped the Northerners during Reconstruction.
3. Because it involves machinery, _____ can produce goods much faster than if these goods were made by hand.
4. Under a system called _____, farmers paid for land they rented with a portion of their crops.
5. The toy _____ is made up of various companies that manufacture toys.

REVIEWING FACTS

1. What was Reconstruction?
2. What was President Lincoln's plan for Reconstruction? What was Congress's plan?
3. What did many Arkansans think of carpetbaggers and scalawags?
4. Name three accomplishments of the Arkansas Reconstruction government.
5. What was the goal of the Freedmen's Bureau?
6. What was the Ku Klux Klan?
7. Name two industries that grew in Arkansas after the Civil War.
8. Why did many Arkansas farmers unite by joining organizations?
9. Who was Charlotte Stephens?
10. Name two changes that occurred in Arkansas during the Progressive Era.

WRITING ABOUT MAIN IDEAS

1. **Writing an Opinion Paragraph:** Do you think that African Americans were helped or hurt by Reconstruction? Write a paragraph giving your opinion and explaining why you feel that way.
2. **Writing a Letter to the Editor:** Newspapers often print letters written by their readers. Each letter tells how the writer feels about some important issue. Write a letter to the editor telling why farmers should join the Agricultural Wheel.
3. **Writing About a Cartoon:** Look closely at the political cartoon of the carpetbagger on page 137. Write a sentence telling the main idea of the cartoon.

BUILDING SKILLS: DRAWING CONCLUSIONS

1. Which steps should you follow when you are trying to draw a conclusion?
2. Read the following facts. Then draw a conclusion from the facts by following the steps you named in Question 1.
   a. Between 1865 and 1900 more than 3,000 miles (4,827 km) of railroad track was laid in Arkansas.
   b. Between 1865 and 1900 coal, lead, and zinc were mined in Arkansas for the first time.
   c. After 1865 many steam-driven sawmills were set up in Arkansas.
3. Why is it helpful to know how to draw conclusions from information?

145

CHAPTER 9

ARKANSAS AND THE NEW CENTURY

FOCUS

Through the turn of the century and World War I, we per-sisted, proud but poor, living in a land rich in potential. . . .

This was part of a speech delivered by Governor Bill Clin-ton, who later became President, to celebrate the one-hundred-fiftieth anniversary of Arkansas's statehood. During the early years of the twentieth century, Arkansans like the woman above enjoyed new freedoms and prosperity.

1 War and Prosperity

READ TO LEARN

Key Vocabulary

World War I
tourism

Key People

Herman Davis
Field Kindley
Scott Joplin
Louise Thaden

Key Places

Smackover

Read Aloud

With 27 newspapers and magazines, 12 banks, railroads running in 7 different directions, and river transportation, Little Rock is no pebble in spite of its name.

This description of Little Rock in 1901, at the dawn of the twentieth century, shows how Arkansas's capital had grown from a small, dusty frontier town to a bustling city. In this lesson you will read about some of the changes that brought our state into the new century.

Read for Purpose

1. **WHAT YOU KNOW:** Why was life difficult for Arkansas's farmers during the late 1800s?
2. **WHAT YOU WILL LEARN:** What was life like in Arkansas during World War I and the Roaring Twenties?

WORLD WAR I

The Progressive Era, which you read about in the last lesson, was interrupted by World War I. This war had begun in Europe in 1914. The Central Powers of Germany, Austria-Hungary, and Turkey opposed the Allied Powers of Great Britain, France, and Russia. On April 6, 1917, the United States joined the war on the side of the Allies.

More than 72,000 Arkansans served in the American army in Europe. New weapons, such as machine guns, tanks, and airplanes, made this war especially deadly. Nearly 2,000 soldiers from our state lost their lives. Some were killed on the battlefield. Others died from diseases that spread quickly through the army camps.

Herman Davis was one of the many Arkansans who fought bravely in World War I. Davis had grown up on a farm in Manila, in Mississippi County. His courage and skill as a marksman won him medals from both the United States government and the government of France. Another hero from our state

147

(*above*) Field Kindley was a World War I "flying ace" from Arkansas. (*below*) Liberty Bonds were sold to support the war effort.

was Field Kindley of Gravette—a "flying ace" who shot down 12 enemy planes during the war.

THE HOME FRONT

Arkansans at home worked hard to support the war effort. People throughout our state bought Liberty Bonds. These bonds were a kind of loan to the government, which would later be repaid with interest. The government used the money to buy weapons and food for the armed forces.

Many other Arkansans volunteered to work for the Red Cross. People across the state worked hard to produce the cotton, bauxite, and coal that were needed to supply the war effort.

In 1918 World War I finally ended. The Allied Powers had defeated the Central Powers. As thousands of soldiers returned home to our state and to our nation, people hoped that this had been "the war to end all wars."

THE ROARING TWENTIES

After the war a mood of excitement spread among many Americans. Business was booming. Recent inventions, such as the car and the radio, were changing the way Americans lived. Because of this fast pace of change, the decade of the 1920s is often called the "Roaring Twenties."

One symbol of this excitement in our state was the discovery of oil near Smackover and El Dorado. A drilling crew struck oil at Busey Well #1 on January 10, 1921. A nearby observer described how a column of gas, water, and oil shot out of the well and "burst into a black mushroom" above it. Soon people were flooding into Smackover. In 7 months the population of this tiny town grew from 100 to 20,000.

People flocked to Arkansas for other reasons, too. Our state became a center for tourism, which is the business of providing services for people on vacation. The scenic beauty of Arkansas's highland regions drew many visitors. In 1926, for example, around 500,000 people visited the Ozarks.

CHANGING LIFE

The discovery of oil and the growth of tourism were typical of the changes that the Roaring Twenties brought to Arkansas. But new inventions also changed the daily lives of many Arkansans. Some of the first radios, telephones, refrigerators, and electric lights appeared in many Arkansas homes during these years.

What do you think it would be like to hear a radio for the first time? When the people of our state turned on their big, boxy radios during the 1920s, they could listen to news reports, sporting events, and detective stories. They might have listened to the ragtime music of composer Scott Joplin, who was born in Texarkana.

The automobile became more popular and inexpensive during the 1920s. In their new Model "T" trucks, farmers could transport their crops much more easily. But the automobile also gave Arkansans the freedom to travel to new places. During their free time, families would drive into town to see a movie or to have a hamburger and a soft drink.

Another method of transportation that Arkansans experienced for the first time was the airplane. Few people actually had a chance to fly. But Louise Thaden of Bentonville was one of the first woman pilots in the United States. Louise M. Thaden Field at Bentonville is named for her.

Many changes came to Arkansas during the Roaring Twenties. (*above*) Oil was discovered in Smackover in 1921. (*below*) Louise Thaden was one of the first Arkansans to fly an airplane.

149

THE FLOOD OF 1927

Flooded areas

MAP SKILL: The Flood of 1927 turned the streets of Little Rock into rivers. Which other cities were flooded during this disaster?

THE FLOOD OF 1927

Not all the excitement of the 1920s was welcome. The Flood of 1927, which you can study on the map on this page, brought disaster to thousands of Arkansas's farmers.

During the summer of 1926 heavy rains began to fall in the upper Mississippi Valley. These rains continued through the end of the year, causing not only the Mississippi River, but most of our state's other rivers, to rise. By January 1927 the Arkansas River had nearly overflowed its banks in Little Rock. The water continued to rise, and soon flooding began. By April 4,200,000 acres (1,699,740 ha) were underwater—almost half of eastern Arkansas! One observer described the mad rush for dry land:

On levees, ridges, and on ancient Indian mounds, wet, miserable man huddles with his domestic animals. Crawling up from the flood come foxes, rabbits, quail, and deer. . . .

The floodwaters ruined crops and destroyed homes. One hundred and twenty-seven people drowned in what President Herbert Hoover called "the greatest peacetime disaster in our history."

A DECADE OF CHANGE

For many Arkansans the 1920s had meant more money, more modern conveniences, and more free time. The Flood of 1927 was a great disaster for our state. Still, the excitement and change that the decade had brought made it deserving of its nickname, the Roaring Twenties.

Check Your Reading

1. How did Arkansans help the country during World War I?
2. Identify Herman Davis and Louise Thaden.
3. Why were the 1920s called the Roaring Twenties?
4. **THINKING SKILL:** Compare and contrast the way that Arkansans lived before and after the 1920s.

150

2 The Great Depression and World War II

READ TO LEARN

Key Vocabulary

economy
stocks
Great Depression
New Deal
World War II

Key People

Franklin D. Roosevelt
Douglas MacArthur

Key Places

England

Read Aloud

We didn't have any dollars
And hardly any dimes,
When the neighbors met up
They talked about hard times.

An Arkansan wrote this rhyme to describe the difficult years of the 1930s. In this lesson you will read about these years. You will also read about the ways in which Arkansans struggled to improve their lives.

Read for Purpose:

1. **WHAT YOU KNOW:** What are some ways in which people in your community earn money?
2. **WHAT YOU WILL LEARN:** What was the Great Depression, and what helped to bring it to an end?

THE GREAT DEPRESSION

In the last lesson you read that the Roaring Twenties were good years for our economy. An economy is the way a state or nation produces and uses money, goods, and natural resources. In the fall of 1929, however, these "good times" came to an end.

During that fall, the prices for stocks had begun to drop. Stocks are shares of ownership in a company. Many stockholders worried. If they held on to their shares too long, they might lose money on them. On October 29, as people across the country rushed to sell their stock, a general panic began. The prices for stocks plunged lower and lower. By the end of the day, the stock market had collapsed in what is called a "crash."

The effects of the crash spread quickly. Banks and factories across the country closed, and many people lost their jobs and savings. The Great Depression had begun.

151

THE DEPRESSION IN ARKANSAS

The Great Depression hit hard in our state. More than 100 of Arkansas's banks closed during 1930. Businesses shut down across the state, leaving thousands of people without work. By 1932 almost four out of ten Arkansans of working age were jobless.

Meanwhile, a long drought crippled Arkansas's farmers throughout 1930 and 1931. As week after week passed, our state's farmers watched the sky, hoping for rain. Hardly any fell. During one period temperatures along the Mississippi Alluvial Plain rose above 110°F. (43°C), killing half the crops in the fields.

Several organizations, such as the Red Cross, tried to help by distributing food. Still, starvation remained a threat for many Arkansans.

In January 1931, for example, hundreds of farmers gathered in the town of **England**, in Lonoke County. Many had not eaten for two or three days. They demanded supplies from the town's merchants, shouting, "Our children want food and we are going to get it!" Although the merchants quickly agreed to distribute food to the crowd, the "England Riot" was reported by newspapers across the nation.

One Arkansan from Elm Springs wrote this desperate letter to the governor: "I went to Fayetteville yesterday . . . and wanted to get more food and was absolutely flatly refused. I left for home hungry, and my wife and child hungry."

As the effects of the Depression deepened, Arkansans looked for new ways to make ends meet. In many areas people bartered goods instead of buying them with cash. A farm couple with a sick child might pay the doctor with one half-dozen eggs. In exchange for fixing somebody's car, a repairman might receive a load of firewood.

The **Great Depression** made life difficult for Arkansans. Many people lost their jobs and had to wait in line for food provided by the government.

President Franklin D. Roosevelt (*seated*) created the programs of the **New Deal** to help America recover. "3-C Boys" were paid by the government to improve parks and plant trees.

GOVERNMENT STEPS IN

In 1932 Franklin D. Roosevelt was elected President. Roosevelt felt that in order for the United States to get back on its feet, the government needed to help businesses, farmers, and the unemployed. He pushed Congress to set up programs offering this help. Roosevelt's programs came to be known as the New Deal.

The first such program to have an effect in Arkansas was called FERA—an abbreviation for the Federal Emergency Relief Administration. FERA workers distributed flour, beans, and milk. They also helped thousands of Arkansans to plant vegetable gardens.

Later on, many Arkansans worked for the CCC, or Civilian Conservation Corps. The "3-C Boys" were paid by the government to plant trees and to build roads and parks. You can still see the letters *CCC* on bridges and even on picnic tables throughout our state.

Another New Deal program resettled sharecropping families on new farms of their own. These farms, located near such communities as Dyess, usually included a house, a barn, and up to 40 acres (16 ha) of land.

Gradually, our state and nation began to recover from the Depression. The recovery was very slow. By 1941 nearly 6 million Americans remained out of work. Still, the New Deal had helped many Americans to survive.

WAR BEGINS

In 1939, while the United States battled with the Depression, war broke out in Europe. In World War II France and Great Britain first fought against Germany, Italy, and Japan. Eventually, the war would spread to almost every part of the world.

153

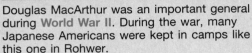
Douglas MacArthur was an important general during **World War II**. During the war, many Japanese Americans were kept in camps like this one in Rohwer.

At first many Arkansans wanted little to do with the faraway war. However, on December 7, 1941, Japanese planes bombed an American naval base at Pearl Harbor, Hawaii. The next day Congress declared war on Japan and its allies.

Once the United States was at war, public opinion in Arkansas changed quickly. Thousands of young Arkansans rushed to volunteer. Eventually, more than 200,000 Arkansans would serve in the armed forces. One Arkansan, General **Douglas MacArthur** of Little Rock, was a great leader in the fight against Japan.

THE WAR AT HOME

The Arkansans at home worked hard to support the war effort. Communities collected scrap metal and old tires to be recycled into military supplies. Many Arkansans used what money they had to purchase war bonds from the government. In Forrest City a group of African Americans bought $47,000 worth of these bonds at a single rally.

The war brought many changes to our state. The national government built two large army training camps in Arkansas—Camp Robinson, near North Little Rock, and Camp Chaffee, near Fort Smith. Workers flocked to new weapons factories in El Dorado, Hope, Hot Springs, and Malvern.

The government built two prisoner-of-war camps in Arkansas, which held 23,000 German and Italian soldiers by the war's end. In Rohwer and Jerome, in southeastern Arkansas, the government also set up two "relocation" camps. Almost 19,000 American citizens of Japanese ancestry were confined to these camps. Victims of fear and suspicion, most of these Japanese Americans had been uprooted from their homes in California. The national government forced them to live in the camps until the war ended.

NEW OPPORTUNITIES

Arkansas's African Americans had suffered the most during the Great Depression. Many had been unable to

154

During World War II Arkansans worked hard on the "home front." People collected scrap metal, women worked in factories, and "ration books" were used to buy scarce foods such as butter.

find work. Now, the sudden demand for labor created by the factories and the army camps brought thousands of new job opportunities. In December 1940 a program was begun at Scipio A. Jones High School in North Little Rock to train African Americans in carpentry. This training gave them the skills for various wartime jobs. However, Arkansas's African Americans continued to be barred from many types of employment.

The war also brought women into the work force. Of course Arkansas women had always worked long hours on their own farms or in their homes. But now they worked at jobs that had traditionally been performed by men. Thousands worked in arms factories. By 1943 women made up 20 percent of our state's industrial work force. They also worked as mechanics, bank tellers, and cab drivers.

THE COMING OF PEACE

In Arkansas, as in the rest of the United States, the Great Depression put an end to the "good times" of the 1920s. Arkansans struggled to find work and to feed their families. The New Deal helped the people of our state through the worst days of the Great Depression. Still, Arkansas's economy did not recover fully until World War II.

In 1945 both Germany and Japan surrendered to the United States and its allies. Arkansans were grateful that the fighting had ended. However, our state's African Americans would continue to fight a different battle during the coming years.

 Check Your Reading

1. Name three ways in which the Great Depression affected Arkansas.
2. How did the New Deal help the people of our state?
3. How did Arkansans contribute to the war at home?
4. THINKING SKILL: How did World War II lead to Arkansas's economic recovery?

Asking Questions

Suppose that your class decides to write an oral history about Arkansans in World War II. Your job is to interview someone who lived during World War II. The first thing you have to do is to make a list of questions to ask your subject. What questions will you ask?

Asking questions is a useful skill. It helps you to learn about a subject. Asking questions also helps you to focus on the information you want or need to know. Sometimes it is hard to figure out just what questions to ask. In these cases begin by asking yourself, "What do I want to learn?"

Trying the Skill

In this chapter you have read about the Great Depression of the 1930s. Which of the following questions would you ask to find out more about how the Great Depression affected Arkansans?

1. What happened to Arkansas's farmers during the Great Depression?
2. Did World War II occur before or after the Great Depression?
3. Why did Arkansans barter goods during the Depression?

How did you decide which questions to ask?

HELPING YOURSELF

The steps on the left will help you to ask questions on any topic. The example on the right shows one way to use these steps to learn more about the Great Depression in Arkansas.

One Way to Ask Questions	Example
1. Identify the topic that you want to find out about.	The topic is how the Great Depression affected Arkansans.
2. Figure out what you want to know about the topic. Review what you already know. Then ask yourself what else you need to learn to understand the topic.	You want to know how the Great Depression affected farmers and why people turned to bartering.
3. List questions you can ask to get this information. The following key words are useful to begin a question: • Use *who*, *what*, *when*, *where*, and *how* for finding facts. • Use *why* for finding cause and effect.	The first question uses the key word *what*. The answer will give you information about how the Depression affected farmers. The third question uses the key word *why*. The answer will let you see how Arkansans tried to solve problems during the Great Depression.
4. Arrange your questions in order, starting with the fact-finding questions and then moving on to those that show cause and effect. End with questions that look for the meaning of what happened.	Fact-finding questions are the easiest, so they should come first. Next ask cause-and-effect questions. At the end, ask questions to try to find out the importance of an event or its meaning.
5. Review your questions. Cross out any that are not related to the information you need.	The second question does not ask anything about how the Great Depression affected Arkansans, so it should be crossed out.
6. Ask your questions and then write down the answers.	By asking questions and recording the answers, you can find out what you need to know.

Applying the Skill

Another topic that you read about in this chapter is the Flood of 1927. Which of these questions would help you to learn about the topic?

1. Who was most affected by the Flood of 1927?
2. Which parts of Arkansas were affected by the flood?
3. How many rivers does Arkansas have?

Check yourself by answering the following questions.

1. Why is the first *Applying the Skill* question useful to you?
2. If you have crossed any of the questions off your list, explain why.

Reviewing the Skill

1. What is the most important purpose of asking questions?
2. What is the first step to take in asking questions?
3. What are some words you can use to come up with good questions?

3 The Struggle for Civil Rights

READ TO LEARN

Key Vocabulary

segregation   unconstitutional
Jim Crow laws   integration
civil rights

Key People

Orval Faubus
Dwight D. Eisenhower
Daisy Bates
Jerry Jewell

Read Aloud

In Stamps the segregation was so complete that most black children didn't really, absolutely know what whites looked like. Other than that they were different, to be dreaded. . . . I remember never believing that whites were really real.

These words were written by Maya Angelou, a famous Arkansas writer who grew up in Stamps, in Lafayette County. They describe the way in which black Arkansans were kept separate from white Arkansans. In this lesson you will read about this harmful separation, and the ways in which our state's African Americans fought against it.

Read for Purpose

1. **WHAT YOU KNOW:** How had Arkansas's African Americans been disappointed during Reconstruction?
2. **WHAT YOU WILL LEARN:** How did the civil rights movement change Arkansas?

SEGREGATION

Imagine that you are traveling on a train, bus, or airplane, and that you are going to visit your grandparents in another part of the United States. How would you feel if the attendant suddenly ordered you to move to the back of the bus, or to another part of the airplane or train? Maybe you would be angry, or hurt, or both.

For many years these kinds of experiences were a part of daily life for most African Americans. They were victims of segregation (seg ri gā′ shən)—that is, laws or practices that keep African Americans and whites separate.

"SEPARATE BUT EQUAL"

In Arkansas, as in many states, segregation dated back to the 1870s. After Reconstruction, many of the people who had run Arkansas's government before the Civil War returned to power.

Like state governments across the South, they adopted a "separate but equal" policy in regard to blacks and whites. By 1891 they had passed laws, called **Jim Crow laws**, to keep the two groups apart. These laws made it a crime for blacks and whites to share train cars, restaurants, hotels, schools, and even drinking fountains.

While Jim Crow laws kept African Americans separate, they didn't make them equal. The train cars or restaurants that were set aside for them were usually of poor quality.

In education, Jim Crow laws called for the creation of separate schools in each community. Black teachers were paid much less than white teachers. In addition, black schools received less money per child from the state than white schools did. For these reasons the "separate but equal" policy prevented African Americans from getting an adequate education.

CIVIL RIGHTS

By denying freedoms and opportunities to African Americans, Jim Crow laws denied them their **civil rights**. Civil rights are the rights of all people to be treated equally under the law. These rights include the right to vote, freedom of speech, and equal protection for all of a nation's citizens.

In 1954, however, the Supreme Court heard a case concerning school segregation, *Brown* v. *Board of Education*. The Court decided that "separate but equal" education was unjust and **unconstitutional**—in other words, not allowed by the Constitution. Therefore, the court ordered that all schools must be open to both black students and white students.

Segregation kept African Americans and whites separate in many Southern states.

159

Governor Orval Faubus (*right*) opposed **integration** of Little Rock Central High School. President Eisenhower sent federal troops to help African Americans enter the school.

CRISIS AT LITTLE ROCK

The Supreme Court's *Brown* decision caused a great deal of disagreement in our state. Orval Faubus, who was elected governor in 1954, favored the "separate but equal" policy in the schools. Although schools such as the University of Arkansas had begun to admit African Americans in the late 1940s, many Arkansans still opposed school integration. Integration means the act of making something available to all racial groups.

This disagreement came to a head in 1957. The state legislature had passed a law opposing the Supreme Court's decision. Meanwhile, Little Rock's Central High School was scheduled to be integrated in September. Would the nine African American students who had registered at Central High be allowed to attend?

As the beginning of the school year approached, tensions rose in Little Rock. Many citizens feared violence. Governor Faubus appeared on television and told the people of Arkansas that "blood will run in the streets" if the African American students tried to enter Central High.

CENTRAL HIGH IS INTEGRATED

On September 4, 1957, the nine students tried to enter Central High for the first time. Angry crowds surrounded the school. Can you imagine how the African American students must have felt? One student, Elizabeth Eckford, remembered the ordeal in this way.

The crowd moved in closer and then began to follow me, calling me names. . . . My knees started to shake all of a sudden and I wondered whether I could make it to the center entrance a block away. It was the longest block I ever walked in my life.

In fact, Elizabeth Eckford didn't enter Central High that day. Under orders from Governor Faubus, members of the Arkansas National Guard blocked her way.

The news from Little Rock made headlines around the world. Many opponents of integration applauded Faubus's actions. So did some Americans who believed that decisions about segregation should be made by the state governments, not the national government. But millions of people were shocked and angered.

On September 24, President Dwight D. Eisenhower decided that the Little Rock crisis had gone on long enough. He sent United States Army troops to restore order. Under the army's supervision, the "Little Rock Nine" were finally allowed to begin the school year at Central High.

The battle for school integration was not over. In 1958 Faubus and the legislature closed down all of Little Rock's high schools for the entire school year. Even after they were reopened, many Arkansans continued to resist the idea of integration. Six years after the crisis, less than 400 African Americans attended integrated schools in the state of Arkansas.

THE CIVIL RIGHTS MOVEMENT

The struggle for civil rights, or the civil rights movement, took place in many other areas besides education.

(*above*) Elizabeth Eckford called her walk to school the "longest block I ever walked in my life." (*below*) Daisy Bates was an important leader in Arkansas's **civil rights** movement.

Leaders such as Daisy Bates urged Arkansas's African Americans to fight for fair treatment. Bates led the Arkansas branch of the NAACP, a civil rights organization. She also published a newspaper, the *Arkansas State Press*, with her husband L. C. Bates.

In several parts of our state African Americans began to challenge segregated businesses and restaurants. A

161

Arkansas's African-Americans staged "sit-ins" as part of the struggle for civil rights.

group of students from Little Rock's Philander Smith College staged "sit-ins" at segregated lunch counters. They also marched on the State Capitol, singing "God Bless America," "The Star-Spangled Banner," and "We Shall Overcome." This last song expressed the hopes and struggles of our nation's African Americans.

Another important part of the civil rights movement was the registration of African American voters. In the face of great danger, Arkansas civil rights workers succeeded in registering 105,000 African Americans by 1966.

Gradually the African Americans of our state have made gains. In 1972 Jerry Jewell of Little Rock became the first African American since Reconstruction to be elected to the Arkansas State Senate. Since then, many others from across the state have held office.

Integration has taken root in many Arkansas schools—including Central High School, which is today made up almost equally of white students and black students. However, the struggle for racial equality continues in our state as it does in our nation.

LOOKING TOWARD THE FUTURE

For many years after Reconstruction our state's African Americans suffered injustice and segregation. In 1954 the Supreme Court decided that school segregation was against the law. This decision prompted the "Little Rock crisis" at Central High School. At the same time, many Arkansans fought against racial injustice in schools, businesses, and politics.

Today many of the young people who fought for civil rights are teachers, doctors, lawyers, and politicians. One of the "Little Rock Nine," Ernest Green, was appointed to a high office in the United States Department of Labor in 1977. These African Americans continue to be an important part of the future of our state and nation.

Check Your Reading

1. What effects did segregation have on our state's African Americans?
2. Explain the idea of civil rights.
3. What kinds of progress have our state's African Americans made because of the civil rights movement?
4. THINKING SKILL: What might have been the consequences if President Eisenhower had not sent United States Army troops to Central High School?

REVIEWING VOCABULARY

Number a sheet of paper from 1 to 5. Beside each number write the letter of the word that best completes the sentence.

1. The _____ was a time when many people lost their jobs.
   a. World War I
   b. World War II
   c. Great Depression
2. _____ became an important part of Arkansas's economy.
   a. Tourism
   b. Stocks
   c. Segregation
3. Because of _____, African Americans received a poorer education than whites did.
   a. integration
   b. segregation
   c. civil rights
4. The _____ movement worked to bring more freedoms to African Americans.
   a. civil rights
   b. Jim Crow
   c. New Deal
5. President Roosevelt's plan to help people during the Great Depression was called the _____.
   a. Jim Crow laws
   b. stock plan
   c. New Deal

REVIEWING FACTS

1. Who were two World War I heroes from our state?
2. In which ways did Arkansans help the war effort during World War I?
3. Which new inventions changed life for many Arkansans during the 1920s?
4. Which natural disaster struck Arkansas in 1927?
5. Support the following statement with three facts: "The Great Depression hit hard in our state."
6. What were the FERA and the CCC?
7. How did World War II affect the lives of African Americans, women, and Japanese Americans?
8. What were Jim Crow laws?
9. How did Governor Orval Faubus feel about school integration?
10. How has the civil rights movement helped African Americans in Arkansas since the 1950s?

WRITING ABOUT MAIN IDEAS

1. **Writing a Radio News Report:** Choose one of the following events and write a radio news story about it: the Flood of 1927, the stock market crash, or the Supreme Court ruling in *Brown* v. *Board of Education*.
2. **Writing a Diary Entry:** Review the information about the CCC. Then write a diary entry in which a "3-C" worker describes a typical day.

BUILDING SKILLS: ASKING QUESTIONS

1. List six key words that can help you to ask questions.
2. List three questions you could ask to learn more about World War II.
3. Why should you ask questions?

REVIEWING VOCABULARY

Number a sheet of paper from 1 to 10. Beside each number write **C** if the underlined word or term is used correctly. If it is not, write the word or term that would correctly complete the sentence.

1. The Civil War was fought between the Union and the <u>Allied Powers</u>.
2. Northerners who traveled to the South during Reconstruction were known as <u>jayhawkers</u>.
3. People who wanted to end slavery were known as <u>abolitionists</u>.
4. During the 1860s the Northern states and the Southern states fought <u>World War I</u>.
5. Jim Crow laws in the South brought about <u>integration</u> of public places.
6. President Roosevelt's plan to help people during the Great Depression was called the <u>Freedmen's Bureau</u>.
7. The Supreme Court decided that the law conflicted with the Constitution. In other words, it was <u>segregated</u>.
8. Manufacturing and agriculture are parts of the Arkansas <u>economy</u>.
9. The stock market crash marked the beginning of the <u>Progressive Era</u>.
10. Many African Americans in the South remained poor because of a farming system called <u>tourism</u>.

◀️▶️ WRITING ABOUT THE UNIT

1. **Writing a Composition:** Many changes came about for African Americans between 1860 and 1960. Write a few paragraphs describing the changes. End your composition by stating one conclusion you can draw from the information you have presented.
2. **Writing a Paragraph of Comparison:** In this unit you have read about two very difficult times for Arkansans—the years after the Civil War and the years of the Great Depression. For each of these periods, think about what caused the hard times, what life was like then, and what was done to improve things. Then write a paragraph comparing the two periods of "hard times."
3. **Writing a Thank-You Letter:** Write a letter to someone who lived in the days of the New South. Tell the person how present-day Arkansas has benefited from the many changes that took place during that time.

ACTIVITIES

1. **Making a Book:** Find out more about the Battle of Pea Ridge. Then make a book about the battle, including a description of the main events, some pictures, and at least one map.
2. **Writing a Book Report:** Read a book about the Great Depression. Choose a book with many pictures or with personal accounts of life at that time. Then write a report about the book.
3. **Working Together to Construct an Illustrated Time Line:** With a group of classmates, make a time line showing the main events discussed in Unit 4. Draw or paint pictures to go with some of the events on the time line. Then display the completed time lines around your classroom.

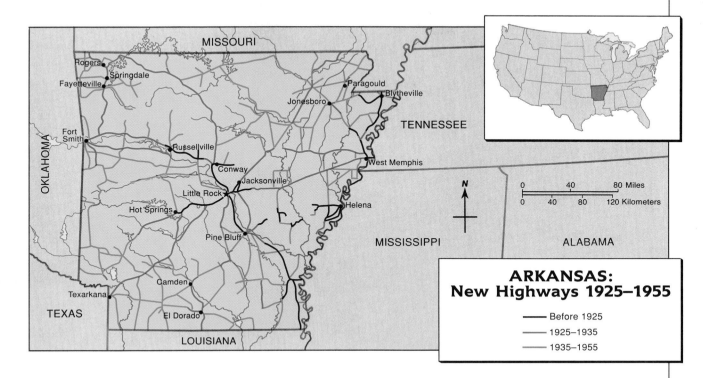

MISSOURI

Rogers
Springdale
Fayetteville
Paragould
Blytheville
Jonesboro

TENNESSEE

Fort Smith
Russellville
Conway
West Memphis
Jacksonville
Little Rock
Hot Springs
Helena
Pine Bluff

MISSISSIPPI

ALABAMA

OKLAHOMA

Camden
Texarkana
TEXAS
El Dorado
LOUISIANA

N

| 0 | 40 | 80 Miles |
| 0 | 40 | 80 | 120 Kilometers |

**ARKANSAS:
New Highways 1925–1955**

——— Before 1925
——— 1925–1935
——— 1935–1955

BUILDING SKILLS:
READING HISTORICAL MAPS

Use the map on this page, "ARKANSAS: New Highways 1925–1955," to answer the following questions.

1. What is the subject of the map?
2. Which color or colors are used to show roads built by 1925? By 1955?

3. Look at the landforms map on page 12. How do you think that Arkansas's landforms affected decisions as to where our state's roads were built?
4. What conclusions can you draw from the rapid growth of road building between 1925 and 1935?
5. Why is it useful to be able to read historical maps?

LINKING PAST, PRESENT, AND FUTURE

In this unit you have read about two occasions on which the world erupted into war. In each case millions of people died, property was lost, and lives were disrupted. Do you think such a war could happen again? If it did, how would it be similar to or different from World War I and World War II?

State tree:
Pine tree

State gem:
Diamond

State bird:
Mockingbird

ARKANSAS

State flower:
Apple blossom

166

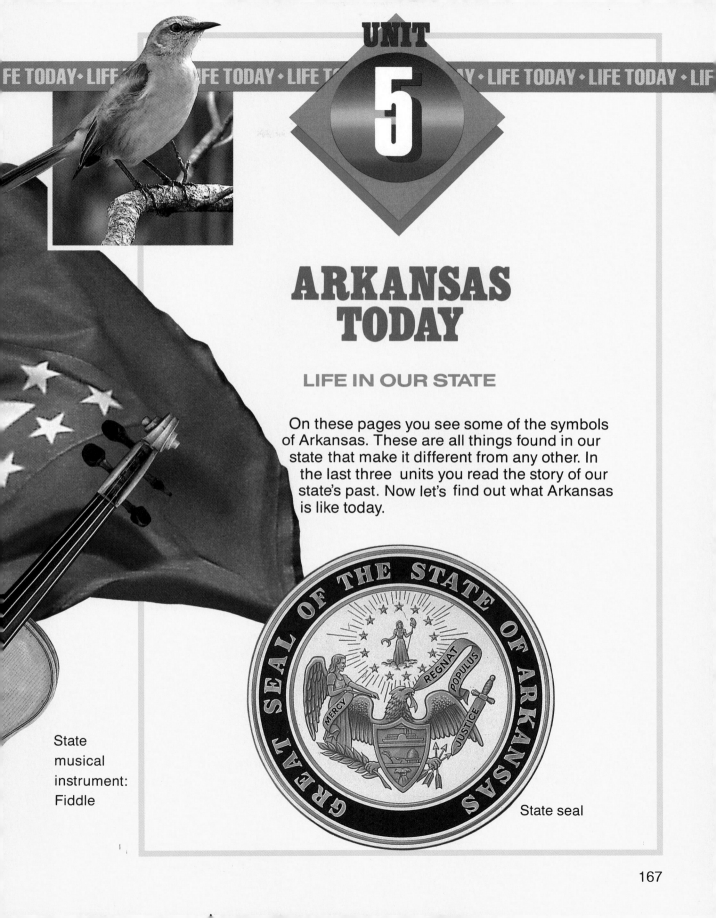

ARKANSAS TODAY

LIFE IN OUR STATE

On these pages you see some of the symbols of Arkansas. These are all things found in our state that make it different from any other. In the last three units you read the story of our state's past. Now let's find out what Arkansas is like today.

State
musical
instrument:
Fiddle

State seal

CHAPTER 10

WORKING IN ARKANSAS

FOCUS

"Good enough" is generally not good enough for most of our people.

This is how one Arkansan described the workers in his company near Jonesboro. People in every part of our state take pride in the jobs they do. In this chapter you will read about some of the ways Arkansans make a living.

1 Farming

READ TO LEARN

Key Vocabulary

subsistence farming
cash crop
livestock
poultry

Read Aloud

No matter where you go in Arkansas you discover that its people are close to the soil.

These words were written by one observer during the 1940s. Many things in Arkansas have changed since that time, but farming remains a key part of our state's life and economy.

Read for Purpose

1. **WHAT YOU KNOW:** How has agriculture been important to the history of Arkansas?
2. **WHAT YOU WILL LEARN:** Which kinds of crops are grown today in Arkansas, and which methods are used to grow them?

PAST AND PRESENT

In Chapter 3 you read that the first Arkansans began to grow crops thousands of years ago. Since that time agriculture has been an important part of life in our state.

Modern-day Arkansans grow corn, squash, and beans, which were grown by the Caddo hundreds of years ago. Arkansans also continue to grow cotton, which was a popular crop with farmers a century ago. But many features of farming in our state have changed. Today's farmers grow these older crops using new tools and methods. They have also discovered newer crops such as rice and soybeans.

Let's take a look at an Arkansas farm of 100 years ago. Although this farm is a fictional one, it is typical of many farms of the time.

The farmer, whose name was James Runyan, owned 10 acres (4 ha) of land south of Harrison, in Boone County. Every year he planted a small crop of cotton on his land, as well as rows of rhubarb, tomatoes, squash, corn, okra, and potatoes.

For some jobs, such as plowing, Runyan used a mule or a horse. But most of the labor on his farm was done by hand. Each April he and his family planted seeds. In late June or early July

The first tractors in Arkansas (*top*) were an improvement over mules and horses. Modern tractors and combines work much faster in producing **cash crops**

they began to pick the crops. They worked at these jobs from early morning until dusk.

James Runyan loaded his small cotton crop onto a wagon and sold it in Harrison. He may have also sold part of his vegetable crop. But he used most of his vegetable harvest to feed his family. This type of farming, which was once very common in Arkansas, is called **subsistence farming**. Rather than make large profits from his crops, a subsistence farmer mostly lives on what he grows.

Today Nancy Runyan is a farmer, too, like her great-grandfather, James. But many things about her farm in White County might surprise James Runyan. For one thing, Nancy grows only a single crop—soybeans—on her

400 acres (162 ha). For another, much of the work is done by machines. At harvest time workers drive huge combines, or harvesting machines, through the fields. While these machines pick and clean the soybeans in the July sun, their operators stay cool inside air-conditioned cabs.

Nancy Runyan's soybeans are a **cash crop**—in other words, she grows them to sell. Her family earns its living from the crop's profits. This, too, shows a great change in our state's agriculture. For many Arkansas farmers today, farming has become a "big business."

SOYBEANS AND RICE

As you have read in earlier chapters, cotton was Arkansas's main crop for many years. Some Arkansans even called it "King Cotton." But today other crops have become more important.

Nancy Runyan's crop, soybeans, was widely introduced in our state during the 1930s and 1940s. Actually, King Cotton had a great deal to do with the introduction of this newer crop in Arkansas. Repeated cotton plantings tended to wear out the soil. Farmers discovered that a planting of soybeans restored the soil, allowing it to "rest."

Gradually soybean farming spread. Over the last ten years soybeans have become one of Arkansas's leading agricultural products. Our state's farmers harvested more than 99 million bushels (35 million hl) of these beans in 1992. Much of this harvest is shipped overseas. But every time you use margarine or cooking oil, it's likely that you're using a product made from soybeans. You may also find soybean oil in paints, soaps, insecticides, and even in ink!

Another major crop is rice. Arkansas farmers began to experiment with rice around 1895. J. M. Fuller, an Arkansas County farmer, planted 40 acres (16 ha) of this new crop in 1905. His first harvest amounted to almost 3,000 bushels (1,000 hl). If you were to line up that many bushel baskets, they would stretch about 1 mile (1.6 km)!

Since that time rice has become very important to our economy. Towering rice elevators dot the countryside of southeastern Arkansas. Millions of bushels are sold overseas. Families in Europe and Africa might well find Arkansas's rice on their dinner tables.

Look at the bar graph on this page to study which crops are grown in our state. Which are the three largest crops produced in Arkansas?

OTHER CROPS

Our long growing season has always encouraged farmers to grow fruits and vegetables. Arkansans raise apples, grapes, and strawberries. Our orchards produce more than 8 million pounds (3.6 million kg) of peaches every year.

The farmers of Hempstead County raise world-famous watermelons. In

GRAPH SKILL: Soybeans are one of Arkansas's most important crops. How many dollars worth of soybeans were grown in our state in 1992?

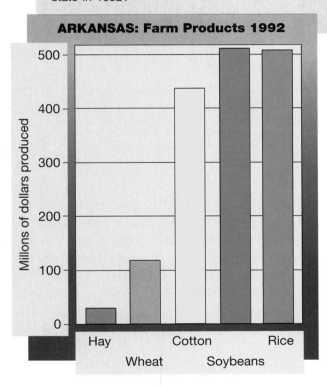

ARKANSAS: Farm Products 1992

fact, 55,000 people flocked to the Hope Watermelon Festival in 1995. There they celebrated this Arkansas farm product with games, races, music, and watermelon-eating contests.

LIVESTOCK

Another growing part of our farm economy is **livestock**. We use this word to describe animals such as cattle,

171

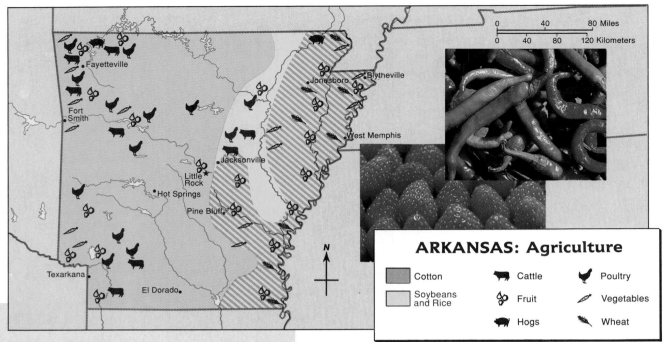

ARKANSAS: Agriculture

▨ Cotton	🐄 Cattle	🐔 Poultry
▧ Soybeans and Rice	🍒 Fruit	🌿 Vegetables
	🐖 Hogs	🌾 Wheat

MAP SKILL: Fresh fruits and vegetables provide a colorful display of Arkansas's agriculture. In which parts of our state are they grown?

horses, and pigs that are raised on a farm. Since Arkansas is sometimes known as the "Razorback State," it is only natural that our farmers raise hogs. Beef cattle and dairy cattle are also an important part of our farm economy. However, the number of cattle in Arkansas has been dropping over the last 15 years.

Our major animal product is poultry—that is, chickens, turkeys, and other birds that are raised for meat and eggs. Arkansas ranks first in the nation in the production of broilers, or small chickens. Our state's poultry farms also produce enormous numbers of eggs.

Look at the map on this page. Which part of our state produces the most cattle? Which part produces the most soybeans?

CHANGING AGRICULTURE

Farming is as important to Arkansas today as it has always been. Soybeans and rice have replaced cotton as the major crops. In many instances, tractors, combines, and computers have replaced human labor. Despite all these changes, though, agriculture remains a key part of the economy of our state.

Check Your Reading

1. How does Nancy Runyan's farm differ from James Runyan's farm?
2. What roles do soybeans and rice play in Arkansas's farm economy?
3. GEOGRAPHY SKILL: Why do you think that soybeans and rice are grown mainly in the eastern part of Arkansas?
4. THINKING SKILL: What are two questions you could ask to learn more about the production of poultry in Arkansas.

LESSON 2 — Manufacturing and Industry

READ TO LEARN

Key Vocabulary

technology   interdependent   free enterprise

service industries   entrepreneur

Key People

Sam Walton

Read Aloud

I believe so much in our state and its possibilities. . . . We live in a complex and challenging time . . . a time in which swift currents of change are sweeping through our state and nation, drawing us into a future very different from even the immediate past.

These words are from a speech by President Bill Clinton when he was governor of Arkansas. This lesson will describe the "currents of change" that industry is bringing to our state.

Read for Purpose

1. **WHAT YOU KNOW:** How has the geography of our state affected the kinds of work that Arkansans do?
2. **WHAT YOU WILL LEARN:** What are some important industries in Arkansas?

LEAVING THE LAND

In Lesson 1 you read that farming has become a big business in Arkansas. Large, single-crop farms produce much bigger harvests than the small farms of a century ago.

At the same time, though, the total number of Arkansans working in agriculture has declined. Why? Modern machinery and methods allow 1 farm worker to do tasks that once required 20 workers. Between 1950 and 1970, three out of four Arkansas farmers left the land for other kinds of work. Many now have found jobs in our state's growing industries.

RESOURCES AND MANUFACTURING

When you are riding in an automobile, have you ever wondered where its parts came from? In fact, the aluminum, the plastic, the stainless steel, and some of the car's electronic parts may have come from Arkansas. Even the gasoline in the tank may have come from our state!

As you have read in Chapter 1, the land of Arkansas is rich in natural resources. Many industries have located here because of these riches. Coal, oil, minerals, timber, and natural gas have all brought businesses to our

173

DIAGRAM SKILL: Cutting trees in the forest is the first step in making paper. What happens to trees after they arrive at the paper manufacturing plant?

state. But locating and collecting these resources is only the first part of such an industry's job.

A bromine company, for example, might mine this valuable mineral in Columbia County. Once the company has mined the bromine, however, someone must still change it into a usable product—plastic, for example. This process usually takes place in a factory and involves machinery. As you read in Chapter 8, we use the word *manufacturing* to describe the process of making things by machinery. Look at the diagram on this page to see how paper is manufactured from wood.

"MADE IN ARKANSAS"

Look at the graph on page 175 to study manufacturing in our state. As you can see, the leading type of manufacturing is food processing. The thousands of people who work in this industry prepare Arkansas's farm products for the market.

Rice, for example, is not ready to be eaten when it is harvested. First it must be cleaned. Then special milling

HOW TREES BECOME PAPER

1. Trucks bring logs to factory
2. Logs chipped into pulp
3. Water added to pulp
4. Pulp sent through rollers
5. Dried on hot rollers
6. Paper taken by truck to printing plant

machines remove the outer layer of the grains. Other machines polish the grains and separate them according to size. In Jonesboro over 500 Arkansans perform these jobs in the world's largest rice mill.

Another important industry is electrical manufacturing. The electric lights, telephone, or refrigerator in your home may all include parts made in our state.

Both of these industries are constantly on the lookout for new ways to improve their products. Some of Arkansas's electronics companies, for example, now use computers to test every product while it is being put together. This use of new ideas and tools to meet people's needs is called technology (tek nol' ə jē).

HIGH-TECH INDUSTRIES

Technology is especially important to a type of industry that is new in our state. These industries require a great deal of scientific experimentation and knowledge. For this reason they are sometimes called "high-technology" industries, or high-tech, for short.

One such industry, located in Camden, manufactures rocket engines and guidance systems. Others produce computer parts, special electronic circuits, or medical equipment.

Some of our state's other high-tech industries use biotechnology—that is, technology involving living things. For instance, some Arkansas scientists have studied the ways in which tiny cells in living things work. They are trying to change these cells in ways that will help people to stay healthy. Other researchers in biotechnology have tried to improve the vegetables and livestock we raise in Arkansas.

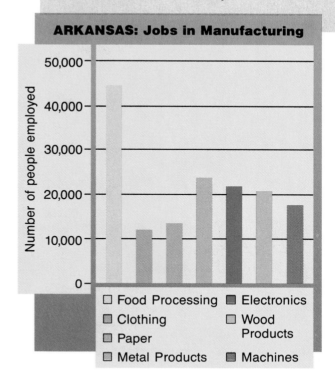

GRAPH SKILL: Technology is an important part of the electronics industry. How many Arkansans work in this industry?

ARKANSAS: Jobs in Manufacturing

☐ Food Processing ■ Electronics
☐ Clothing ☐ Wood Products
☐ Paper
☐ Metal Products ■ Machines

These kinds of research are very difficult to perform. A single speck of dust or dirt may ruin an experiment. For this reason these industries often use special areas called "clean rooms." The workers in these rooms wear special clothes and must also go through a machine that "vacuums" them clean before they enter. Would you like it if your room at home had to be as clean as a "clean room"?

SERVICE INDUSTRIES

Not all of Arkansas's industries make products. Instead, some may offer a service—that is, a useful or necessary kind of work. These industries, which "serve" people, are called service industries

ARKANSAS: Manufacturing

👕 Clothing	⚙️ Machines	✏️ Paper
⌇ Electronics	▰ Metal products	▭ Wood products
🥫 Food processing		

MAP SKILL: Arkansas workers make everything from frozen dinners to airplanes. Which manufacturing industries are located in Jonesboro?

You see many service industry workers every day. The service industries include education, health care (doctors, nurses, and workers in hospitals and home health care), and government. The plumber who fixes your sink is part of a service industry. So are the school bus driver and the cook who prepares your sandwich at a local restaurant. Can you think of other examples of service industry workers in your community?

In Arkansas, as in the rest of the United States, the number of people who work in service industries is on the rise. In fact, the majority of Americans may be employed by these industries within 50 years.

INTERDEPENDENCE

As you have read, service industries and manufacturing operate in different ways. However, these two parts of our economy rely on each other for help.

A timber company near Hot Springs sends wood to a paper factory near Pine Bluff. The paper factory turns the wood into paper. From there, a truck-

ing company takes the paper to a printer near Jonesboro, who prints a magazine that you buy. These different businesses are interdependent (in tər di pen' dənt). In other words, they depend on one another to help meet the needs and wants of our state.

ENTREPRENEURS IN ARKANSAS

How do you think businesses are started? Some service industries, such as your school system, fire department, or police department, are set up by the government. However, many businesses are created by individuals who hope to earn money from them. A person who creates a business for profit is called an entrepreneur (än trə prə nûr'). Free enterprise is the economic system in which people own and run their own businesses.

Many Arkansans have created businesses. One Arkansan, Sam Walton, opened his first "five-and-ten-cent" store in Newport in 1945. That store grew into a business of more than 1,735 stores in 42 states. During his lifetime, Sam Walton became a billionaire and received a Presidential Medal of Freedom.

WORKING IN ARKANSAS

One hundred years ago a young person looking for a job in Arkansas had few choices. Most people did farm work. Today, however, things are very different. You can now choose among the state's many manufacturing industries, or get a job in a service industry. You might also become an entrepreneur and start your own business!

Sam Walton was an entrepreneur who started in business with one small store. Wal-Mart is one of many stores he founded.

Check Your Reading

1. Why has the number of Arkansans working on farms grown smaller?
2. Define the terms *technology* and *high-tech*, and give two examples of high-tech industries that are located in our state.
3. What are our state's three largest industries?
4. **GEOGRAPHY SKILL:** Why do you think that Jonesboro, on Crowley's Ridge, makes a good location for a rice mill?
5. **THINKING SKILL:** Can you think of any jobs that might exist when you will be an adult that do not exist now?

Comparing Local Maps

In this book you have studied many kinds of maps. Each map gives different information, and often you can find the information you need by looking at just one map. Sometimes, however, you want information that does not appear on a single map. In such cases you may have to look at two or more maps and compare them.

For example, look at the agriculture map on page 172. Notice that rice, soybeans, and cotton are grown in eastern Arkansas but not in western Arkansas. To find out the reason, look at the physical map on page 233. Notice that eastern Arkansas has rivers and low-lying land that are good for growing these crops.

Making Comparisons

The first step in comparing maps is to figure out what you are comparing. Ask yourself the following questions.

• Am I comparing maps that show different information *about the same place*?
• Am I comparing maps that show similar information *about two different places*?

You can answer these questions by looking at the title and labels on each map. Study the two maps on these pages. Do they show the same place? How can you tell? What does the map below show? What does the map on page 179 show?

Next decide which information each map gives. Use the map keys to find out

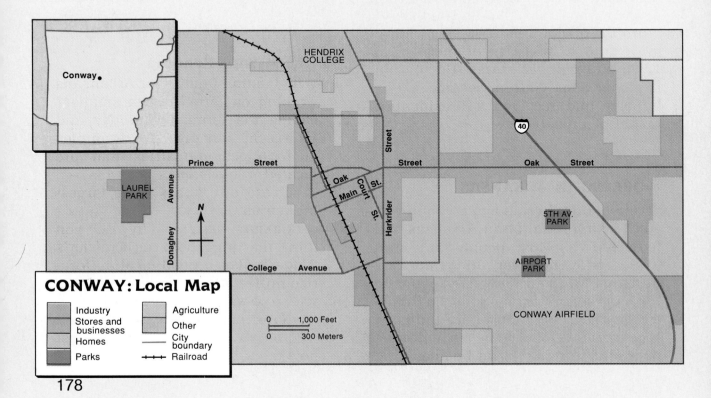

CONWAY: Local Map

Key:
- Industry
- Stores and businesses
- Homes
- Parks
- Agriculture
- Other
- City boundary
- Railroad

Map labels: Conway. HENDRIX COLLEGE, LAUREL PARK, Prince Street, Donaghey Avenue, Oak, Main, Court St., Harkrider, Street, Oak Street, 40, 5TH AV. PARK, AIRPORT PARK, College Avenue, CONWAY AIRFIELD

0 — 1,000 Feet
0 — 300 Meters

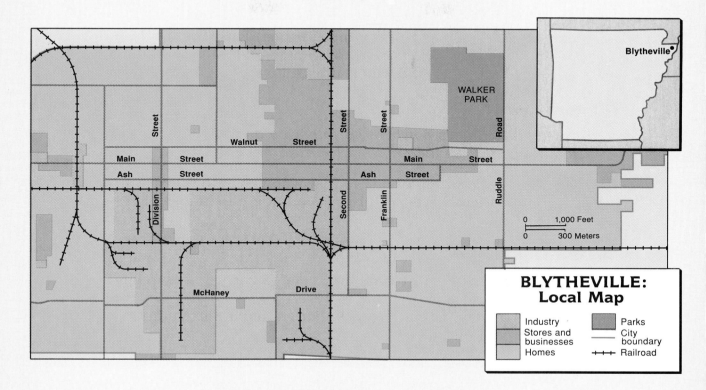

The map shows streets including Street, Walnut Street, Main Street, Ash Street, Division, McHaney, Drive, Second, Franklin, Ash Street, Main Street, Ruddle, Road, and WALKER PARK.

Inset map shows Blytheville location in Arkansas.

Scale: 0 — 1,000 Feet; 0 — 300 Meters

**BLYTHEVILLE:
Local Map**

Industry
Stores and businesses
Homes
Parks
City boundary
+++ Railroad

what the different colors stand for. Which color shows agriculture in Conway? What does the color pink stand for in both Conway and Blytheville?

Then look for similarities and differences between information on the two maps. Which city has the larger business area? Does Conway or Blytheville have more industry?

Finally, make statements based on the information on the two maps. Based on the information presented on page 178, which of the following statements about Conway is true?

- Conway is mostly a city of farmers.
- Conway has a larger residential area than business area.

Reviewing the Skill

Compare the maps to answer the following questions.

1. What are the three main uses of land in Blytheville?
2. What is most of the land in Conway used for? What is most of the land in Blytheville used for?
3. Why do you think that many of the railroads in Blytheville are located near areas of industry?
4. Which city has more parks?
5. What can you learn from comparing maps that give similar information about two different places?
6. How is it helpful to compare two or more maps?

3 Tourism

Key Vocabulary

architecture

Key Places

Hot Springs National Park
Prairie Grove Battlefield
Buffalo National River

Read Aloud

In early fall, there's nowhere I'd rather be than the Ouachita Mountains, just as the trees start to turn red and gold.

These are the words of one tourist who visited Arkansas in 1989. In this lesson you will read about the importance of tourism to our state.

Read for Purpose

1. **WHAT YOU KNOW:** Have you ever taken a car trip to another part of Arkansas?
2. **WHAT YOU WILL LEARN:** How is tourism important to the economy of our state?

VACATIONING IN ARKANSAS

The sun was just coming up when Hester Baker carried her suitcase out to the driveway of her home in Magnolia. Her mother and father were packing the car with tents, sleeping bags, and other camping equipment.

"Don't forget the maps, Hester," reminded her mother. "You're going to be our navigator."

Hester helped her father strap the canoe onto the roof of the car.

"Which way to Hot Springs?" asked Mr. Baker.

"It's north on Route 79," Hester answered, and soon the Baker family was off for their summer adventure.

TOURISM AND THE ECONOMY

By spending their vacation in Arkansas, the Baker family was contributing to one of our state's most important industries—tourism. As you read in Chapter 9, tourism is the business of providing services to people who are on vacation.

The Bakers, of course, are Arkansans themselves. But many people come to our state from different states and countries. Every year more than 15 million people visit Arkansas to enjoy its many attractions.

These visitors stay at hotels, motels, and campgrounds. They eat Arkansas food and buy souvenirs. In order to provide services for these tourists, 50,000 Arkansans work in the tourism industry—a greater number than all the fifth-grade students in our state! Their jobs range from park ranger to fiddle player, but they all work to make sure that tourists really enjoy their visit to Arkansas.

HOT SPRINGS

The Baker family's first stop was Hot Springs. Visitors have been coming to the hot, bubbly springs here for thousands of years. Many people believe that if they bathe in these soothing, natural waters, they will stay healthy. In 1921 Congress created Hot Springs National Park. Because it is a national park, the area is protected by our government, so that people will be able to enjoy its natural splendor forever.

In Hot Springs the Bakers hiked through the scenic hills. They listened to a ranger discuss the wildlife living in the park. There were once so many bears in our state that Arkansas was known as the "Bear State." Bears, deer, and bobcats still live in this area, but today's tourists know our state as the "Natural State."

Later in the day, Hester's family strolled down Bathhouse Row and looked at the interesting architecture (är' ki tek chər) of Hot Springs. Architecture is the style of a building. Look at the photograph on this page. How would you describe the architecture of Hot Springs?

The Hot Springs area is also famous for its many different minerals. Hester bought a large piece of stone, called quartz, for her collection. These pieces of clear quartz are also known as "Hot Springs Diamonds."

THE OZARKS

Now the Bakers drove north through the steep, winding roads of the Ouachita Mountains. The next stop on their trip was Arkansas's most popular tourist area—the Ozarks. People from around the world tour these mountains every year. They visit historical sites such as the Prairie Grove Battlefield and scenic places such as the Buffalo National River.

The Ozark region is also famous for the many craftspeople who work there. These people preserve the traditions and culture of the Ozarks. They make pottery, baskets, quilts, and even musical instruments in the way they have been made for hundreds of years. Many festivals are held in the Ozarks every summer. Musicians, actors, dancers, and singers join the craftspeople in entertaining at these events.

People visit Hot Springs to look at the architecture and to soak in the baths.

State Parks
1. Crater of Diamonds
2. Crowley's Ridge
3. Devil's Den
4. Lake Frierson
5. Lake Ouachita
6. Mammoth Spring
7. Millwood
8. Moro Bay
9. Old Washington
10. Petit Jean
11. Prairie Grove
12. Queen Wilhelmina
13. Toltec Mound
14. Withrow Springs

Festivals
A. Apple Festival
B. Arkansas Folk Festival
C. Arkansas Rice Festival
D. Autumnfest
E. Brickfest
F. Championship Grape Stomp
G. Oktoberfest
H. Peach Festival
I. Pine Bluff Air Festival
J. Pink Tomato Festival
K. Riverfest
L. Rodeo Round-up
M. Watermelon Festival
N. Wings Over the Prairie

ARKANSAS: Places to Visit

★ State capital

National park, forest, or river

State park

• Other city

▲ Festival

MAP SKILL: Tourists come every spring to see musicians perform at the Arkansas Folk Festival. In which town does this festival take place?

ATTRACTIONS EVERYWHERE

Tourists can find beauty and excitement in every corner of our state. Many communities hold annual festivals or celebrations, which you can study above and on pages 248–249 of the Arkansas Almanac. Other attractions continue all year long. Visitors can go fishing in Millwood Lake or discover geological wonders at Blanchard Springs Cavern. They can explore the ancient ruins at Toltec or canoe down the wild rapids of the White River.

The tourist industry is important for many reasons. It helps people to enjoy the natural attractions and interesting sites that make Arkansas special. It provides many jobs for the people of our state. And finally, it helps us to preserve our heritage as Arkansans.

Check Your Reading

1. How does tourism help the economy of Arkansas?
2. Why did Congress establish Hot Springs National Park?
3. How do craftspeople of the Ozarks help to preserve the heritage of our state?
4. **GEOGRAPHY SKILL:** Which parts of our state would be enjoyable for tourists who like hiking?
5. **THINKING SKILL:** What can you conclude from the fact that Arkansas is today called the "Natural State"?

REVIEWING VOCABULARY

cash crop   poultry
interdependent   technology
livestock

Number a sheet of paper from 1 to 5. Beside each number write the word from the list above that best matches the definition.

1. Animals raised on a farm, such as pigs and cattle
2. Depending on each other to help meet needs and wants
3. The use of new ideas and tools to meet people's needs
4. Birds raised for their meat or eggs
5. A crop grown to be sold

REVIEWING FACTS

1. What is subsistence farming?
2. What are three of Arkansas's leading agricultural products?
3. In which part of Arkansas are the most soybeans grown?
4. Which crop is Hempstead County famous for?
5. Give an example of interdependence between farmers and service workers.
6. What are two major types of manufacturing in Arkansas?
7. What is a "clean room"?
8. How does an entrepreneur make money?
9. Name two places in Arkansas where tourism is an important business.
10. How do craftspeople help to preserve our traditions?

WRITING ABOUT MAIN IDEAS

1. **Preparing an Interview:** Choose a job in a service industry that interests you. Plan an interview with a person who holds that job. Write at least five questions that you would ask the person about his or her job.
2. **Writing a Letter:** Choose one tourist attraction in Arkansas. Imagine that you want to plan a vacation there. To help you plan the vacation, write a letter to get information about that place.
3. **Planning a Menu:** Study the map of farm products on page 172. Then plan a meal to be made completely from foods that are produced in Arkansas. Identify places where each farm product might have come from.

BUILDING SKILLS: COMPARING MAPS

1. Why is it useful to compare maps?
2. What is the first step you should take when comparing maps?
3. How can the information in the map key be helpful in comparing maps?
4. Look at the maps of Arkansas in the Atlas on pages 232 and 233. How are these maps similar? How are they different?

CHAPTER 11

ARKANSAS'S GOVERNMENT

FOCUS

I met the governor in Center Point, and he gave a speech to us. The speech was about freedom.

These are the words of Leah Clark, a fifth-grade student from Howard County. Upholding the freedom of every Arkansan is part of the governor's duty as head of our state government. In this chapter you will read about the different parts of our state government. You will also read about other kinds of government that affect our lives in Arkansas.

1 State Government

READ TO LEARN

Key Vocabulary

tax
budget
General Assembly
legislative branch

bill
executive branch
veto
judicial branch

Key People

Bill Clinton

Read Aloud

I am proud of my state. I will uphold its constitution, obey its laws, and work for the good of all its citizens.

These words come from the "Arkansas Creed." A creed is a formal statement of a person's beliefs or opinions. When you say these words out loud, you are expressing a belief about Arkansas, its laws, and its government. How would you explain this belief in your own words?

Read for Purpose

1. WHAT YOU KNOW: Why are rules important in your school and classroom?
2. WHAT YOU WILL LEARN: How does our state government provide services for its citizens?

OUR STATE AND YOU

You have probably seen many photographs of our State Capitol in Little Rock. You may have even visited it during a class trip. Have you ever wondered about the activities that go on inside the Capitol? Every day, decisions are made there that affect the daily lives of every single Arkansan—including you.

In the last chapter you read that services are useful or necessary kinds of work. Certain of these services, such as running hospitals or taking care of Arkansas's parks, are provided to us by the state government. Of course, the government must pay for these services. Our state is able to pay because it collects money from the people of Arkansas. This money is called taxes.

Suppose that you were given a sum of money as a birthday present. What would you do with it? You might go to the movies and then use the remaining money to buy a record. Perhaps you would put aside a portion of the money in your savings account.

In a way, our state government makes similar decisions regarding our

185

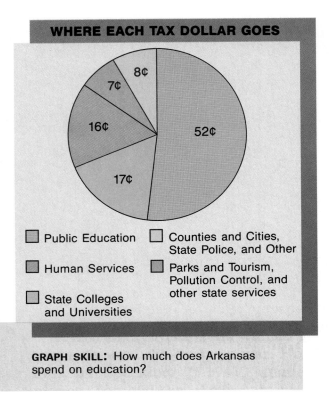

WHERE EACH TAX DOLLAR GOES

8¢

7¢

16¢

52¢

17¢

☐ Public Education

☐ Human Services

☐ State Colleges and Universities

☐ Counties and Cities, State Police, and Other

☐ Parks and Tourism, Pollution Control, and other state services

GRAPH SKILL: How much does Arkansas spend on education?

tax dollars. The leaders of our government must decide which services these dollars should pay for. Then they must determine how much money should be spent on each service. This plan for the ways in which money will be spent is called a budget.

Look at the circle graph on this page. It shows how Arkansas spends each tax dollar. According to the graph, what is our state's biggest expense?

Sometimes people may argue about the amount of money that should be spent on a particular service. How are these decisions finally made? In order to answer this question, you need to know more about the way in which our state government works.

THE LEGISLATIVE BRANCH

Dennis Taylor lives in Harrison, high in the Ozarks. Ever since he was a child, he has loved the folk music of the Ozark region. He learned to play the fiddle at age four, and this instrument always seemed to him to express something of the beauty of these jagged mountains.

In 1985 an idea occurred to Dennis. Arkansas already had a state flower, a state gem, and a state bird. You will read about these symbols of our state later on. Dennis thought that the fiddle would be a good choice for the state instrument. He realized that to make this choice official, the state would have to pass a law. How did this work?

Dennis first brought his idea to the General Assembly, which is the legislative (lej' is lā tiv) branch of the Arkansas government. A branch is a part of government. The members of the General Assembly meet and make laws. In Arkansas the legislative branch is made up of two different parts: the House of Representatives and the Senate. The 100 representatives and 35 senators are chosen by the voters of our state.

Dennis discussed his idea with Bob Watts, his state representative. Representative Watts agreed to write a bill to make the fiddle our state instrument. A bill is a plan for a law.

The "fiddle bill," now officially called House Bill 749, was presented to the House of Representatives. The representatives liked Dennis's idea and voted to pass the bill.

Next, the bill was sent to the Senate. Sometimes the senators disagree with the representatives and refuse to pass a bill. But in this case they agreed that Dennis's idea was a good one. Now just one more person had to be convinced in order for the bill to become a law—the governor of Arkansas.

THE EXECUTIVE BRANCH

The governor is elected by the people of Arkansas to head the executive (eg zek' yə tiv) branch of our government. He or she makes sure that the laws are carried out. The governor also plays an important role in making laws. On page 246 of the Arkansas Almanac you can study a list of all the governors in our state's history.

After both houses of the General Assembly had passed Dennis's bill, it went to then Governor Bill Clinton for approval. Governor Clinton had two choices. He could sign House Bill 749, which would make it a state law, or he could veto the bill—that is, refuse to sign it. However, if more than half of the members of the General Assembly still favored the bill, they would be

CHART SKILL: The "fiddle bill" started with Dennis Taylor's idea. What is the next step for a bill to become a law?

HOW A BILL BECOMES A LAW

1. Idea for the Bill

2. Concerned citizen goes to the State Legislature

3. Member of the House of Representatives writes the bill

4. The House of Representatives approves the bill

5. The Senate approves the bill

6. The Governor signs the bill

OR The Governor vetoes the bill

7. More than ½ of the House and more than ½ of the Senate vote for the bill.

8. The bill becomes a law

187

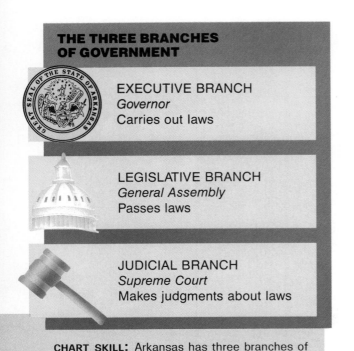

THE THREE BRANCHES OF GOVERNMENT

EXECUTIVE BRANCH
Governor
Carries out laws

LEGISLATIVE BRANCH
General Assembly
Passes laws

JUDICIAL BRANCH
Supreme Court
Makes judgments about laws

CHART SKILL: Arkansas has three branches of government. What is the function of the **executive branch**?

able to "override," or set aside, the governor's veto.

Governor Clinton thought about Dennis's idea. He finally decided that the fiddle would be a good symbol for our state. Dennis was invited to a special ceremony at the State Capitol in Little Rock. There, on March 7, 1985, he watched Governor Clinton sign the bill into law.

THE JUDICIAL BRANCH

Dennis's bill had become a law. But one more branch of our state government may become involved with this law. This branch is called the **judicial** (jü dish′ əl) **branch**. The word *judicial* means "relating to courts of law and to justice."

In our state the judicial branch has many judges, as well as several different kinds of courts. The highest court

in the state is the Supreme Court. It is made up of a chief justice and six associate justices, all of whom are elected by the people.

No Arkansan has suggested that Dennis's law disagrees with the Arkansas constitution. But suppose that somebody did challenge the law in court. The case might go through the lower courts and finally reach the Supreme Court of Arkansas. If that were to happen, the Supreme Court justices would decide whether the law was constitutional. If they decided that it was not constitutional, then the law would be thrown out.

OUR GOVERNMENT

Arkansas's government is our government. By electing the members of each of the three branches, the people of Arkansas decide who will serve them in our capital city, Little Rock. They decide who will make the laws.

When you are older, you might become a member of the General Assembly, or even governor of Arkansas. But even by voting you will be playing a part in our state government. You will be making choices about how people will live in Arkansas.

Check Your Reading

1. What are taxes?
2. Name the three branches of state government and explain the job that each branch performs.
3. What happens to a bill if the governor decides to veto it?
4. What is Arkansas's highest court?
5. **THINKING SKILL:** Beginning with Dennis Taylor's idea, list the steps that the "fiddle bill" went through on its way to becoming a law.

188

LESSON

2 Local Government

READ TO LEARN

Key Vocabulary

quorum court
county judge
municipal
mayor
city council
city manager

Key Places

Pulaski County
Paragould
Brinkley

Read Aloud

Heavens, we're here to serve the public, not us.

These are the words of Bill Carter, the mayor of West Fork in Washington County. Like other leaders in local government, Bill Carter believes in serving the people of his community. You will read about local government in this lesson.

Read for Purpose

1. **WHAT YOU KNOW:** What are some of the services that are provided by your county, city, or town government?
2. **WHAT YOU WILL LEARN:** How is a local government different from a state government?

GOVERNMENT IN OUR COMMUNITY

In the last lesson you read about the three branches that make up our state government. The three branches work together to make decisions about laws. They also decide what kinds of services the state should provide to the people of Arkansas.

These decisions affect everybody in our state. But what if somebody in your town suggested that there should be another traffic light on the main street? What if your fire department wanted to hire two more firefighters?

Decisions like these do not affect all Arkansans. They are local decisions—that is, they have to do with one place. For this reason, such decisions are made by local government.

COUNTY GOVERNMENT

As you know, the United States is divided into states. In the same way, Arkansas is divided into smaller parts. Each of these parts is called a county.

Arkansas has 75 counties, which you can learn more about by looking at pages 242–244 of the Arkansas Almanac. Each of these counties has its own local government. Like the state government, county governments are divided into several different parts. Each part has its own role in serving Arkansans like yourself.

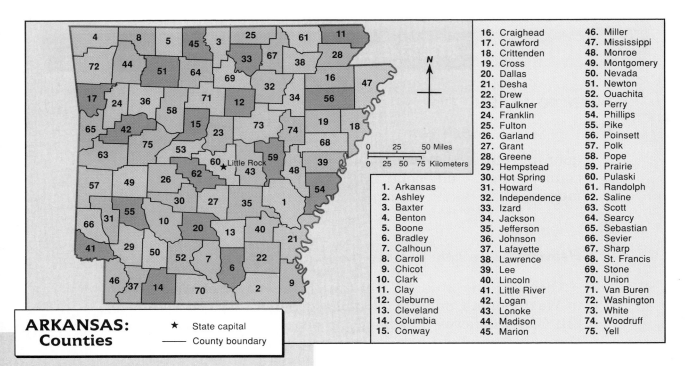

16. Craighead	46. Miller
17. Crawford	47. Mississippi
18. Crittenden	48. Monroe
19. Cross	49. Montgomery
20. Dallas	50. Nevada
21. Desha	51. Newton
22. Drew	52. Ouachita
23. Faulkner	53. Perry
24. Franklin	54. Phillips
25. Fulton	55. Pike
26. Garland	56. Poinsett
27. Grant	57. Polk
28. Greene	58. Pope
29. Hempstead	59. Prairie
30. Hot Spring	60. Pulaski
31. Howard	61. Randolph
32. Independence	62. Saline
33. Izard	63. Scott
34. Jackson	64. Searcy
35. Jefferson	65. Sebastian
36. Johnson	66. Sevier
37. Lafayette	67. Sharp
38. Lawrence	68. St. Francis
39. Lee	69. Stone
40. Lincoln	70. Union
41. Little River	71. Van Buren
42. Logan	72. Washington
43. Lonoke	73. White
44. Madison	74. Woodruff
45. Marion	75. Yell

1. Arkansas	
2. Ashley	
3. Baxter	
4. Benton	
5. Boone	
6. Bradley	
7. Calhoun	
8. Carroll	
9. Chicot	
10. Clark	
11. Clay	
12. Cleburne	
13. Cleveland	
14. Columbia	
15. Conway	

ARKANSAS: Counties

★ State capital
—— County boundary

MAP SKILL: Arkansas has 75 counties, each with its own government. In which county is our state capital located?

The **quorum court** (kwôr′ əm kôrt) is the legislative branch of county government. Although it is called a "court," the quorum court has nothing to do with trials or juries. It is actually a group of people who have been elected to make laws for the county. The quorum court is like a smaller, more local version of Arkansas's General Assembly.

County government also has an executive branch. The head of this branch, who is elected by the people of the county, is called the **county judge**. Again, the county judge is not actually a judge. Instead, he or she has the same duties in a county as the governor has in a state.

A county judge's job can be very complicated. For this reason, all of the state's 75 county judges meet 4 times a year. Together, they talk about the problems facing them.

Rita Gruber, a former county judge for **Pulaski County**, says, "The county government must work together with all the other levels of government to get things done." Therefore, she thinks that the most important things for a county judge to keep in mind are the "three *C*s"—"coordination, cooperation, and communication." The current county judge for Pulaski County is Floyd G. "Buddy" Villines.

As county judge, Buddy Villines works with other officials to make sure that the county roads are maintained. He oversees the work of Pulaski County's garbage and waste disposal system. In addition, he is responsible when an emergency occurs. If a flood, earthquake, tornado, or some other disaster were to strike Pulaski County, he would decide how to control the damage and whether people needed to leave their homes.

County judges, like Floyd G. "Buddy" Villines, oversee healthcare and public safety in their counties.

Like our state government, county governments collect taxes from their citizens. They use this money to help run schools, to build county roads, and to pay salaries to police officers. Some county governments may also build campgrounds or pay for machinery to recycle bottles and newspapers. Which of these county services have you made use of recently?

Look at the map on page 190 that shows all of our state's counties. Can you find the county in which you live?

MUNICIPAL GOVERNMENT

County governments are especially important in those parts of our state where there are no cities. Today, however, more than half of the population of Arkansas lives in cities and towns. These communities also have a second kind of local government, called municipal (mū nis' ə pəl) government. This word is related to the word *municipality* (mū nis ə pal' i tē), which we sometimes use to describe a town or city that has its own government.

Almost 500 towns and cities are located in Arkansas. Most of them have a form of municipal government made up of a mayor and a city council. Like the different branches of the county government, these branches are similar to those of the state government. The mayor is the head of the executive branch. The city council is the legislative branch of a town or city. All of these leaders are elected by the people of the town or city. Does your community have a mayor? Do you know his or her name?

Charles Partlow has been the mayor of Paragould, in Greene County, since 1978. Before 1978 he served on the city council. "I like to do things to help people," he says. "I'm trying to make Paragould a better town."

191

A big part of Charles Partlow's job as mayor is preparing the city budget for Paragould. "I'm an accountant by trade," he says, "and that helps."

In 1980 he worked to persuade the state legislators to pass a new law concerning sales taxes, or taxes on the purchase of particular goods. This law, which was finally passed by the General Assembly, allows people in cities like Paragould to determine which goods should be taxed. But Charles Partlow also does many other things, from answering schoolchildren's questions to performing weddings.

A mayor's job, especially in a large city, can be both difficult and rewarding. Lottie Shackelford, a former mayor of Little Rock, calls the job "an honor and a privilege."

A CITY MANAGER'S JOB

Some towns and cities in Arkansas, such as Maumelle, Little Rock, Hot Springs, and Arkadelphia, have chosen another type of municipal government. In these communities the voters elect a city council, but they may not elect a mayor. The council then hires a person to serve as city manager.

The city manager performs some of the same tasks as a mayor would. But mainly, the city manager keeps track of the amount of money that the city collects and spends.

Horace Smith served as the city manager for Brinkley, in Monroe County. He said that what he did as city manager was "not all that different from what the head of an industry does." Horace Smith prepared an annual budget and oversaw the various departments of the government.

The city council writes laws for the city and makes sure that many services are provided to the public.

MUNICIPAL SERVICES

Both kinds of municipal government provide a large variety of services. One way to understand the kinds of services provided is to try to imagine what your life would be like if these services were to stop. When you turned on a faucet in your kitchen, no water would come out. If you wanted to play baseball or some other outdoor sport, there might be no parks available in your community. Nobody would come to pick up your garbage. If you wanted to read a book, you would have to buy it, because there would be no library in your town or city.

GOVERNMENTS WORK TOGETHER

As our state, county, and city populations grow, the role of government becomes more complicated. Certain problems cannot be solved entirely at either the state, county, or municipal level. In such areas as education and programs to fight drug abuse, the three different levels of government work closely together.

Many problems facing Arkansans also affect people in other states. These problems often involve still another level of government—the national government. In the next lesson you will read about how the United States government and the Arkansas government work together.

Check Your Reading

1. What is the role of local government in our state?
2. Name two parts of our county government and explain what they do.
3. How does a mayor's job differ from that of a city manager?
4. Why is local government important to the people of a town or city?
5. **THINKING SKILL:** List three questions you could ask to learn about your own community's municipal government.

Reading a Newspaper

Key Vocabulary
news article
feature article
editorial
classified ad
headline
byline
dateline

Suppose that you had to find out which topics your county government is discussing this year. How would you begin to find such information? One answer is by reading newspapers. Many towns and cities in Arkansas have newspapers. These papers print stories about local, state, and national events. Reading newspapers is important because it keeps you informed about what is happening.

The Parts of a Newspaper
Newspapers often have several sections, or parts. The front section usually has news articles. A news article is a story about an important event that has just taken place. News articles can be about local, state, national, or world events. What might be the subject of a local news story in your area?

Another part of the newspaper has feature articles. A feature article reports in detail on a person, subject, or event. For example, the local newspaper of Osceola, in Mississippi County, might report on how a new textile factory is affecting the town.

Newspapers also have sports sections, cartoons, and editorials. An editorial is an article in which the editors give their opinion on an important issue. Unlike a news article, which reports only facts, an editorial gives opinions. In an election year the editors might write an editorial telling which candidate they support for governor and why they support him or her.

Another part of the newspaper has classified ads. Classified ads are short advertisements that appear in small print. They might list job openings, homes for rent, or cars for sale. People place classified ads in a newspaper to let other people know that they want to buy or sell something.

The Parts of a News Article
News stories begin with headlines like those below. Headlines are sentences or phrases printed in large type at the top

LITTLE ROCK FLEXES ZONING MUSCLE OUTSIDE CITY

BENTON LIFTS FREEZE ON RURAL WATER USAGE

RAZORBACKS CLIMB TO NO. 7

Arkansas Daily News

December 10, 1989

REOPENING PROMISES NEW JOBS

By Joan Ryan

OSCEOLA, December 10 — Residents of this Delta town have been hoping that a buyer would be found for the Crompton plant. In 1984 Crompton closed its Osceola textile plant, leaving 800 people without jobs. Now a clothing manufacturer has bought the plant and will reopen it in the next few months. A company spokesperson said that the company will begin by hiring 600 workers. That number is expected to grow to 2,000 in a few years. The factory in Osceola will be used to manufac... both men's and wom... clothing. ... st of these g...ds, howe... will...

of a news story. These headlines appeared in the *Arkansas Democrat*, one of the many newspapers that keep Arkansans informed about what is going on. Newspapers use headlines to catch readers' attention. Headlines also let readers know what an article is about.

Many news articles have a byline. A byline gives the name of the reporter who wrote the article. Does the news story above have a byline?

Some news articles have a dateline. A dateline tells where and when the story was written. What is the dateline on this news article?

A well-written news article begins by answering four basic questions. News writers sometimes call these questions the "four *W*s" since they all begin with that letter. *Who* was involved in the story? *What* happened? *When* did it happen? *Where* did it happen? As you read the news article above, decide if the reporter has answered these questions.

Reviewing the Skill

1. Name three parts of a newspaper.
2. According to the headline, what is the subject of the article above?
3. Does the article above answer the questions *Who? What? When? Where?* Explain.
4. What is one difference between a news article and an editorial?
5. How does reading a newspaper help you to be a better citizen?

3 National Government

READ TO LEARN

Key Vocabulary
democracy

Key People
Hattie Caraway   Dale Bumpers
J. William Fulbright   David Pryor
John L. McClellan

Read Aloud

We were brought up with the work ethic, encouraged to get an education, and we were told we could do anything we wanted.

Dale Bumpers, from Charleston in Franklin County, used these words to describe his childhood. His family taught him to value hard work, education, and opportunity. These values have helped Bumpers to serve in our national government as a United States senator. You will read about our national government in this lesson.

Read for Purpose

1. **WHAT YOU KNOW:** Have you ever visited our nation's capital?
2. **WHAT YOU WILL LEARN:** How does the national government work to help the people of our state?

OUR COUNTRY'S GOVERNMENT

In this chapter you have read about our state and local governments. However, there is one level of government we have not talked about. This is the government of the United States, or our national government.

Do you remember the three branches of our state government? Our national government is divided into three similar branches.

The legislative branch is called Congress. Like Arkansas's own General Assembly, Congress is made up of two "houses," or parts—the House of Representatives and the Senate. Arkansas voters elect people to represent our state in both houses.

The members of the House of Representatives are elected every two years. These officials are usually called congressmen or congresswomen. The number of people that a state sends to the House of Representatives depends on the size of its population. Arkansans elect four representatives. States with larger populations, such as California, may send over 40 people to the House of Representatives.

The members of the Senate, or senators, are elected every six years. However, the number of senators that represents each state has nothing to do with population. Every state, including Arkansas, elects two senators.

The voters of Arkansas also help to choose the head of our nation's executive branch—the President of the United States. The President is elected every four years. Like the governor of a state, he makes sure that the laws are carried out.

The third branch of the national government is the United States Supreme Court. This is the highest court in the United States. Its members decide whether laws passed by Congress and by the state legislatures follow the United States Constitution.

ARKANSANS IN WASHINGTON

As one of the 50 states, Arkansas has played an important part in our national government. The people of our state have sent many leaders to Washington, D.C.

In 1932 Hattie Caraway of Jonesboro became the first woman to be elected to the United States Senate. Caraway worked hard to help Arkansans during the Depression. She also tried to pass laws protecting the rights of women.

Another important Arkansas senator was J. William Fulbright (fùl' brīt). He was first elected to the Senate in 1944 and he served there for 30 years. Fulbright helped to pass many important laws during his years in the Senate. He also founded the Fulbright Exchange Program. This famous program sends students from the United States to study in other countries, and it brings students from other countries here for the same purpose.

Another Arkansan, John L. McClellan (mə klel' ən), served in the United States Senate during the same years as Fulbright. You have actually read about one of his projects in Chapter 2—the system of dams and locks on the Arkansas River. This river system, which is officially called the McClellan-Kerr Navigation Project, is one of the many programs and laws that McClellan helped to pass.

Arkansas's Hattie Caraway (*left*), the first woman senator, and J. William Fulbright (*right*) served our state for many years in the United States Senate.

United States Senators Dale Bumpers (*right*) and David Pryor (*left*) represent Arkansas in Washington, D.C.

Today, Arkansans such as Senator Dale Bumpers and Senator David Pryor continue to make contributions to our national government. They and other Arkansans will carry the tradition of service to our country's government into the future.

NATIONAL GOVERNMENT IN ARKANSAS

Earlier in this chapter you read about the many services provided by our state and local governments. You may wonder whether any services remain for the national government to provide. In fact, there are many.

Have you ever visited the Ozark National Forest, which you read about in Chapter 2? This national forest is one of several places in our state that are run by the national government.

Maintenance of the Interstate Highway System is another service provided to us by the national government. The government makes sure that roads like Interstate Highway 30, which connects Little Rock and Texarkana, are kept in good shape. Other services provided to us by the national government include the postal service and our nation's military services.

YOUR GOVERNMENT

In this chapter you have read that the purpose of government is to serve all its citizens. Our type of government, which we often call a democracy (di mok′ rə sē), is run by the people it governs. Through the process of electing our leaders, the people of our state and nation make their ideas and opinions known.

In a few years, when you become 18 years old, you will be able to vote. Voting will be your right, but it will also be your duty. Another right you will have in our democracy is the right to run for public office. Perhaps years from now, students will read about your accomplishments as an Arkansas leader!

 Check Your Reading

1. How many members does Arkansas elect to each house of Congress?
2. What are the roles of the President and the members of the United States Supreme Court?
3. Tell what is important about Hattie Caraway, J. William Fulbright, and John L. McClellan.
4. What are some of the services that the national government provides to the people of Arkansas?
5. THINKING SKILL: Based on your reading of this lesson, what conclusions can you draw about the role of Arkansas's citizens in our national government?

REVIEWING VOCABULARY

bill   tax
budget   veto
democracy

Number a sheet of paper from 1 to 5. Beside each number write the word from the list above that best completes the sentence.

1. Each local homeowner paid a ____ to the city government.
2. The senator suggested the ____ that eventually became a law.
3. The state ____ included spending $1 million to repair the government office building.
4. The governor does not approve of the bill, so he will ____ it.
5. We live in a ____, so the people elect most government officials.

REVIEWING FACTS

Number a sheet of paper from 1 to 10. Beside each number write whether the word or phrase relates to state, county, municipal, or national government. Some of the words and phrases may relate to more than one level of government.

1. General Assembly
2. executive branch
3. mayor
4. quorum court
5. city manager
6. Congress
7. taxes
8. governor
9. the three branches
10. Senate

WRITING ABOUT MAIN IDEAS

1. **Writing About Government in Your Life:** List ten ways that the local, state, or national government has affected your life. Find a way to organize the list into categories. Then write a paragraph with this topic sentence: "My life is greatly affected by government."
2. **Writing a Paragraph:** Arkansas's government depends on the participation of people. For example, adults must take the time to vote. In what other ways can people be good citizens? Write a paragraph explaining how you can be a good citizen.
3. **Writing a Plan for a Government Tour:** Imagine that you are going to lead a "state government tour" in Little Rock. Write out a plan for the tour, including all the buildings you will visit. Then list the stops in order, and explain how each stop will help people to understand how our state government works.

BUILDING SKILLS: READING A NEWSPAPER

1. Name four parts of a newspaper.
2. Which part of a news story is supposed to catch the reader's interest?
3. Where in a newspaper can you read the editors' opinions?
4. How can reading a newspaper help you in school?

CHAPTER 12

ENJOYING ARKANSAS

FOCUS

I've been traveling around Arkansas taking photographs for 15 years. It's really a labor of love. I get the chance to meet people from many different backgrounds and enter their worlds for a few moments.

These are the words of Matt Bradley, who took many of the photographs in this book. His photographs capture something special about Arkansas's land and people. In this chapter you will learn more about what it means to be an Arkansan today.

1 Who We Are

READ TO LEARN

Key Vocabulary
immigrant
rural
urban

Key Places
Tontitown
Stuttgart
Slovak

Read Aloud

Mr. Austin Corbin of New York . . . says he has sold to 250 Italian families a large plantation he owns in Chicot County, Arkansas, opposite Greenville, comprising 4,000 acres of cultivated land. The colonists are expected to arrive during the winter.

This is part of an article that appeared in the *Arkansas Gazette* in 1895. The group of Italian "colonists" was one among many groups that have come to our state from different countries. In this lesson you will learn about the varied people of Arkansas today.

Read for Purpose

1. **WHAT YOU KNOW:** Why did settlers come to Arkansas in the 1800s?
2. **WHAT YOU WILL LEARN:** Who are the people of today's Arkansas?

ARKANSAS'S POPULATION

Today 2,453,000 Arkansans live in our state. This figure makes Arkansas the thirty-third largest in population of the 50 United States. In other words, 32 states in our nation have more people than Arkansas, and 17 states have fewer people.

Compared to some states, our population may seem small. But don't be fooled by numbers—2,453,000 is a great many people. If you had to count every single Arkansan at the rate of one person per second, it would take you almost 28 days without a break!

What does it mean to be one out of today's 2,453,000 Arkansans? Our state's people are as varied as our land. They come in all ages, colors, and sizes. And they have come from many different parts of the world.

EARLY ARRIVALS

As you read in Chapter 3, the first people to live in the land of Arkansas

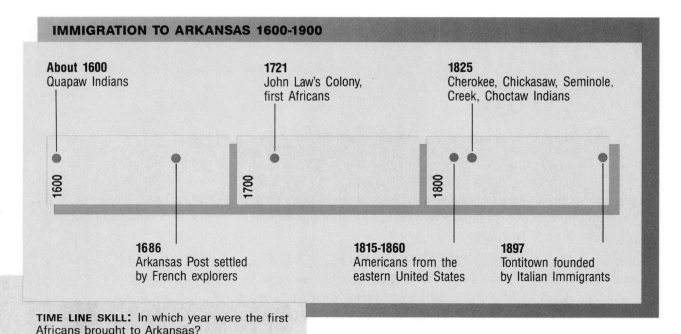

IMMIGRATION TO ARKANSAS 1600-1900

About 1600
Quapaw Indians

1721
John Law's Colony,
first Africans

1825
Cherokee, Chickasaw, Seminole,
Creek, Choctaw Indians

1600   1700   1800

1686
Arkansas Post settled
by French explorers

1815-1860
Americans from the
eastern United States

1897
Tontitown founded
by Italian Immigrants

TIME LINE SKILL: In which year were the first Africans brought to Arkansas?

were hunters and gatherers. These hunters were the ancestors of our state's Native American groups.

Spanish and French explorers were the next arrivals in the land of Arkansas. None of these early expeditions stayed for long in our state. However, you can still find traces of the French in many Arkansas place-names, such as Antoine in Pike County and Des Arc in Prairie County. Magazine Mountain, in the Arkansas River Valley, probably got its name from the French word for a barn or warehouse—*magasin*.

Next came the arrival of pioneer settlers about whom you read in Chapter 6. Many of these settlers were of English, Scotch-Irish, or German descent. The majority of today's Arkansans claim these settlers as their ancestors.

During the early 1800s, still another important group arrived in our state—Africans. Unlike most groups in our state's history, these new arrivals had been forced to come to Arkansas.

However, they brought many African customs to our state. African languages, music, arts, and even foods have become part of Arkansas life.

RECENT ARRIVALS

Do you remember the Italian "colonists" you read about earlier in this lesson? They were part of a "second wave" of immigrants (im' i grənts) who arrived in Arkansas from Europe during the late 1800s and early 1900s. An immigrant is a person who leaves one country in order to come and live in another.

Our state government encouraged many people to settle in Arkansas during these years. So did the railroad companies and other industries, which often advertised for workers in American and European newspapers.

Many people from the United States and Europe responded to these efforts. In 1884 one Arkansan spoke of the "stream of immigration [that] has poured into our borders." Much of this stream came from other southern

202

states. However, people from Italy, Germany, and Switzerland also arrived here to start a new life.

The 250 Italian families soon gave up their plantation in Chicot County. They moved north and founded a new town in the Ozarks—Tontitown in Washington County. Today some of Tontitown's citizens still speak Italian as well as English. On the steep Ozark slopes they grow grapes, just as their ancestors in Italy did. For whom do you think these Italian immigrants named Tontitown?

A glance at the map of Arkansas on page 233 in the Atlas will give you some idea of the other European groups who arrived around the beginning of the century. German-American immigrants in Arkansas County named Stuttgart after a city in Germany. Immigrants from Central Europe founded Slovak in Prairie County. Can you think of the names of other towns in Arkansas that may tell you about the towns' founders?

In more recent years Arkansas has become home for many immigrants from Southeast Asia and the Middle East. Other immigrants have arrived from the countries of Latin America.

WHERE WE LIVE

The number of people living in Arkansas has remained fairly stable during the last 50 years. What has changed, however, is *where* we live.

Look at the graph on this page. Before the 1950s most Arkansans lived in rural areas. The word *rural* means "having to do with the country or agriculture." As you have read in Chapter 10, though, the number of Arkansans who work on farms has fallen sharply.

Between 1975 and 1976 alone, almost 7,000 people left the fields and orchards of our state. Many of the Arkansans who no longer do farm work have moved to urban areas—that is, to our state's cities.

As you can tell from the graph on this page, 9 out of 10 Arkansans lived in rural areas in 1900. By 1980 this figure had dropped to less than 5 out of 10. Does your family live in an urban or rural area of Arkansas?

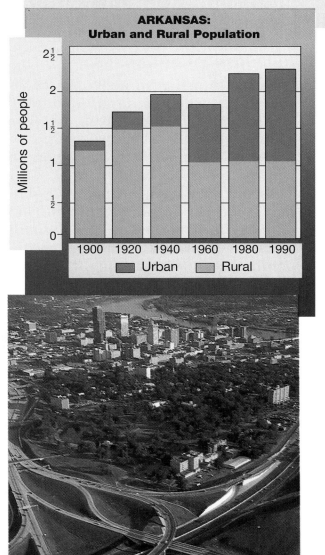

GRAPH SKILL: Many Arkansans have moved from rural to urban areas such as Little Rock. In which year did more than half of the population first live in urban areas?

ARKANSAS: Urban and Rural Population

Millions of people

Urban   Rural

from all over the world settle in Arkansas. What are some of the reasons that these people come to our state?

RELIGION IN ARKANSAS

You have just read about the countries from which today's Arkansans come, and in which areas we live. These facts tell us about who we are as a people. Another important part of who we are is our religion.

As you have read in Chapter 5, religion is the way people worship the God or gods in whom they believe. For millions of Arkansans, religion is an important part of everyday life. They may attend church services every week and sing in a choir. They may volunteer with religious groups to help senior citizens or to teach people to read.

Most Arkansans are members of the Methodist church or the Baptist church, which are both Christian churches. Some Arkansans practice Roman Catholicism, another Christian faith, while others practice the Jewish or Islamic faiths. All these faiths make life in our state richer.

LIVING TOGETHER

Arkansas's population and culture have always been made up of many different parts. Native Americans, European Americans, and African Americans have all made key contributions. Today, groups from Asia, Latin America, and the Middle East are adding their voices to this "chorus." The richness of life in our state owes much to its many voices.

Check Your Reading

1. What is the population of Arkansas?
2. Name four groups of immigrants who have made contributions to life in our state.
3. In what ways is religion important to the people of Arkansas?
4. **GEOGRAPHY SKILL:** Where did the name "Magazine Mountain" come from?
5. **THINKING SKILL:** What are three questions you could ask an immigrant to learn more about the place that he or she came from?

2 Culture and the Arts

READ TO LEARN

Key Vocabulary

folk art
country music
jazz
gospel music

Key People

Johnny Cash
Glen Campbell
Al Green
Maya Angelou
John Gould Fletcher
Fay Jones

Read Aloud

Arkansas has . . . places for an artist to grow and work. . . . We love it where we are, and we stay or we come back to it. There are adventures to be made here, room to get your ideas going and people to listen to you.

These are the words of one writer who has written about growing up in our state. In this lesson you will read about some of the musicians, writers, and other artists who have found Arkansas a place "to get your ideas going."

Read for Purpose

1. **WHAT YOU KNOW:** What kinds of books, music, and art do you enjoy?
2. **WHAT YOU WILL LEARN:** What are some of the arts that are important to our state?

ART IN OUR STATE

In Chapter 3 you read that a culture is the way of life of a group of people. Culture includes a people's customs and beliefs. It also includes the art that these people create—the books they write, the pictures they paint, or the music they play. All these art forms tell us important things about the people who make them. And, just as important, these arts are here to be enjoyed.

FOLK ART

One particular type of art has a long and rich history in Arkansas. This is **folk art**—things made by everyday people like you. As one Ozark farmer has recalled, "You take people livin' on a homestead out in the woods—why, there wasn't a store right across the road to go and get whatever you need. And so if you needed somethin' why you went and made it." Folk art can

205

Johnny Cash (*below*) and Glen Campbell (*right*) are two popular **country music** singers who were born in our state.

include a quilt that you have sewn, or a song that you have made up, or even a recipe for a cake.

Perhaps these things don't seem like "art" to you. But just as a painting or a book can express something about the person who has created it, so can folk art. This kind of art can also express something special about Arkansas.

THE MUSIC OF OUR STATE

Our state has a rich tradition of music. Much of this tradition goes back to the early 1800s. It might surprise you to learn that much of the music you listen to today has roots in our state's history.

Do you remember the Smith family, about whom you read in Chapter 6? Pioneer families like the Smiths sang songs for pleasure or while working. Pioneers wrote some of these songs.

Others may have been brought to our state by Scotch-Irish, English, or other immigrants. Even the words of these songs from other countries were sometimes changed to fit the rugged life of the Arkansas frontier.

Often the Arkansas pioneers would combine music with dancing. Around 1840 the German writer Friedrich Gerstäcker (ger′ stek ər) described a Fourth of July picnic in Arkansas.

Even before I reached the house I could hear the wailing of music from a single fiddle. In one wing of the house the young people were dancing the gay and strenuous dances of the people here. . . .

The songs of the Arkansas pioneers gradually changed over the years. Many of them later influenced the sound of **country music**. Have you ever heard **Johnny Cash** sing "I Walk The Line" or **Glen Campbell** sing "Rhinestone Cowboy"? Did you know that both of these country musicians are from our state?

Africans, who were brought to Arkansas throughout the early 1800s, contributed still other kinds of music. Some songs began in the fields as the captives called out to one another at work. Others reflected the desire for freedom. Although most of these songs were sung in English, many showed the strong influence of African rhythms and styles.

By the early 1900s these African rhythms began to appear in a new kind of music—jazz. You have already read about one of the first great jazz composers, Scott Joplin. The son of an enslaved person, this African American was born in Texarkana in 1868. Around 1900 Joplin invented a form of jazz music called ragtime. Some of his songs, such as "Maple Leaf Rag," are still played by musicians today.

Another kind of music also grew out of the experiences and religious feelings of African Americans. This type of music is called gospel music. One famous gospel singer, Al Green, was born in Forrest City in St. Francis County. He has written many gospel songs and has performed them on stages throughout the world.

You may not listen to jazz, country music, or gospel music. But almost all of today's music, especially rock and roll, would never have existed without these musical "ancestors." In this sense, you probably hear echoes of Arkansas's history every time you turn on the radio!

(*above*) Al Green, from Forrest City, performs **gospel music** throughout our country.
(*below*) Scott Joplin composed many early **jazz** tunes, such as "Maple Leaf Rag."

207

ARKANSAS WRITERS

Of course, music is not the only way in which Arkansans have expressed themselves. You have already read the words of one Arkansas writer, Maya Angelou, in Chapter 9. Angelou was raised by her grandparents in Stamps, in Lafayette County. Although she has spent much of her adult life in other parts of the world, many of her books describe her childhood in our state. In her most famous book, *I Know Why the Caged Bird Sings*, she remembered one feature of her life in Stamps.

> *On Saturdays, barbers sat their customers in the shade on the porch of the Store, and troubadours* [musicians] *on their ceaseless crawlings through the South leaned across its benches and sang their sad songs. . . .*

(*above*) Maya Angelou has written books about her experiences growing up in Arkansas. (*below*) Fay Jones has designed many buildings that remind us of the natural beauty of our state.

Another famous writer from our state is the poet John Gould Fletcher of Little Rock. Fletcher won the Pulitzer Prize for his work. More recently, novelists such as Donald Harington, Ellen Gilchrist, and Jack Butler have written about life in our state. Have you ever seen the movie *True Grit*? It was based on the work of still another Arkansas writer, Charles Portis.

ARKANSAS ARCHITECTURE

You might not think of the buildings that you see every day as works of art. But buildings, too, can express an architect's feelings about a place.

Fay Jones of Fayetteville has built some of our state's most beautiful houses and chapels. Jones likes to draw his ideas from the surrounding land, so that each building "blends into its environment." Have you ever visited Thorncrown Chapel in Eureka Springs? Buildings such as this one have earned Fay Jones many honors and prizes. In February 1990 President

People throughout our state, like these performers at the Children's Theater in Little Rock, enjoy participating in the arts.

George Bush presented him with a gold medal for his contribution to American architecture.

ART FOR EVERYONE

After reading about our state's artists, you may be curious to see, hear, or read their works. You can find books by John Gould Fletcher or Maya Angelou at your local public library. But where can you see paintings, plays, or examples of folk art?

Some good places to start are the Arkansas Art Center in Little Rock and the University of Arkansas Museum in Fayetteville. Both of these museums include works by artists who have been inspired by our land. Arkansas also has many theaters and performance halls throughout the state. Perhaps there is one in your own town or city.

You can see examples of folk art at local arts and crafts fairs. But in Mountain View, in Stone County, an entire museum is dedicated to preserving the arts and crafts of our state. At the Ozark Folk Center you can see a blacksmith making horseshoes, a potter crafting a vase, or a banjo player "dueling" with a mountain fiddler.

Whether you are reading the novel *True Grit* or watching a performance of Ozark jig-dancing, you are learning something about our state. You are learning something about what it means to be an Arkansan.

Check Your Reading

1. Why are the arts important to us?
2. Name one writer, one musician, and one architect from our state.
3. How can folk art tell us about life in Arkansas?
4. **THINKING SKILL:** What conclusion can you draw from the information included in the last section of this lesson?

209

Decision Making

Every time you make a decision you are shaping your life in some way. As you learned in Chapter 3, making decisions means choosing from alternatives. Will you play a video game in your spare time, or will you read a good book? Will you spend your allowance on a snack today, or save it to buy something special later on?

Sometimes your decisions affect other people as well as yourself. Which friends will you invite to your party? Will you keep a friend's secret or tell it to someone else?

Because you make decisions all the time, it is helpful to know how to make a good decision. The chart on page 211 lists five steps you can use when you have to make a decision.

HELPING YOURSELF

The steps below show one way to make a decision.

1. Define the goal you want to achieve.

2. Identify alternatives by which you can achieve your goal.

3. Predict the likely results of each alternative.

4. Evaluate each outcome by determining its costs and deciding whether or not it would help you and others involved.

5. Choose the best alternative—the one that is most likely to help you reach your goal.

Applying the Skill

Have you ever been asked, "What are you going to do when you grow up?" That decision is still a long way off, but what you decide to do today may affect your future. In Lesson 2 you read about Arkansans who have become musicians, writers, poets, and architects. Some of them decided early on in life what they wanted to do. Others did not choose a career until they were older.

You can use the chart above to help make important decisions, such as which career you should choose. If you follow these steps carefully, you will learn to make better decisions.

Suppose that you love sports. You are especially good at gymnastics, track, and basketball. Your goal, you decide, is to become a world-class star in one of these sports. However, this year you must choose the sport to which you will devote the most time and effort. How could you go about making this decision?

1. Which step might you take first?
   a. Ask your friends what they think you should do.
   b. Choose the sport that has the most television coverage.
   c. Talk to athletes in all three sports to find out what it takes to excel in that sport.
2. If you enjoy being outdoors, which of the three alternatives would you probably eliminate?
   a. gymnastics
   b. track
   c. basketball
3. Who, besides yourself, might be affected by your decision? Explain.
4. List two other things you might do to help you make a decision about which sport to pursue.
5. Why might a decision like this one be hard to make?

Reviewing the Skill

1. What does making a decision involve?
2. Why do you need a goal in order to make a decision?
3. Why do you think it is a good idea to identify and evaluate the alternatives by which you can achieve your goal?
4. Why are some decisions more difficult to make than others?

211

3 Sports and Recreation

READ TO LEARN

Key Vocabulary

recreation
professional

Key People

Dizzy Dean   Sidney Moncrief
Bear Bryant

Read Aloud

When I put on that Arkansas uniform, I am proud and I mean business. . . . Everything I do is for Arkansas. Man, I love this place.

These are the words of Ernie Murry from Wabbaseka in Jefferson County. Ernie played basketball for the University of Arkansas in 1990. He and his teammates worked hard to become one of the "final four" best college teams during that year. In this lesson you will read about the many different types of sports and outdoor activities that people in our state enjoy.

Read for Purpose

1. **WHAT YOU KNOW:** Which sporting events have you attended in our state?
2. **WHAT YOU WILL LEARN:** What kinds of recreational activities do people in Arkansas enjoy?

ENJOYING OUR STATE

As the canoe slipped between the rocks in the churning river, white water rushed past both sides of the prow. A sheet of foam splashed up over Anita and Robin Snider, making them gasp. Their parents laughed and struggled to steer the canoe through the rapids.

Soon the excitement had passed, and the Sniders floated into a more peaceful stretch of the Buffalo River. Robin stared up at the huge cliffs along the banks. As the current grew gentler,

Anita dropped a fishing line over the side of the canoe. Later that evening the Sniders would camp by the river and prepare for their hiking trip into the hills of the Buffalo National River.

Canoeing, camping, fishing, and hiking are just a few of the many kinds of **recreation** (rek rē ā′ shən) that the people of our state enjoy. Recreation is something that people do for amusement or relaxation. What are some kinds of recreation that you like?

Arkansas's climate, geography, and natural beauty provide many opportunities for all kinds of recreation.

THE GREAT OUTDOORS

Every time you step outside in Arkansas, there are dozens of ways in which you can enjoy yourself. Our state's many lakes, rivers, fields, and forests are all reasons that we call Arkansas "The Natural State." People take advantage of our state's natural riches by doing everything from bass fishing to hang gliding.

You read in Chapter 10 about the many interesting places that people can visit in our state. Most of Arkansas's 44 state parks are especially suited to outdoor recreation.

In addition, our national government has set aside five national parks and three national forests in Arkansas.

Thousands of Americans of all ages enjoy the Buffalo National River and Hot Springs National Park every year. Have you visited any of the national or state parks in Arkansas?

You can pitch a tent at nearly 2,000 campsites, and hundreds of miles of hiking trails crisscross every region of our state. Arkansas's lakes, such as Lake Ouachita and Beaver Lake, provide some of the most beautiful spots for water recreation in the world. If we treat these special places with care, Arkansans will be able to enjoy them for many years to come.

RAZORBACK EXCITEMENT

"Wooooooo Pig! Sooiee!" The huge crowd at War Memorial Stadium was on its feet cheering for the University of Arkansas football team. It was the final quarter of the Razorbacks' big game against the Longhorns of the University of Texas.

The center snapped the ball. The quarterback threw a pass. Touchdown! The "Hogs" had scored with only a few seconds left in the game. They had beaten the "Horns"! Jumping, shouting, and waving pennants, the Razorbacks' fans went wild with excitement.

People throughout our state enjoy watching the Razorbacks play football. So do football fans all over the United States. But do you know where the name "razorback" came from? A razorback is a wild hog with a sharp, narrow back. According to legend, the explorer Hernando de Soto brought the ancestors of these hogs to Arkansas from Europe more than 400 years ago. Today the razorback, which has become part of Arkansas's folklore, may still live in the mountains and forests of our state. The University of Arkansas chose this tough, resourceful animal as its mascot in 1909.

SPORTS IN ARKANSAS

Watching the Razorbacks is not the only way that Arkansans enjoy sports. Most of the colleges and universities in Arkansas offer a variety of athletic programs—from football and swimming

The University of Arkansas football team, the Razorbacks, attracts fans from all corners of our state.

to basketball and tennis. Many communities offer opportunities in parks and schools for a wide range of sporting activities. Have you participated in any sports at your school?

Arkansas is also home to the Arkansas Travelers, a **professional** (prə fesh′ ə nəl) baseball team. A professional is a person who is paid to do a job. For professional athletes, playing sports is their work.

Over the years, Arkansas has produced many gifted professional athletes. Dizzy Dean, from Ash Flat in Sharp County, became famous as an all-star pitcher for the St. Louis Cardinals. Bear Bryant was a football player who later coached the University of Alabama football team. He won more games than any other coach in history. Sidney Moncrief, known as "Super Sidney," grew up in Little Rock. After playing basketball for the University of Arkansas, he went on to a long career with the Milwaukee Bucks.

ENJOYING LIFE IN ARKANSAS

Whether you are hiking or swimming, watching sports or taking part in them, Arkansas is a wonderful place for recreation. From the rushing water of the Buffalo River to the 50-yard line at War Memorial Stadium, the people of our state find many ways to enjoy life in Arkansas.

 Check Your Reading

1. What are some of the ways in which people can enjoy Arkansas's state parks?
2. Where might the first "razorback" hogs have come from?
3. Which important record does Bear Bryant hold?
4. GEOGRAPHY SKILL: Look at the map on page 182 and locate five state parks in Arkansas.
5. THINKING SKILL: In what ways does the geography of Arkansas shape the kinds of recreation that people enjoy in our state?

215

How Should We Use Our National Forests?

You have read about the natural beauty of Arkansas's forests and how people throughout our state use these places for a variety of purposes. You have also read about the timber and paper industries and their importance to our state's economy.

Some of the largest forests in Arkansas are national forests—that is, areas set aside by our national government for the use of all people. Today, people in Arkansas are in disagreement about how these areas should be used. Some people feel that certain types of tree harvesting, like clearcutting, should be allowed. Clearcutting is a process in which patches of forest are completely cut down and later replanted with pine seedlings or left to regrow naturally.

The industries that buy this wood to make paper and other products feel that clearcutting helps our economy without harming the environment. Other Arkansans argue that clearcutting is harmful and destroys the beauty of our forests. Should clearcutting take place in our national forests?

Two DIFFERENT Viewpoints

Clearcutting Should Be Allowed

One person who thinks that clearcutting should be allowed in our national forests is Merf Pavlovich, director of the Arkansas Forestry Association.

One of the major uses of our national forests has always been to produce timber, Arkansas's number one renewable resource. Timber companies pay the Forest Service for the trees they cut. This money helps to provide services to the people of our state. Twenty-eight counties receive money for schools and roads from the cutting in national forests. Harvesting trees also creates many jobs for the people who live in those areas. In fact, one out of every five people in our state works in the wood products industry.

Years ago, natural fires cleared out large areas of older trees and helped young ones sprout. Clearcutting is a modern way to copy nature's cycle. Only small areas are clearcut, every hundred years or so. People can still enjoy the national forests for a wide variety of outdoor activities. Clearcutting gives the best balance between helping the economy of our state and preserving our National Forest.

- According to Merf Pavlovich, how are the effects of clearcutting similar to those of a natural forest fire?

Clearcutting Should Not Be Allowed

Jerry Williams is a member of OWL, or the Ouachita Watch League. He feels that clearcutting should not be allowed in our national forests.

My grandfather logged right here. He had a sawmill here in Hot Springs. My dad was a logger, too. They both had a desire to get the timber out, but they had no desire to ruin the forest.

You don't have to be an expert in forestry to know what is happening here. When the Forest Service allows clearcutting, mixed forests of pines and hardwoods are replaced by "pine plantations"—vast areas with nothing but pine trees. Dogwoods, redbuds, red maples, oaks and hickories are all cleared out.

Who wants to hike through a forest of pine plantations? But it is not just the beauty of the forests at stake. The homes of animals such as woodpeckers are destroyed. There are other ways to provide timber to industry without ruining our national forests. By cutting some trees and leaving others standing, we can preserve a natural forest where pines and hardwoods grow together.

- According to Jerry Williams, do the same kinds of trees that grow in forests before clearcutting grow there afterwards?

BUILDING CITIZENSHIP

1. Instead of clearcutting, Jerry Williams says that some trees can be cut and others left alone. Does Jerry Williams's way of harvesting timber still allow for jobs and money for the state?
2. Why do you think the timber industry supports clearcutting?
3. Do you think clearcutting should be allowed? Explain your answer.

4 Arkansas and the World

READ TO LEARN

Key Vocabulary

pollute

Read Aloud

We close our story of the bittersweet earth, its rivers, its caves, and its people. Men, women, girls, and boys—taking, giving, struggling, working, playing, loving—all continually leave their marks on the land. This story has no end, but recurs like the seasons. . . .

These are the words of one writer from our state. They express her ideas about Arkansas's history and land. In this lesson you will read about recent changes in our state.

Read for Purpose

1. WHAT YOU KNOW: How is your life different from the lives of early Arkansans?
2. WHAT YOU WILL LEARN: How is Arkansas more involved in the world around it?

FIRST PRESIDENT FROM ARKANSAS

On November 3, 1992, Arkansas Governor Bill Clinton became the forty-second President of the United States. The first President from Arkansas, Bill Clinton won with 43 percent of the vote. Senator Albert Gore of Tennessee became the new Vice President.

During his campaign, Clinton spoke about issues such as the economy and the environment. Arkansans and other Americans were worried about the changing economy. Workers were facing competition for jobs with people in other countries. Clinton promised to try and find solutions to these issues.

ARKANSAS AND THE WORLD

Advances in technology allow businesses anywhere in the world to meet the needs and wants of different people. As a result, Arkansas must now compete with other countries and states to attract new business and industry. For its efforts, by 1996 Arkansas led the country in new manufacturing jobs created every year.

The Great Arkansas Cleanup is one way that Arkansans work to fight pollution in our state.

Agriculture in Arkansas also stretches beyond the boundaries of the United States. Arkansans ship rice, soybeans, and other agricultural goods all over the world. In fact, 40 percent of the rice grown in Arkansas is sold overseas.

The growth of these industries in Arkansas has also caused problems. The waste produced pollutes air, water, and soil. Pollution not only harms nature but also the economy. For example, pollution harms tourism, a strong industry in "The Natural State." We must work together to support industry and protect the environment.

YOU ARE THE FUTURE

In two earlier lessons you read about a Quapaw Indian boy, Kugee, and Hannah Smith, a pioneer girl in Arkansas. Although their lives were very different from your own, you may see some similarities, too. Both of these early Arkansans worked, played, and lived as part of a community.

However, there is an important difference between the lives of these early Arkansans and your own. Kugee and Hannah Smith had very few choices about their own futures. For you, and for other young Arkansans of today, these choices are almost limitless.

What will you make of tomorrow's Arkansas—with its beauty, its resources, and its inventive, friendly people? Perhaps when other students are studying Arkansas's history 20 or 30 years from now, they will read your name among our state's "Key People"!

Check Your Reading

1. Name two reasons voters liked Bill Clinton.
2. What are some of the problems that Arkansans face today?
3. How is Arkansas becoming more involved with the world?
4. **THINKING SKILL:** Predict how you think Arkansas will be different 100 years from now.

YOU
Can Make a Difference

Throughout this book you have read about people who make a difference. These people have helped their community and state with their effort, their enthusiasm—and their hope.

Calvin King helps African Americans who live in the Delta by showing them how to make their farms more productive. His organization has allowed hundreds of family farmers to preserve a vanishing way of life in our state.

Ellen Neaville makes a difference by helping young Arkansans to become more aware of our environment. The more we learn about our state's precious natural resources, the better we will be able to guard them for the future.

King and Neaville are only two of the many fine citizens who are helping their fellow Arkansans. If you look around, you will probably see somebody who is working hard to solve a problem in your own community. That person could be an adult. But he or she could also be a young person like you.

There are many ways in which you can help people in your community. Each September many Arkansans clean our lakeside and riverside parks as part of the Great Arkansas Cleanup. In some communities the government may sponsor recycling projects.

If your school or place of worship has a canned-food drive, you could give something to support it. If a neighbor needs help carrying groceries or planting a vegetable garden, you could offer to help. If you live near a park or historical site, you could keep one of its areas clean of litter. Can you think of other ways to help your fellow Arkansans?

You might be able to help solve a problem, or you might think of other ways to help your community. The important thing to remember is that *you* can make a difference!

REVIEWING VOCABULARY

folk art   professional
immigrant   recreation
pollute

Number a sheet of paper from 1 to 5. Beside each number write the word or term from the list above that best matches the definition.

1. A person who is paid to do a job
2. Things made by ordinary people
3. To make dirty or impure
4. A person who leaves one country in order to live in another
5. Something that people do for amusement or relaxation

REVIEWING FACTS

1. Who were the first immigrants to Arkansas?
2. From where did the ancestors of most Arkansans come?
3. If you were to visit Tontitown, how could you tell that it was founded by Italian immigrants?
4. Is Little Rock an urban area or a rural area? Explain your answer.
5. Name three kinds of music that are part of our state's history.
6. Who is Maya Angelou?
7. Name two Arkansas sports teams that the people of our state like to watch.
8. Name three types of places to which Arkansans can go for recreation.
9. Who was Dizzy Dean? Who is "Super Sidney" Moncrief?
10. Which problems have been caused by manufacturing in Arkansas?

WRITING ABOUT MAIN IDEAS

1. **Writing a Paragraph:** Imagine that you are an immigrant coming to the United States from another country. What might be some of the reasons that you would want to settle in Arkansas? Write a paragraph explaining why you would choose Arkansas as your new home.
2. **Writing a Diary Entry:** Choose a recreational activity that you like to do or enjoy watching. Write a diary entry about one of your experiences with it. Tell where and when the activity took place and why you enjoyed it.
3. **Writing a Description:** Choose a picture in this book that shows a piece of folk art, or choose an example from another source. Write a paragraph describing the piece you chose. What do you think the piece expresses about the artist or about Arkansas?

BUILDING SKILLS: DECISION MAKING

1. Name some steps that you can take to make a good decision.
2. List three decisions that you made this week. Explain how you made each decision.
3. Why is it important to be able to make good decisions?

REVIEWING VOCABULARY

cash crop
democracy
interdependent
tax
technology

Number a sheet of paper from 1 to 5. Beside each number write the word or term from the list above that best completes the sentence.

1. Thanks to _____, people can now use computers to solve difficult problems.
2. The farmer grew rice as a _____. He planned to sell it and make money to buy things that he needed.
3. Because we live in a _____, we can elect our leaders.
4. Farmers and factory workers need each other; they are _____.
5. The money raised from the _____ on gasoline will be used by the government to repair the highways.

 WRITING ABOUT THE UNIT

1. **Making a List:** Think about the past week. What things did you do that brought you in touch with a person in a service industry? List five service workers that you met.
2. **Writing a Paragraph:** Think of a state law relating to recreation in Arkansas that you would like to see passed. Write a paragraph describing the steps that would have to take place in order for your idea to become a law.
3. **Writing About Starting a Company:** Think of a company that you might want to start. Would you provide a product or a service? Use the maps and other information in the unit to decide where your company should be located. Write a few paragraphs about your plans for the company.

ACTIVITIES

1. **Being a Folk Artist:** Choose one folk art practiced in Arkansas. Find out how it is done. Then try to do it yourself. Display your piece of art to the class.
2. **Working Together to Study Your Own Community:** Make a chart about government in your community. Include information about local government and about the people who represent you in state government.

LINKING PAST, PRESENT, AND FUTURE

You have read about the many jobs that a person in Arkansas can have. What job do you think you would like to have when you grow up? Is it a job that has been important in the past? Or is it a job in a new industry?

REFERENCE SECTION

ARCTIC OCEAN

GREENLAND) (DENMARK)

80°N

160°W 140°W 120°W 100°W 80°W 60°W

Arctic Circle

ALASKA (U.S.)

60°N

CANADA

NORTH

AMERICA

40°N

UNITED STATES

BERMUDA (U.K.)

ATLANTIC OCEAN

MIDWAY ISLANDS (U.S.)

See inset below

Tropic of Cancer

MEXICO

20°N

HAWAII (U.S.)

Caribbean Sea

GUYANA

SURINAME

VENEZUELA

FRENCH GUIANA (FRANCE)

PACIFIC OCEAN

COLOMBIA

0° Equator

GALÁPAGOS ISLANDS (ECUADOR)

ECUADOR

SOUTH

AMERICA

PERU

BRAZIL

WESTERN SAMOA

AMERICAN SAMOA (U.S.)

FRENCH POLYNESIA (FRANCE)

BOLIVIA

TONGA

PARAGUAY

20°S

Tropic of Capricorn

URUGUAY

CHILE ARGENTINA

40°S

FALKLAND ISLANDS (U.K.)

60°S

Antarctic Circle

80°S

ANTARCTICA

160°W 140°W 120°W 100°W 80°W 60

Central America and West Indies

90°W 80°W

FLORIDA (U.S.)

Gulf of Mexico

THE BAHAMAS

70°W

Tropic of Cancer

TURKS AND CAICOS IS. (U.K.)

ATLANTIC OCEAN

60°W

20°N

CUBA

20°N

VIRGIN ISLANDS (U.K.)

ST. KITTS AND NEVIS

CAYMAN ISLANDS (U.K.)

MEXICO

JAMAICA

HAITI

DOMINICAN REPUBLIC

ANTIGUA AND BARBUDA

BELIZE

PUERTO RICO (U.S.)

GUADELOUPE (FRANCE)

GUATEMALA

VIRGIN ISLANDS (U.S.)

DOMINICA

HONDURAS

MARTINIQUE (FRANCE)

ST. LUCIA

EL SALVADOR

Caribbean Sea

ST. VINCENT AND THE GRENADINES

PACIFIC OCEAN

NICARAGUA

ARUBA (NETHERLANDS)

NETHERLANDS ANTILLES (NETHERLANDS)

BARBADOS

GRENADA

10°N

TRINIDAD AND TOBAGO

COSTA RICA

10°N

PANAMA

VENEZUELA

0 250 500 Miles

0 250 500 Kilometers

90°W

80°W

70°W

COLOMBIA

GUYANA

ARCTIC OCEAN

80°N

Arctic Circle

60°N

SPITSBERGEN
(NORWAY)

SVALBARD IS.
(NORWAY)

ICELAND

See inset below

North
Sea

RUSSIA

ASIA

EUROPE

40°N

AZORES IS.
(PORTUGAL)

GEORGIA
ARMENIA
TURKEY

KAZAKHSTAN

UZBEKISTAN
KYRGYZSTAN

MONGOLIA

NORTH
KOREA

JAPAN

MOROCCO

CANARY IS.
(SPAIN)

TUNISIA

LEBANON

SYRIA

TURKMENISTAN

TAJIKISTAN

SOUTH
KOREA

PACIFIC OCEAN

WESTERN SAHARA
(MOROCCO)

ALGERIA

LIBYA

EGYPT

ISRAEL
JORDAN

IRAQ

KUWAIT

QATAR

AZERBAIJAN

AFGHANISTAN

IRAN

PAKISTAN

CHINA

NEPAL BHUTAN

HONG KONG

TAIWAN

Tropic of Cancer

20°N

BAHRAIN

SAUDI
ARABIA

UNITED
ARAB
EMIRATES

INDIA

MACAU (PORT.)

WAKE ISLAND
(U.S.)

MAURITANIA

CAPE VERDE

MALI

NIGER

CHAD

SUDAN

OMAN

BANGLADESH

MYANMAR
(BURMA)

LAOS

NORTHERN
MARIANA IS. (U.S.)

MARSHALL ISLANDS

SENEGAL

GAMBIA

GUINEA-BISSAU

GUINEA

SIERRA LEONE

BURKINA
FASO

NIGERIA

BENIN

AFRICA

ERITREA

YEMEN

DJIBOUTI

THAILAND

VIETNAM

PHILIPPINES

GUAM (U.S.)

FEDERATED STATES
OF MICRONESIA

CENTRAL
AFRICAN REP.

ETHIOPIA

CAMBODIA

BRUNEI

PALAU

KIRIBATI

LIBERIA

GHANA

CÔTE D'IVOIRE

TOGO

CAMEROON

UGANDA

SOMALIA

SRI
LANKA

MALAYSIA

NAURU

SÃO TOMÉ AND PRÍNCIPE

EQUATORIAL GUINEA

GABON

CONGO

RWANDA

ZAIRE

KENYA

BURUNDI

MALDIVES

SINGAPORE

INDONESIA

PAPUA
NEW
GUINEA

SOLOMON
ISLANDS

Equator

0°

ATLANTIC
OCEAN

TANZANIA

SEYCHELLES

INDIAN
OCEAN

TUVALU

ANGOLA

MALAWI

ZAMBIA

MOZAMBIQUE

COMOROS

VANUATU

FIJI

20°S

NAMIBIA

ZIMBABWE

BOTSWANA

MADAGASCAR

MAURITIUS

RÉUNION (FR.)

NEW
CALEDONIA
(FRANCE)

N
W   E
S

SOUTH
AFRICA

SWAZILAND

LESOTHO

AUSTRALIA

0   1,000   2,000 Miles
0   1,000   2,000 Kilometers
Scale accurate at Equator

**NEW
ZEALAND**

60°S

Antarctic Circle

80°S

W   20°W   0°   20°E   40°E   60°E   80°E   100°E   120°E   140°E   160°E

ANTARCTICA

30°E   40°E   50°E

20°N

10°W

North
Sea

FINLAND

60°W

NORWAY

SWEDEN

ESTONIA

10°E

IRELAND

UNITED
KINGDOM

DENMARK

Baltic Sea

LATVIA

RUSSIA

NETHERLANDS

LITHUANIA

RUSSIA

BELARUS

ATLANTIC
OCEAN

BELGIUM

GERMANY

POLAND

50°N

LUXEMBOURG

CZECH
REPUBLIC

UKRAINE

FRANCE

LIECHTENSTEIN

SLOVAKIA

MOLDOVA

SWITZERLAND

AUSTRIA

HUNGARY

50°N

SLOVENIA

ROMANIA

MONACO

CROATIA

BOSNIA AND
HERZEGOVINA

Black Sea

GEORGIA

PORTUGAL

ANDORRA

SAN
MARINO

ITALY

YUGOSLAVIA

BULGARIA

40°N

SPAIN

CORSICA
(FR.)

BALEARIC IS.
(SP.)

ALBANIA

MACEDONIA

TURKEY

GIBRALTAR (U.K.)

SARDINIA
(IT.)

Mediterranean
Sea

GREECE

ASIA

0   250   500 Miles
0   250   500 Kilometers

SICILY
(IT.)

MALTA

CRETE (GR.)

CYPRUS

SYRIA

LEBANON

0°   10°E   20°E   30°E

RUSSIA

ARCTIC OCEAN

70°N

ALASKA

CANADA

Nome

Yukon

Fairbanks

180°

60°N

Anchorage

Juneau★

PACIFIC OCEAN

170°W

0   250   500 Miles
0   250   500 Kilometers

160°W   150°W   140°W

CANADA

40°N

Seattle   River   Spokane

★
Olympia   WASHINGTON

Great Falls   Missouri River

Helena ★   MONTANA

Columbia

Portland

★ Salem   IDAHO   Billings

Eugene   OREGON   WYOMING

Boise   Snake River   Casper

Pocatello

Great
Salt
Lake   Ogden

Reno   NEVADA   Salt Lake City ★   Cheyenne ★

Carson City   Provo   COLORADO

San Francisco   ★ Sacramento   UTAH   Denver ★

Oakland   Colorado
San Jose   Springs
Pueblo

PACIFIC OCEAN

CALIFORNIA   Las
Vegas

30°N

Los Angeles   Santa
Fe

Long Beach   ARIZONA   Albuquerque

San Diego   Colorado River   NEW MEXICO

Phoenix ★

130°W   Tucson   El Paso

Rio Grande

N
W   E
S

MEXICO

160°W   PACIFIC   155°W
OCEAN

Kauai   N
W   E
Niihau   Oahu   S

Honolulu ★   Molokai

Lanai   Maui   20°N

HAWAII   Kahoolawe

Hawaii   Hilo

0   100   200 Miles
0   100   200 Kilometers

120°W   110°W

CANADA

NORTH DAKOTA
Grand Forks
★ Bismarck Fargo

MINNESOTA
Duluth
Minneapolis • St. Paul

SOUTH DAKOTA
★ Pierre

Lake Superior

WISCONSIN
Green Bay
Madison Milwaukee

MICHIGAN
Grand Rapids Lansing
Detroit

Lake Michigan
Lake Huron
Lake Ontario
Lake Erie

MAINE
★ Augusta

Burlington • Montpelier
VERMONT **NEW HAMPSHIRE** ★ Portland
★ Concord

NEW YORK
Buffalo Albany ★
MASSACHUSETTS
★ Boston
Providence

Hartford ★ **CONNECTICUT**
RHODE ISLAND

PENNSYLVANIA
Pittsburgh Harrisburg ★
Newark Trenton • New York
NEW JERSEY
Philadelphia
Dover ★
DELAWARE

IOWA
Cedar Rapids Rockford
Davenport
★ Des Moines

NEBRASKA
Omaha
Lincoln ★

Platte River
Missouri River

KANSAS
Kansas City
Topeka ★
Kansas City

Arkansas River

Wichita •

Chicago Gary Fort Wayne
Peoria

INDIANA
★ Indianapolis

ILLINOIS
★ Springfield
St. Louis
Evansville

Jefferson City ★

MISSOURI

Mississippi River

Toledo Cleveland

OHIO
Wheeling
• Columbus
Cincinnati

WEST VIRGINIA
★ Charleston

Baltimore
Washington, D.C. ★ Annapolis
MARYLAND

VIRGINIA
Richmond ★
Norfolk

KENTUCKY
Frankfort ★
Louisville

Nashville • Knoxville •

NORTH CAROLINA
• Raleigh
• Charlotte

TENNESSEE

Ohio River
Tennessee River

OKLAHOMA
Tulsa •
Oklahoma City ★
Fort Smith

Red River

ARKANSAS
Little Rock ★

Memphis

MISSISSIPPI
Birmingham •
★ Jackson

Mississippi River

ALABAMA
Columbus
Montgomery ★

GEORGIA
Atlanta ★

SOUTH CAROLINA
★ Columbia
Charleston •

Savannah •

TEXAS
Fort Worth • Dallas
★ Austin
• San Antonio
Laredo Corpus Christi

Shreveport •
LOUISIANA
Baton Rouge ★
New Orleans
Houston

Biloxi • Mobile

★ Tallahassee Jacksonville •

FLORIDA
Tampa •
Miami •

ATLANTIC OCEAN

Gulf of Mexico

THE BAHAMAS

CUBA

★ National capital   ★ State capital   • Other city

0   150   300 Miles
0   150   300 Kilometers

50° N
40° N
70° W
30° N
80° W
90° W
100° W

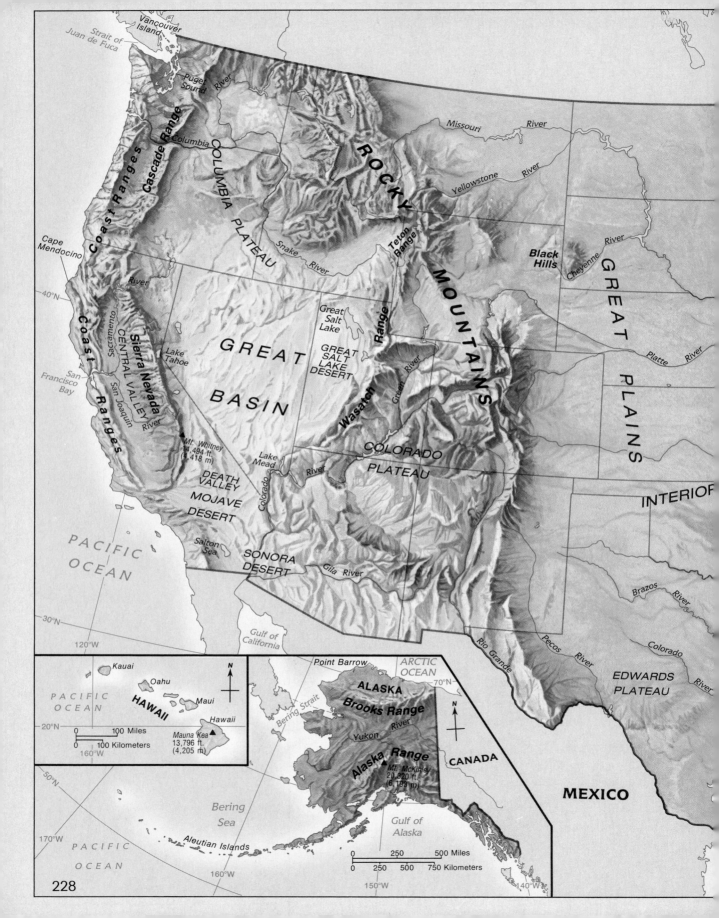

Vancouver
Island
Strait of
Juan de Fuca
Puget
Sound
Columbia
River
COLUMBIA
PLATEAU
ROCKY
Missouri
River
Yellowstone
River

Coast Ranges
Cascade Range
Cape
Mendocino
Snake
River
Teton
Range
Black
Hills
Cheyenne
River
GREAT
40°N

Coast Ranges
River
Sacramento
CENTRAL
VALLEY
Sierra Nevada
Lake
Tahoe
GREAT
BASIN
Great
Salt
Lake
GREAT
SALT
LAKE
DESERT
Range
MOUNTAINS
Platte
River
PLAINS

San
Francisco
Bay
San
Joaquin
River
Mt. Whitney
14,494 ft.
(4,418 m)
Lake
Mead
Wasatch
Green River
COLORADO
PLATEAU

DEATH
VALLEY
MOJAVE
DESERT
Colorado
River
INTERIOR

PACIFIC
OCEAN
Salton
Sea
SONORA
DESERT
Gila River

30°N
Gulf of
California
Rio Grande
Pecos
River
Colorado
River
EDWARDS
PLATEAU

120°W
Brazos
River

Kauai
N
Point Barrow
ARCTIC
OCEAN
70°N
MEXICO

Oahu
PACIFIC
OCEAN
Maui
HAWAII
Hawaii
ALASKA
Brooks Range
N

20°N
0   100 Miles
0   100 Kilometers
Mauna Kea
13,796 ft.
(4,205 m)
Bering Strait
Yukon
River
Alaska Range
Mt. McKinley
20,320 ft.
(6,193 m)
CANADA

160°W
50°N
170°W
Bering
Sea
Aleutian Islands
Gulf of
Alaska

PACIFIC
OCEAN
160°W
150°W
0   250   500 Miles
0   250   500   750 Kilometers
140°W

228

CANADA

Lake of
the Woods

Mesabi Range

Lake Superior

GREAT

LAKES

CENTRAL   PLAINS

Mississippi

Lake Michigan

Lake Huron

River

Wabash   River

Lake Ontario

Lake Erie

St. Lawrence River

Adirondack
Mts.

Green Mts.

White Mts.

Bay of
Fundy

Hudson River

Cape
Cod

ALLEGHENY
PLATEAU

Susquehanna

Delaware R.

Long Island

40°N

70°W

Missouri

River

Ohio   River

Allegheny   Mountains

APPALACHIAN   MOUNTAINS

Potomac   R.

Delaware Bay

Chesapeake Bay

PLAINS

OZARK
PLATEAU

River

Kentucky
Lake

PIEDMONT

ATLANTIC   COASTAL   PLAIN

Cape Hatteras

ATLANTIC

OCEAN

Arkansas

River

Ouachita
Mountains

Mississippi

River

Tennessee   River

Savannah River

Alabama   River

Chattahoochee   River

Red   River

GULF   COASTAL   PLAIN

30°N

Mobile Bay

Galveston Bay

Mississippi Delta

Gulf of Mexico

90°W

Lake
Okeechobee

N

THE UNITED STATES
Physical

0   100   200   300 Miles

0   100   200   300   400 Kilometers

Florida Keys

Straits of Florida

80°W

WEST INDIES

229

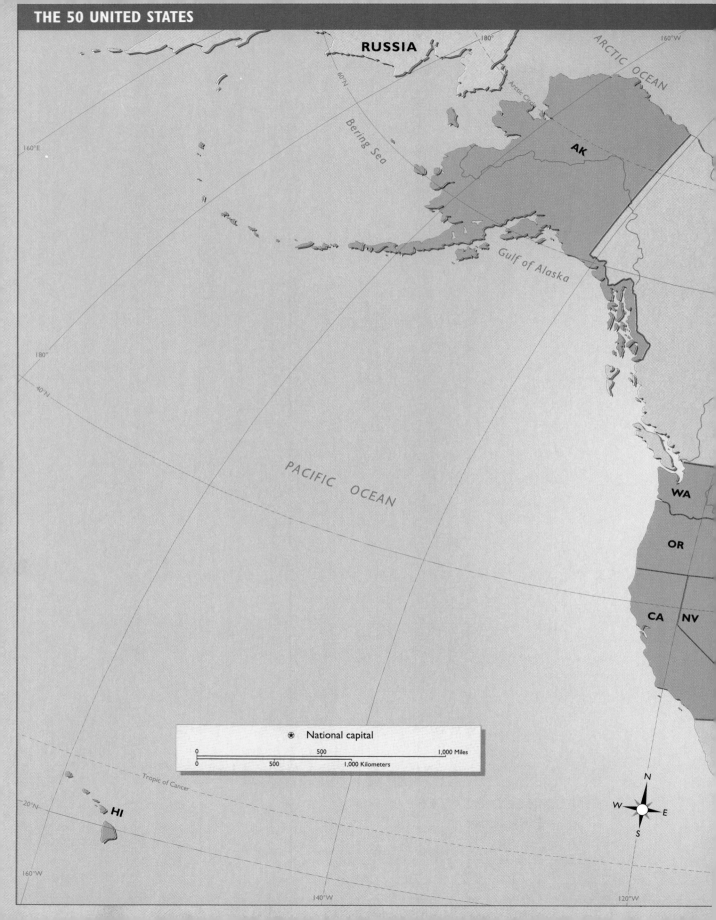

RUSSIA

ARCTIC OCEAN

Bering Sea

AK

Arctic Circle

Gulf of Alaska

180°

160°E

60°N

40°N

PACIFIC OCEAN

WA

OR

CA NV

Tropic of Cancer

20°N

HI

160°W

140°W

120°W

⊛ National capital

| 0 | 500 | 1,000 Miles |
| 0 | 500 | 1,000 Kilometers |

N
W ⊛ E
S

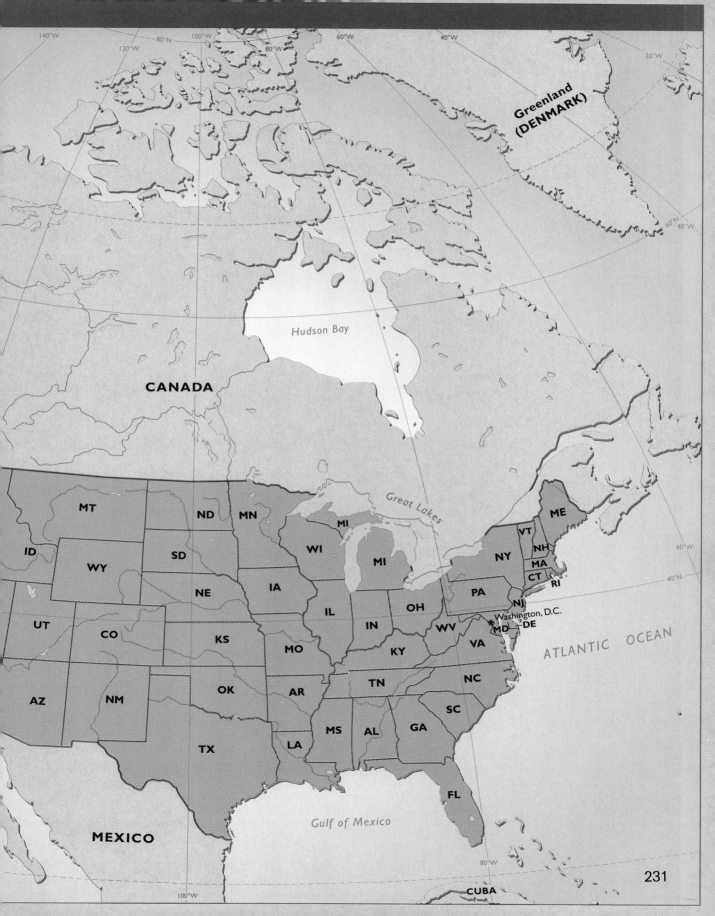

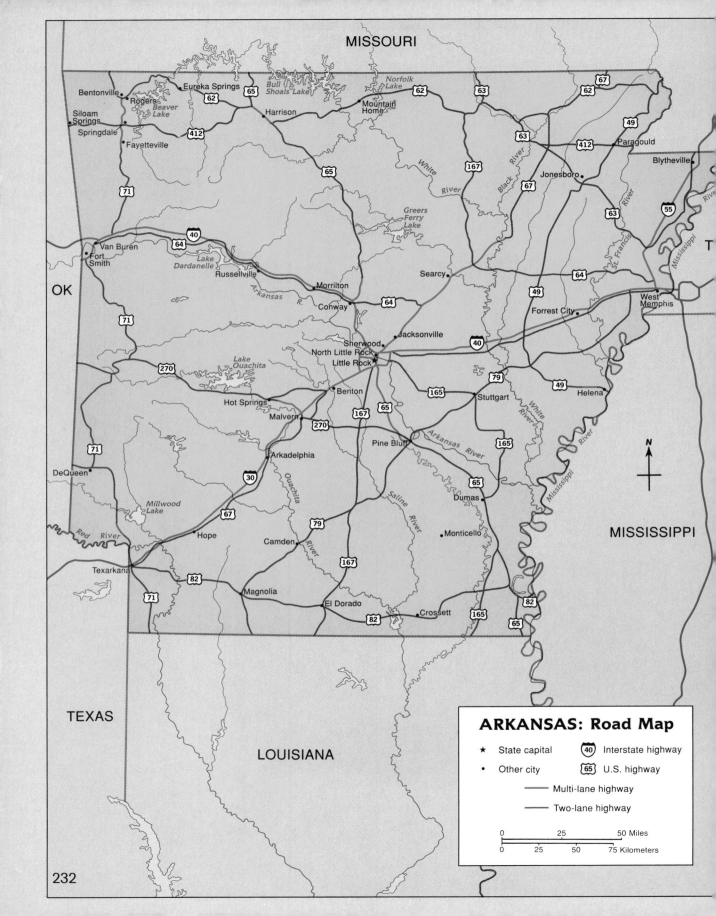

MISSOURI

Bentonville
Rogers
Siloam
Springs
Springdale
Fayetteville

Beaver
Lake

Eureka Springs

62

65

Harrison

Bull
Shoals Lake

Norfolk
Lake

Mountain
Home

62

63

62

67

49

412

63

Paragould

Blytheville

412

Jonesboro

167

63

67

55

63

65

White
River

Black
River

Greers
Ferry
Lake

71

Van Buren
Fort
Smith

OK

64

40

Lake
Dardanelle

Russellville

Arkansas R.

Morrilton

Conway

64

Searcy

64

St. Francis
River

Mississippi River

T

West
Memphis

49

Forrest City

40

71

270

Lake
Ouachita

Sherwood
North Little Rock
Little Rock

Jacksonville

79

165

Stuttgart

49

Helena

Benton

167

65

165

White
River

Hot Springs
Malvern

270

Pine Bluff

Arkansas River

Mississippi River

71

DeQueen

Millwood
Lake

Arkadelphia

30

Ouachita River

Saline River

65

Dumas

MISSISSIPPI

Monticello

Red River

67

Hope

Camden

79

167

N

82

Magnolia

El Dorado

82

Crossett

165

82

65

Texarkana

71

TEXAS

LOUISIANA

232

ARKANSAS: Road Map

★ State capital

40 Interstate highway

• Other city

65 U.S. highway

Multi-lane highway

Two-lane highway

0   25   50 Miles

0   25   50   75 Kilometers

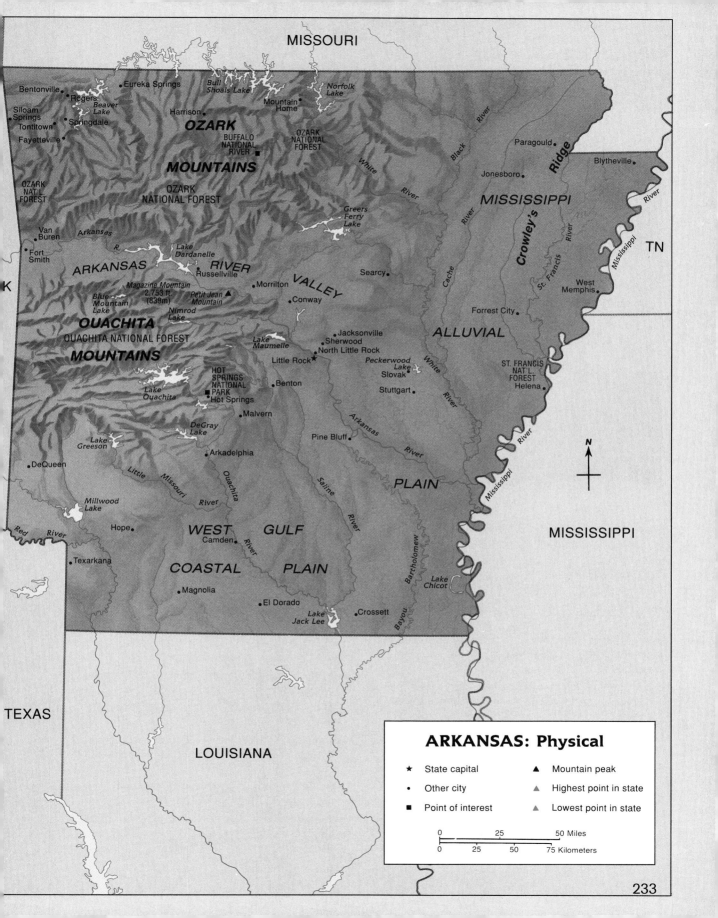

MISSOURI

Bentonville
Rogers
Siloam
Springs
Tontitown
Fayetteville

Eureka Springs

Beaver
Lake

Harrison

Bull
Shoals Lake

Mountain
Home

Norfolk
Lake

OZARK

BUFFALO
NATIONAL
RIVER ■

OZARK
NATIONAL
FOREST

MOUNTAINS

OZARK
NAT'L
FOREST

OZARK
NATIONAL FOREST

Van
Buren
Fort
Smith

Arkansas
R.

Lake
Dardanelle

Russellville

ARKANSAS

Magazine Mountain
2,753 ft.
(839m)

Petit Jean ▲
Mountain

Blue
Mountain
Lake

Nimrod
Lake

RIVER

VALLEY

Morrilton

Conway

Greers
Ferry
Lake

Searcy

Paragould

Jonesboro

Black

River

River

River

Cache

St. Francis

Crowley's Ridge

MISSISSIPPI

Blytheville

River

Mississippi

TN

West
Memphis

OUACHITA

OUACHITA NATIONAL FOREST

MOUNTAINS

Lake
Ouachita

HOT
SPRINGS
NATIONAL
PARK ■
Hot Springs

DeGray
Lake

Lake
Maumelle

Little Rock ★

Benton

Malvern

Lake
Greeson

DeQueen

Arkadelphia

Little
Missouri

River

Ouachita

River

Millwood
Lake

Hope

Camden

WEST

GULF

COASTAL

River

Saline

River

PLAIN

Magnolia

El Dorado

Lake
Jack Lee

Crossett

Bartholomew

Bayou

Lake
Chicot

Red
River

Jacksonville
Sherwood
North Little Rock

Peckerwood
Lake
Slovak

Stuttgart

ALLUVIAL

White

River

Forrest City

ST. FRANCIS
NAT'L
FOREST
Helena

Pine Bluff

Arkansas

River

PLAIN

Mississippi

River

MISSISSIPPI

N

TEXAS

LOUISIANA

ARKANSAS: Physical

★ State capital

• Other city

■ Point of interest

▲ Mountain peak

▲ Highest point in state

▲ Lowest point in state

0   25   50 Miles

0   25   50   75 Kilometers

233

DICTIONARY OF GEOGRAPHIC TERMS

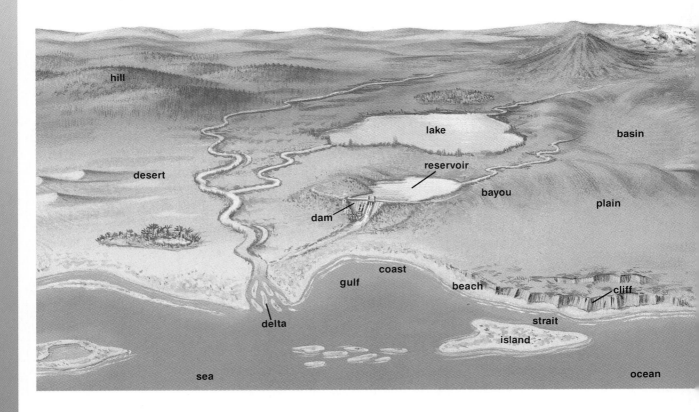

basin (bā′ sin) A low, bowl-shaped landform surrounded by higher lands. *See also* **river basin.**

bay (bā) A part of an ocean, sea, or lake that extends into the land. A bay is usually smaller than a gulf.

bayou (bī′ ü) A sluggish inlet or outlet of a river, lake, or gulf.

beach (bēch) The gently sloping shore of an ocean or other body of water, especially that part covered by sand or pebbles.

canal (kə nal′) A waterway built to carry water for navigation or irrigation. Navigation canals usually connect two other bodies of water.

canyon (kan′ yən) A deep, narrow valley with steep sides.

cape (cāp) A projecting part of a coastline that extends into an ocean, sea, gulf, bay, or lake.

cliff (klif) A high, steep face of rock or earth.

coast (kōst) Land along an ocean or sea.

dam (dam) A wall built across a river to hold back flowing water.

delta (del′ tə) Land at the mouth of a river, made of silt, sand, and pebbles. A delta is usually shaped like a triangle.

desert (dez′ ərt) A very dry area where few plants grow.

gulf (gulf) A part of an ocean or sea that extends into the land. A gulf is usually larger than a bay.

harbor (här′ bər) A protected place along a shore where ships can safely anchor.

hill (hil) A rounded, raised landform that is not as high as a mountain.

island (ī′ lənd) A body of land completely surrounded by water.

isthmus (is′ məs) A narrow strip of land bordered by water and connecting two larger bodies of land.

lake (lāk) A body of water completely surrounded by land.

mountain (mount′ ən) A high, rounded, or pointed landform with steep sides. A mountain is higher than a hill.

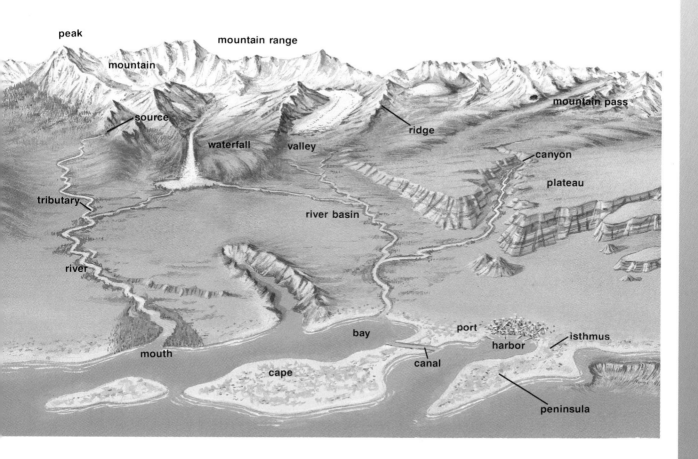

peak
mountain range
mountain
source
waterfall
valley
ridge
mountain pass
canyon
plateau
tributary
river basin
river
port
isthmus
bay
harbor
mouth
canal
peninsula
cape

mountain pass (mount′ ən pas) An opening or gap through a mountain range.

mountain range (mount′ ən rānj) A row or chain of mountains.

mouth (mouth) The part of a river where it empties into another body of water.

ocean (ō′ shən) One of the earth's four largest bodies of water. The four oceans are really a single body of salt water that covers about three fourths of the earth's surface.

peak (pēk) The pointed top of a mountain or hill.

peninsula (pə nin′ sə lə) A body of land nearly surrounded by water.

plain (plān) A large area of flat or nearly flat land.

plateau (pla tō′) A high, flat landform raised above the surrounding land.

port (pôrt) A place where ships load and unload goods.

reservoir (rez′ ər vwär) A natural or artificial lake used to store water.

ridge (rij) A long and narrow chain of hills or mountains.

river (riv′ ər) A large stream of water that flows in a natural channel across the land and empties into a lake, ocean, or another river.

river basin (riv′ ər bā′ sin) All the land drained by a river and its tributaries.

sea (sē) A large body of water partly or entirely surrounded by land; another word for *ocean*.

source (sôrs) A spring, lake, or other body of water where a river or stream begins.

strait (strāt) A narrow waterway or channel connecting two larger bodies of water.

tributary (trib′ yə târ ē) A river or stream that flows into a larger river or stream.

valley (val′ ē) An area of low land between hills or mountains.

waterfall (wô′ tər fôl) A flow of water falling from a high place.

GAZETTEER

This Gazetteer is a geographical dictionary that will help you to pronounce and locate the places discussed in this book. Latitude and longitude are given for cities and some other places. The page number tells you where the name of each place appears in the text for the first time.

PRONUNCIATION KEY

a	cap	hw	where	oi	coin	ü	moon
ā	cake	i	bib	ôr	fork	ū	cute
ä	father	ī	kite	ou	cow	ûr	term
är	car	îr	pierce	sh	show	ə	about, taken,
âr	dare	ng	song	th	thin		pencil, apron,
ch	chain	o	top	th	those		helpful
e	hen	ō	rope	u	sun	ər	letter, dollar,
ē	me	ô	saw	ù	book		doctor

A

Arkadelphia (är kə del′ fē ə) A city in west-central Arkansas; 34°N, 93°W. (p. 61)

Arkansas (är′ kən sô) A state in the south-central part of the United States; the subject of this textbook. (p. 9)

Arkansas Post (är′ kən sô pōst) The first permanent European settlement in Arkansas; 84°N, 91°W. (p. 88)

Arkansas River (är′ kən sô riv′ ər) A river that flows through the center of Arkansas. (p. 13)

Arkansas River Valley (är′ kən sô riv′ ər val′ ē) A highland region of Arkansas, located between the Ozarks and the Ouachitas. (p. 28)

Arkansas Territory (är′ kən sô ter′ i tôr ē) The territory established by Congress in 1819 that included all of present-day Arkansas and most of present-day Oklahoma. (p. 97)

B

Bartholomew Bayou (bär thäl′ ə mü bi′ ü) A bayou in the southern area of the West Gulf Coastal Plain, near the Louisiana border. (p. 35)

Beaver Lake (bē′ vər lāk) A lake in northwestern Arkansas. (p. 213)

Bentonville (ben′ tən vil) A town in northwestern Arkansas; the location of Louise M. Thaden Field; 36°N, 94°W. (p. 149)

Bering Strait (bîr′ ing strāt) A narrow waterway connecting the Bering Sea and the Arctic Ocean. (p. 50)

Beringia (bîr′ ən gē ə) A land bridge that connected Asia with North America between 12,000 and 20,000 years ago. (p. 50)

Blytheville (blīth′ vil) An important town in the Mississippi Alluvial Plain; center for cotton and soybeans; 36°N, 90°W. (p. 33)

Brinkley (brink′ lē) A town in east-central Arkansas; 35°N, 91°W. (p. 192)

Buffalo National River (buf′ ə lō nash′ ə nəl riv′ ər) A site of scenic beauty in the Ozarks, visited by many people each year. (p. 181)

Bull Shoals Lake (bəl shōlz lāk) An important lake in northern Arkansas. (p. 14)

C

Caddo River (kad′ ō riv′ ər) A river in west-central Arkansas. (p. 61)

Camden (kam′ dən) A city in southern Arkansas, located along the Ouachita River; 33°N, 93°W. (p. 110)

Charleston (chärlz′ tən) The hometown of Dale Bumpers, located in west-central Arkansas; 35°N, 94°W. (p. 196)

Crowley's Ridge (krou′ lēz rij) The smallest natural region of Arkansas, located in the eastern part of the state. (p. 28)

D

Des Arc (dez′ ärk) A community in central Arkansas; 35°N, 92°W. (p. 143)

E

El Dorado (el də rād′ ō) A city in south-central Arkansas where oil and gas were discovered in the 1920s; 33°N, 93°W. (p. 23)

England (ing′ glənd) The town in central Arkansas where the "England Riot" took place during the Great Depression; 35°N, 92°W. (p. 152)

Eureka Springs (yu̇ rē′ kə springz) An important tourist center in the Ozark Mountains; 36°N, 94°W. (p. 38)

F

Fayetteville (fā′ ət vil) A city in northwestern Arkansas, home of the University of Arkansas; 36°N, 94°W. (p. 131)

Florida (flôr′ i də) The southernmost state in the southeastern United States; the name given by the Spanish to the southeastern United States during the 1500s. (p. 79)

Forrest City (fôr′ ist sit′ ē) A city in east-central Arkansas, hometown of Al Green; 35°N, 91°W. (p. 154)

Fort Smith (fôrt smith) The second-largest city in Arkansas; 35°N, 94°W. (p. 39)

Fort Sumter (fôrt sum′ tər) A Union fort off the coast of South Carolina, the site of the opening battle of the Civil War; 33°N, 80°W. (p. 125)

G

Gravette (grə vet′) A community in northwestern Arkansas; 36°N, 94°W. (p. 16)

Greers Ferry Lake (grîrz fer′ ē lāk) A major lake in north-central Arkansas. (p. 14)

H

Harrison (har′ ə sən) A town in the Ozark Mountains; 36°N, 93°W. (p. 186)

Helena (hel′ ə nə) A community at the southern tip of Crowley's Ridge, important in food packing and shipping; 35°N, 90°W. (p. 35)

Hope (hōp) A town in Hempstead County in southwestern Arkansas, home of the Hope Watermelon Festival; 34°N, 94°W. (p. 171)

Hot Springs (hot springz) The largest city in the Ouachita Mountains, famous for its natural hot springs; 35°N, 93°W. (p. 41)

Hot Springs National Park (hot springz nash ə nəl pärk) A national park created by Congress in 1921, where visitors can hike, bathe in the natural hot springs, and enjoy the scenery. (p. 181)

I

Indian Territory (in′ dē ən ter′ i tôr ē) An area of land west of Arkansas, set up in the 1830s as a place to relocate Native American groups; it later became the state of Oklahoma. (p. 107)

J

Japan (jə pan′) A country off the coast of Asia that fought against the United States during World War II. (p. 153)

Jonesboro (jōnz′ bər ə) A city in northeastern Arkansas, location of the world's largest rice mill; 36°N, 91°W. (p. 175)

K

Kappa (kap′ ə) A Quapaw village that flourished about 300 years ago; 34°N, 91°W. (p. 65)

L

Lafayette County (laf ē et′ koun′ tē) The county in southwestern Arkansas in which author Maya Angelou grew up. (p. 158)

Lake Chicot (lāk chē′ kō) An "oxbow lake" in southeastern Arkansas. (p. 14)

Lake Hamilton (lāk ham′ əl tən) A man-made lake in central Arkansas, near Hot Springs. (p. 14)

Lake Ouachita (lāk wäsh′ ə tô) A major lake in west-central Arkansas. (p. 14)

Little Rock (lit′ əl rok) The capital of Arkansas; 35°N, 92°W. (p. 16)

Louisiana (lü ē zē an′ ə) The state just south of Arkansas. (p. 11)

Louisiana Territory (lü ē zē an′ ə ter′ i tôr ē) The land bought from France in 1803 that covered most of the western Mississippi Valley; Arkansas was part of this territory. (p. 96)

M

Magnolia (mag nōl′ yə) A town in southwestern Arkansas; 33°N, 93°W. (p. 180)

Manila (mə nil′ ə) A community in northeastern Arkansas; birthplace of Arkansas war hero Herman Davis; 36°N, 90°W. (p. 147)

Maumelle River (mō mel′ riv′ ər) A tributary of the Arkansas River, located in the Arkansas River Valley. (p. 39)

Mena (mē′ nə) A small community in southwestern Arkansas; 35°N, 94°W. (p. 27)

Millwood Lake (mil′ wŭd lāk) A lake in southwestern Arkansas. (p. 182)

Mississippi (mis ə sip′ ē) A state just east of Arkansas. (p. 12)

Mississippi Alluvial Plain (mis ə sip′ ē ə lü′ vē əl plān) The largest of Arkansas's six regions, forming roughly the eastern third of the state. (p. 28)

Mississippi River (mis ə sip′ ē riv′ ər) The river that forms the eastern border of Arkansas. (p. 11)

Missouri (mi zùr′ ē) The state just north of Arkansas. (p. 11)

Monticello (mon tə sel′ ō) A small community in southeastern Arkansas; 34°N, 92°W. (p. 27)

Mountain View (moun′ tən vū) The site of a museum of Arkansas arts and crafts in north-central Arkansas; 36°N, 92°W. (p. 209)

N

New France (nü frans) The French colony of the 1600s that came to include much of present-day Canada. (p. 82)

North America (nôrth ə mer′ i kə) One of the earth's seven continents, the one on which the United States is located. (p. 50)

North Little Rock (nôrth lit′ əl rok) A city in central Arkansas, located across the Arkansas River from Little Rock; the site of job-training programs for African-Americans during World War II; 35°N, 92°W. (p. 155)

O

Oklahoma (ō klə hō′ mə) A state just west of Arkansas. (p. 12)

Orleans Territory (ôr′ lē ənz ter′ i tôr ē) The territory bought from France in 1803 that covered most of present-day Louisiana. (p. 96)

Ouachita Mountains (wäsh′ ə tô moun′ tənz) A mountain range in western Arkansas; one of the highland regions of Arkansas. (p. 13)

Ouachita River (wäsh′ ə tô riv′ ər) An important river that flows through southern Arkansas. (p. 13)

Ozark Mountains (ō′ zärk moun′ tənz) A mountain range in northwestern Arkansas; one of the highland regions of Arkansas. (p. 13)

P

Paragould (par′ ə güld) A city in northeastern Arkansas; 36°N, 90°W. (p. 191)

Pea Ridge (pē rij) The site of the first major battle in Arkansas during the Civil War; 36°N, 94°W. (p. 130)

Petit Jean River (pə′ tē jēn riv′ ər) A tributary of the Arkansas River, located in the Arkansas River Valley. (p. 39)

Pine Bluff (pīn bluf) A city in south-central Arkansas; an important center of the paper and wood products industry; 34°N, 92°W. (p. 176)

Prairie Grove Battlefield (prâr′ ē grōv bat′ əl fēld) The site of the Civil War Battle of Prairie Grove; 36°N, 94°W. (p. 181)

Pulaski County (pə las′ kē koun′ tē) The county in central Arkansas in which Little Rock is located. (p. 190)

R

Red River (red riv′ ər) An important river that flows through southwestern Arkansas. (p. 13)

S

St. Francis River (sānt fran′ səs riv′ ər) An important river that flows through eastern Arkansas. (p. 13)

Slovak (slō′ väk) A town in central Arkansas; 35°N, 92°W. (p. 203)

Smackover (smak′ ō vər) A town in south-central Arkansas where oil was discovered in the 1920s; 33°N, 93°W. (p. 148)

South America (south ə mer′ i kə) One of the earth's seven continents, located south of North America. (p. 51)

South Carolina (south kar ə lī′ nə) A state in the southeastern United States along the Atlantic coast; the first state to secede from the Union in 1860. (p. 123)

Stamps (stamps) A community in southwestern Arkansas; the hometown of Maya Angelou; 33°N, 93°W. (p. 158)

Stuttgart (stut′ gärt) A town in east-central Arkansas; 34°N, 92°W. (p. 203)

T

Tennessee (ten ə sē′) A state just east of Arkansas. (p. 12)

Texarkana (tek sär kan′ ə) A city in southwestern Arkansas on the Texas border; 33°N, 94°W. (p. 149)

Texas (tek′ səs) A state just west of Arkansas. (p. 12)

Toltec Mounds State Park (tōl′ tek moundz stāt pärk) A state park where it is possible to see mounds built by Native Americans about 1,000 years ago; 35°N, 92°W. (p. 55)

GAZETTEER

Tontitown (tän′ tē toun) A town in northwestern Arkansas, founded by Italian immigrants in the late 1800s; 36°N, 94°W. (p. 203)

U

United States (ū nī′ tid stātz) The country located in North America of which Arkansas is one of 50 states. (p. 79)

V

Van Buren (van byùr′ ən) A city in northwestern Arkansas; 35°N, 95°W. (p. 27)

W

Washington (wô′ shing tən) The town in southwestern Arkansas that served as the Confederate state capital during the Civil War; 34°N, 94°W. (p. 131)

Washington, D.C. (wô′ shing tən dē sē) The capital of the United States; 39°N, 77°W. (p. 136)

West Fork (west fôrk) A community in northwestern Arkansas; 36°N, 94°W. (p. 189)

West Gulf Coastal Plain (west gulf kōs′ təl plān) A natural lowland region of Arkansas. (p. 28)

West Memphis (west mem′ fis) A city in northeastern Arkansas, located along the Mississippi River; 35°N, 90°W. (p. 80)

White River (hwīt riv′ ər) An important river in eastern Arkansas. (p. 13)

---

a cap; ā cake; ä father; är car; âr dare; ch chain; e hen; ē me; hw where; i bib; ī kite; îr pierce; ng song; o top; ō rope; ô saw; oi coin; ôr fork; ou cow; sh show; th thin; th those; u sun; ù book; ü moon; ū cute; ûr term; ə about, taken, pencil, apron, helpful; ər letter, dollar, doctor

GAZETTEER

BIOGRAPHICAL DICTIONARY

This Biographical Dictionary will help you to pronounce and identify the Key People discussed in this book. The page number tells you where each person first appears in the text.

PRONUNCIATION KEY

a	cap	hw	where	oi	coin	ü	moon
ā	cake	i	bib	ôr	fork	ū	cute
ä	father	ī	kite	ou	cow	ûr	term
är	car	îr	pierce	sh	show	ə	about, taken,
âr	dare	ng	song	th	thin		pencil, apron,
ch	chain	o	top	th	those		helpful
e	hen	ō	rope	u	sun	ər	letter, dollar,
ē	me	ô	saw	u̇	book		doctor

A

Angelou, Maya (an′ jə lü, mī′ ə), 1928– Author who grew up in Lafayette County. (p. 158)

B

Bates, Daisy (bāts), 1920– Civil rights leader in Arkansas who headed the state chapter of the NAACP and published a newspaper. (p. 161)

Bryant, Bear (brī′ ənt), 1913–1983 Former coach of the University of Alabama football team. (p. 215)

Bumpers, Dale (bum′ pərz), 1925– United States senator from Arkansas. (p. 198)

C

Campbell, Glen (kam′ bəl), 1936– Country singer from Arkansas. (p. 206)

Caraway, Hattie (kar′ ə wā), 1878–1950 United States senator from Arkansas, 1931–1945; the first woman to be elected to the United States Senate. (p. 197)

Cash, Johnny (cash), 1932– Country singer from Arkansas. (p. 206)

Clayton, Powell (klāt′ ən), 1833–1914 Governor of Arkansas during Reconstruction. (p. 137)

Cleburne, Patrick (klē′ bərn), 1828–1864 Arkansas military hero during the Civil War. (p. 132)

Clinton, Bill (klint′ ən), 1946– Governor of Arkansas, 1979–1981 and 1983–1993. Forty-second President of the United States. (p. 173)

Crittenden, Robert (krit′ ən dən), 1797–1834 First territorial secretary of Arkansas. (p. 97)

D

Davis, Herman (dā′ vis), 1888–1923 Arkansas military hero during World War I. (p. 147)

De Soto, Hernando (də sō′ tō, er non′ dō), 1500?–1542 Spanish explorer who crossed the Mississippi River and wandered throughout Arkansas in search of gold. (p. 79)

De Tonti, Henri (dā tōn′ tē, on rē′), 1650–1704 Italian explorer who started Arkansas's first permanent European settlement at Arkansas Post. (p. 88)

Dean, Dizzy (dēn), 1911–1974 All-star pitcher for the St. Louis Cardinals who was born in Sharp County. (p. 215)

Dodd, David O. (dod), 1846–1864 Confederate spy from Arkansas who was hanged for refusing to betray the source of his information. (p. 132)

E

Eisenhower, Dwight D. (īz′ ən hou ər), 1890–1969 United States President from 1953 to 1961; sent federal troops to Little Rock to help bring about the integration of the public schools. (p. 161)

F

Faubus, Orval (fô′ bəs), 1910–1994 Governor of Arkansas, 1955–1967, who tried to prevent integration of the public schools during the 1950s. (p. 160)

Flanagin, Harris (flan′ i gən), 1817–1875 Confederate governor of Arkansas during the Civil War. (p. 131)

Fletcher, John Gould (flech′ ər), 1886–1950 Pulitzer Prize-winning poet from Arkansas. (p. 208)

Fulbright, J. William (fu̇l′ brīt), 1905–1995 Powerful United States senator from Arkansas from the 1940s through the 1970s. (p. 197)

G

Green, Al (grēn), 1946– World-famous gospel singer from Forrest City. (p. 207)

Grey, William H. (grā), 1830–1888 African American who served in the Arkansas State Senate during Reconstruction. (p. 138)

J

Jefferson, Thomas (jef' ər sən), 1743–1826 Third President of the United States; agreed to the Louisiana Purchase. (p. 95)

Jewell, Jerry (jü' əl), 1930– First African American to serve in the Arkansas State Senate since Reconstruction. (p. 162)

Johnson, Andrew (jon' sən), 1808–1875 Seventeenth President of the United States; tried to bring about a smooth Reconstruction after the Civil War. (p. 136)

Joliet, Louis (jō' lē et, lü' ē), 1645–1700 French explorer who, together with Jacques Marquette, sailed down the Mississippi River as far south as Arkansas. (p. 82)

Jones, Fay (jōnz), 1921– Architect who designed some of Arkansas's most famous houses and chapels. (p. 208)

Joplin, Scott (jop' lən), 1868–1917 Composer of jazz music who was born in Texarkana. (p. 149)

K

Kindley, Field (kind' lē), 1896–1920 Flying ace from Arkansas during World War I. (p. 148)

L

La Harpe, Bernard de (lä ärp', ber' nar də), 1683–1765 French explorer who found and named the "little rock" that later became the site of Little Rock. (p. 90)

La Salle, Robert (lə sal'), 1643–1687 French explorer who reached the mouth of the Mississippi River in 1682 and claimed the entire Mississippi Valley for France. (p. 83)

Law, John (lô), 1671–1729 Businessman from Scotland whose attempt to start a colony in Arkansas became known as the "Mississippi Bubble." (p. 89)

Lincoln, Abraham (ling' kən), 1809–1865 Sixteenth President of the United States; issued the Emancipation Proclamation and led the Union during the Civil War. (p. 123)

M

MacArthur, Douglas (mə kär' thər), 1880–1964 General in the fight against Japan during World War II. (p. 154)

Marquette, Jacques (mär ket', zhäk), 1637–1675 French priest who, together with Louis Joliet, sailed down the Mississippi River as far south as Arkansas. (p. 82)

McClellan, John L. (mə klel' ən), 1896–1977 United States senator from Arkansas from the 1940s through the 1970s; sponsored the McClellan-Kerr Navigation Project. (p. 197)

Miller, James (mil' ər), 1776–1851 First territorial governor of Arkansas. (p. 97)

Moncrief, Sidney (mon krēf'), 1957– "Super Sidney," who had a long career as a player for the University of Arkansas Razorbacks and the Milwaukee Bucks basketball teams. (p. 215)

Murphy, Isaac (mûr' fē), 1799–1882 Governor of Arkansas, 1864–1868, who was the only delegate at the Arkansas state convention of 1861 to vote against secession. (p. 125)

N

Nuttall, Thomas (nət' ôl), 1786–1859 Traveler and scientist who visited Arkansas in 1819. (p. 11)

P

Pryor, David (prī' ər), 1934– United States senator from Arkansas. (p. 198)

R

Rector, Henry (rek' tər), 1816–1899 Governor of Arkansas, 1860–1862, who favored seceding from the Union. (p. 124)

Robinson, Joe T. (rob' in sən), 1872–1937 Served as United States representative and as United States senator from 1903 to 1937; served briefly as governor of Arkansas in 1913. (p. 144)

Roosevelt, Franklin D. (rōz' velt), 1882–1945 President of the United States during the Great Depression and World War II. (p. 153)

S

Sarasen (sar' ə sin), 1735–1832 Quapaw chief during the early 1830s who tried to help his people stay on their land. (p. 106)

Sequoyah (si kwoi' ə), 1770?–1843 A Cherokee who lived in Arkansas during the early 1800s and who invented the Cherokee alphabet. (p. 106)

Sevier, Ambrose (sə vîr'), 1801–1848 The Arkansas Territory's delegate to Congress; asked that the territory be granted statehood. (p. 101)

Stephens, Charlotte (stē' vənz), 1854–1951 First African American to teach in a Little Rock public school. (p. 144)

T

Thaden, Louise (tha' dən), 1909–1975 An Arkansan who was one of America's first woman airplane pilots. (p. 149)

W

Walton, Sam (wôlt' ən), 1918–1992 Successful Arkansas entrepreneur. (p. 177)

Woodruff, William (wùd' rəf), 1795–1885 Founded the *Arkansas Gazette* in 1819. (p. 100)

ARKANSAS ALMANAC

An almanac is a collection of facts and figures. This almanac
will help you to learn more about your state.

ARKANSAS'S COUNTIES

County Name	County Seat	County Population (1990)	Area in Sq Miles	Named For	Year Formed
Arkansas	DeWitt and Stuttgart	24,989	1,006	The District of Arkansas	1813
Ashley	Hamburg	27,916	934	U.S. Senator Chester Ashley	1848
Baxter	Mountain Home	32,635	546	Governor Elisha Baxter	1873
Benton	Bentonville	92,418	843	State Senator Thomas Benton	1836
Boone	Harrison	29,335	584	Daniel Boone	1869
Bradley	Warren	14,389	654	Captain Hugh Bradley, hero of the War of 1812	1840
Calhoun	Hampton	6,452	628	John C. Calhoun, U.S. senator from South Carolina	1850
Carroll	Eureka Springs and Berryville	17,813	634	Charles Carroll, signer of the Declaration of Independence	1823
Chicot	Lake Village	18,251	649	Point Chicot on the Mississippi River	1823
Clark	Arkadelphia	24,848	867	William Clark, governor of Missouri Territory	1818
Clay	Piggot and Corning	21,328	641	State Senator John Clayton	1873
Cleburne	Heber Springs	20,357	551	Confederate General Patrick Cleburne	1883
Cleveland	Rison	8,543	599	U.S. President Grover Cleveland	1873
Columbia	Magnolia	27,623	767	another name for America	1852
Conway	Morrilton	20,910	558	Henry Conway, territorial delegate to Congress	1823
Craighead	Jonesboro and Lake City	71,071	713	State Senator Thomas Craighead	1859
Crawford	Van Buren and Fort Smith	43,483	594	U.S. Secretary of War William Crawford	1820
Crittenden	Marion	53,353	599	Territorial Secretary Robert Crittenden	1825
Cross	Wynne	21,329	622	Colonel David Cross, Confederate hero	1862
Dallas	Fordyce	11,020	668	U.S. Vice President George Dallas	1845
Desha	Arkansas City	21,282	746	Captain Benjamin Desha, hero of War of 1812	1838
Drew	Monticello	19,943	831	Governor Thomas Drew	1846

County Name	County Seat	County Population (1990)	Area in Sq Miles	Named For	Year Formed
Faulkner	Conway	56,963	645	Sanford Faulkner, early settler	1873
Franklin	Ozark and Charleston	16,276	609	Benjamin Franklin	1837
Fulton	Salem	10,857	616	Territorial Governor Wm. Fulton	1842
Garland	Hot Springs	78,503	657	Governor Augustus Garland	1873
Grant	Sheridan	14,865	633	U.S. President Ulysses S. Grant	1869
Greene	Paragould	34,045	579	Nathanael Greene, hero of the American Revolution	1833
Hempstead	Hope	26,168	725	Edward Hempstead, delegate to Congress	1818
Hot Spring	Malvern	29,469	615	local hot springs	1829
Howard	Nashville	14,393	574	State Senator James Howard	1873
Independence	Batesville	34,370	763	in honor of Ark. independence	1820
Izard	Melbourne	11,728	581	Territorial Governor George Izard	1825
Jackson	Newport	22,572	633	U.S. President Andrew Jackson	1829
Jefferson	Pine Bluff	98,670	882	U.S. President Thomas Jefferson	1829
Johnson	Clarksville	19,105	676	Benjamin Johnson, judge	1833
Lafayette	Lewisville	10,444	518	Marquis de Lafayette	1827
Lawrence	Walnut Ridge	19,466	589	Captain James Lawrence, hero of War of 1812	1815
Lee	Marianna	15,071	602	General Robert E. Lee	1873
Lincoln	Star City	14,330	562	U.S. President Abraham Lincoln	1871
Little River	Ashdown	15,336	516	the Little River	1867
Logan	Paris and Booneville	21,630	717	James Logan, early settler	1871
Lonoke	Lonoke	39,715	783	from "Lone Oak"	1873
Madison	Huntsville	12,214	837	U.S. President James Madison	1836
Marion	Yellville	13,575	587	General Francis Marion, hero of the American Revolution	1835
Miller	Texarkana	41,375	619	Territorial Governor James Miller	1820
Mississippi	Blytheville and Osceola	61,862	896	Mississippi River	1833
Monroe	Clarendon	13,839	609	U.S. President James Monroe	1829
Montgomery	Mount Ida	8,563	774	Richard Montgomery, hero of the American Revolution	1842

County Name	County Seat	County Population (1990)	Area in Sq Miles	Named For	Year Formed
Nevada	Prescott	11,618	620	State of Nevada	1871
Newton	Jasper	8,822	823	Congressman Thomas Newton	1842
Ouachita	Camden	34,037	737	Ouachita Mountains	1842
Perry	Perryville	8,084	550	Commodore Oliver Perry, hero of War of 1812	1840
Phillips	Helena	34,694	685	Sylvanus Phillips, early settler	1820
Pike	Murfreesboro	11,213	598	Zebulon Pike, explorer	1833
Poinsett	Harrisburg	28,036	762	Secretary of War Joel Poinsett	1838
Polk	Mena	18,426	860	U.S. President James Polk	1844
Pope	Russellville	45,197	820	Territorial Governor John Pope	1829
Prairie	Des Arc and De Valls Bluff	10,324	656	grand prairie country	1846
Pulaski	Little Rock	393,150	767	Count Casimir Pulaski, hero of the American Revolution	1818
Randolph	Pocahontas	19,028	656	John Randolph, statesman	1835
Saline	Benton	64,072	725	local salt deposits	1835
Scott	Waldron	10,254	896	Andrew Scott, territorial judge	1833
Searcy	Marshall	9,355	668	Richard Searcy, territorial judge	1838
Sebastian	Greenwood and Forth Smith	106,075	535	U.S. Senator William Sebastian	1851
Sevier	DeQueen	15,451	560	U.S. Senator Ambrose Sevier	1828
Sharp	Ash Flat	17,644	606	Representative Ephraim Sharp	1868
St. Francis	Forrest City	32,437	638	St. Francis River	1827
Stone	Mountain View	10,181	606	local hills	1873
Union	El Dorado	51,404	1,053	honoring the Union of the United States	1829
Van Buren	Clinton	15,767	709	U.S. President Martin Van Buren	1833
Washington	Fayetteville	114,504	951	U.S. President George Washington	1828
White	Searcy	56,725	1,040	White River	1835
Woodruff	Augusta	11,409	592	William Woodruff, founder of the Arkansas Gazette	1862
Yell	Danville and Dardanelle	18,098	930	Governor Archibald Yell	1840

ARKANSAS'S CITIES

City Name	City Population (1990)
Little Rock	175,795
Fort Smith	72,798
North Little Rock	61,741
Pine Bluff	57,140
Jonesboro	46,535
Fayetteville	42,099
Hot Springs	32,462
Springdale	29,941
Jacksonville	29,101
West Memphis	28,259
Conway	26,481
Rogers	24,692
El Dorado	23,146
Bytheville	22,906
Texarkana	22,631
Russellville	21,260
Sherwood	18,893
Paragould	18,540
Benton	18,177
Searcy	15,180
Van Buren	14,979
Camden	14,380
Forrest City	13,364
Bentonville	11,257
Magnolia	11,151
Stuttgart	10,420
Arkadelphia	10,014
Harrison	9,922
West Helena	9,695
Hope	9,643
Malvern	9,256
Batesville	9,187
Mountain Home	9,027
Osceola	8,930
Cabot	8,319
Wynne	8,187
Siloam Springs	8,151
Monticello	8,116
Helena	7,491
Newport	7,459
Morrilton	6,551
Warren	6,455
Trumann	6,304

City Name	City Population (1990)
Crossett	6,282
Pocahontas	6,151
Marian	5,910
Heber Springs	5,628
Dumas	5,520
Mena	5,475
Bryant	5,269
Ashdown	5,150
McGehee	4,997
Fordyce	4,729
Dermott	4,715
Nashville	4,639
Beebe	4,455
Barling	4,078
Lonoke	4,022
Marion	4,391
Walnut Ridge	4,388
Brinkley	4,234
Greenwood	3,984
Whitehall	3,849
Gosnell	3,783
Piggott	3,777
Dardanelle	3,722
Prescott	3,673
De Witt	3,553
Earle	3,393
Ozark	3,330
Corning	3,323
Eudora	3,155
Marked Tree	3,100
Hamburg	3,098
Sheridan	3,098
Waldron	3,024
Alma	2,959
Salem	2,950
Atkins	2,834
Lake Village	2,791
Augusta	2,759
Hoxie	2,676
Bald Knob	2,653
Rockwell	2,514
Piney	2,500

Source: 1990 U.S. Census, Arkansas, Table 10.

ARKANSAS'S GOVERNORS

GOVERNOR	TERM	GOVERNOR	TERM
James Miller	1819-1825	George W. Donaghey	1909-1913
George Izard	1825-1829	Joseph T. Robinson	1913-1913
John Pope	1829-1835	George W. Hays	1913-1917
William Fulton	1835-1836	Charles H. Brough	1917-1921
James S. Conway	1836-1840	Thomas C. McRae	1921-1925
Archibald Yell	1840-1844	Tom J. Terrai	1925-1927
Thomas S. Drew	1844-1849	John E. Martineau	1927-1928
John S. Roane	1849-1852	Harvey Parnell	1928-1933
Elias N. Conway	1852-1860	J. M. Futrell	1933-1937
Henry M. Rector	1860-1862	Carl E. Bailey	1937-1941
Harris Flanagin	1862-1864	Homer M. Adkins	1941-1945
Isaac Murphy	1864-1868	Ben T. Laney	1945-1949
Powell Clayton	1868-1871	Sid McMath	1949-1953
Elisha Baxter	1873-1874	Francis Cherry	1953-1955
Augustus H. Garland	1874-1877	Orval E. Faubus	1955-1967
William R. Miller	1877-1881	Winthrop Rockefeller	1967-1971
Thomas J. Churchill	1881-1883	Dale L. Bumpers	1971-1975
James H. Berry	1883-1885	Davis H. Pryor	1975-1979
Simon P. Hughes	1885-1889	Bill Clinton	1979-1981
James P. Eagle	1889-1893	Frank White	1981-1983
William Fishback	1893-1895	Bill Clinton	1983-1993
James P. Clarke	1895-1897	Jim Guy Tucker	1993-
Dan W. Jones	1897-1901		
Jeff Davis	1901-1907		
John S. Little	1907-1909		

The Arkansas State Capitol building in Little Rock was completed in 1915. The building is about one quarter the size of the Capitol in Washington, D.C. It is made from Arkansas marble which was brought from the area around Batesville.

ARKANSAS ALMANAC

TOURISM IN ARKANSAS

WHERE TOURISTS COME FROM
(Out of every 100 people)

TX 19
AR 8
MO 7
LA 6
OK 10

OTHER STATES AND FOREIGN COUNTRIES

MOST VISITED COUNTIES

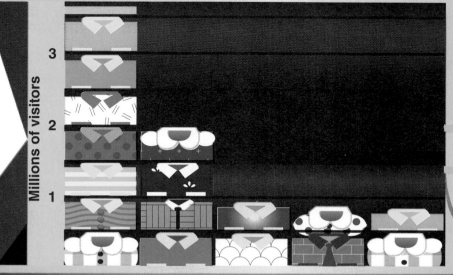

Millions of visitors

3

2

1

Pulaski   Garland   Washington   Carroll   Sebastian

 = 1/2 million people

ANNUAL EVENTS IN ARKANSAS

SUMMER

JUNE
Diamond Festival, Murfreesboro
Oil Town, Smackover
Pink Tomato Festival, Warren
Bat-O-Rama, Devil's Den State Park, West Fork
Big Dig, Toltec Mounds State Park, Scott
Old Fort River Festival, Fort Smith
*Purple Hull Pea and World Championship
   Rotor Tiller Race*, Emerson

JULY
Fourth of July, statewide
Chicken and the Egg Festival, Prescott

AUGUST
White River Carnival, Batesville
Watermelon Festival, Hope
Grape Festival, Tontitown
Bluegrass Festival, Harrison
Old Settlers Reunion, Mena

FALL

SEPTEMBER
Great Arkansas Cleanup, statewide
International Fest, Little Rock
County Fairs, statewide
Pioneer Day, St. Paul

OCTOBER
Oktoberfest, Hot Springs
Autumnfest, Fayetteville
Frontier Days, Washington
Arkansas State Fair, Little Rock
Prairie Grove Battle Reenactment, Prairie Grove
Livin' on the Levee, West Memphis
Arkansas Rice Festival, Weiner

NOVEMBER
Wings Over the Prairie, Stuttgart
Delta Arts and Crafts Festival, Dumas
Downtown Christmas Parade, Little Rock

WINTER

DECEMBER
Candlelight Tour of Homes, Eureka Springs
Ozark Christmas, Mountain View
Pioneer Christmas, Rison
Christmas Parades and Celebrations, statewide

JANUARY
Eagle Awareness Day, De Gray State Park, Bismarck

FEBRUARY
Walleye Contest, Fairfield Bay

SPRING

MARCH
Jonquil Festival, Washington
Mid-South Gospel Quartet Convention, Jonesboro
Pioneer Craft Festival, Rison
Arkansas State Fiddlers Jamboree, Harrison
Wild Turkey Calling Contest, Marshall
Young Arkansas Artists Exhibition, Little Rock
Governor Conway Days, Bradley

APRIL
Ozark Scottish Festival, Batesville
Wildflower Weekend, statewide
Arkansas Folk Festival, Mountain View
Spinach Festival, Alma
Dogwood Festival, Siloam Springs
Fordyce on the Cotton Belt Festival, Fordyce

MAY
Arkansas-Oklahoma Rodeo, Fort Smith
Riverfest, Little Rock
Craft and Folk Music Festival, Little Rock
Catfish Festival, Eudora

GLOSSARY

This Glossary will help you to pronounce and understand the meanings of the Key Vocabulary in this book. The page number at the end of the definition tells where the word first appears.

PRONUNCIATION KEY

a	cap	hw	where	oi	coin	ü	moon
ā	cake	i	bib	ôr	fork	ū	cute
ä	father	ī	kite	ou	cow	ûr	term
är	car	îr	pierce	sh	show	ə	about, taken,
âr	dare	ng	song	th	thin		pencil, apron,
ch	chain	o	top	th	those		helpful
e	hen	ō	rope	u	sun	ər	letter, dollar,
ē	me	ô	saw	u̇	book		doctor

A

abolitionists (ab ə lish′ ə nists) People who believed that slavery should be ended. (p. 123)

agriculture (ag′ ri kul chər) Farming. (p. 17)

alluvium (ə lü′ vē əm) The mud, sand, or other material left behind by a flowing river. (p. 32)

alternative (ôl tûr′ nə tiv) A choice between two or more things; one of the things that may be chosen. (p. 56)

ancestors (an′ ses tərz) Relatives who lived long before you. (p. 72)

archaeologist (är kē ol′ ə jist) A scientist who studies ancient or prehistoric people. (p. 50)

Archaic (är kā′ ik) The time period that lasted from about 10,000 years ago to about 3,000 years ago. (p. 52)

architecture (är′ ki tek chər) The style of a building; the art of designing buildings. (p. 181)

artifact (är′ tə fakt) An object that people of the past have left behind. (p. 50)

B

barter (bär′ tər) To trade goods for other goods. (p. 89)

bayou (bī′ ü) A sluggish inlet of water. (p. 35)

Big Dipper (big dip′ ər) A group of seven stars in the sky, shaped like a bowl. (p. 68)

bill (bil) A plan for a law. (p. 186)

budget (buj′ it) A plan for the way in which money will be spent. (p. 186)

bushwhackers (bush′ hwak ərz) Bands of thieves, supportive of the Confederacy, who used the Civil War as an excuse to rob people and destroy property. (p. 131)

byline (bī′ līn) The words at the beginning of a newspaper article that tell who wrote the story. (p. 195)

C

carpetbagger (kär′ pit bag ər) A Northerner who settled in the South after the Civil War. (p. 137)

cash crop (kash krop) A crop grown to be sold. (p. 170)

census (sen′ səs) A count of the population in a certain area. (p. 92)

century (sen′ chə rē) A period of 100 years. (p. 87)

ceremony (ser′ ə mō nē) An act or set of acts performed on a special occasion. (p. 54)

city council (sit′ ē koun′ səl) The legislative branch of a town or city government. (p. 191)

city manager (sit′ ē man′ i jər) A person hired by a city council to head the executive branch, and to keep track of the money collected and spent by the city. (p. 192)

civil rights (siv′ əl rīts) The rights of all people to be treated equally under the law. (p. 159)

Civil War (siv′ əl wôr) The war fought between the Northern states and the Southern states between 1861 and 1865. (p. 125)

classified ad (klas′ ə fīd ad) A short advertisement that appears in small print in a newspaper, usually offering goods, services, or jobs. (p. 194)

climate (klī′ mit) The weather that a place has over many years. (p. 15)

colony (kol′ ə nē) A settlement that is ruled by another country. (p. 82)

compass (kum′ pəs) An instrument with a magnetic needle that always points north when the compass is held level. (p. 69)

conclusion (kən klü′ zhən) An end point of a process, such as a statement that pulls together pieces of information but does not restate the information. (p. 140)

Confederacy (kən fed′ ər ə sē) The Confederate States of America, or the group of states that fought against the Union in the Civil War. (p. 123)

constitution (kon sti tü′ shən) A plan of government. (p. 101)

country music (kun′ trē mū′ zik) A type of American music which grew out of folk music. (p. 206)

county judge (koun′ tē juj) The head of the executive branch of county government. (p. 190)

culture (kul′ chər) The way of life of a group of people. (p. 53)

D

dateline (dāt′ līn) The words at the beginning of a newspaper article telling when and where the article was written. (p. 195)

decade (dek′ ād) A period of ten years. (p. 86)

decision (di sizh′ ən) A choice. (p. 56)

degree (di grē′) A unit of measurement for latitude and longitude. (p. 18)

democracy (di mok′ rə sē) A government that is run by the people it governs. (p. 198)

E

economy (i kon′ ə mē) The way in which a state or a nation produces and uses money, goods, and natural resources. (p. 151)

editorial (ed i tôr′ ē əl) A newspaper article in which editors give their opinion about an issue. (p. 194)

elevation (el ə vā′ shən) The height of land above sea level. (p. 30)

Emancipation Proclamation (i man sə pā′ shən prok lə mā′ shən) The document issued by President Abraham Lincoln in 1863 that freed all the slaves in the Southern states. (p. 131)

entrepreneur (än trə prə nûr′) A person who creates a business for profit. (p. 177)

erosion (i rō′ zhən) The wearing away of land by wind or water. (p. 37)

executive branch (eg zek′ yə tiv branch) The part of a government that carries out the laws. (p. 187)

expedition (ek spi dish′ ən) A journey made for a special purpose. (p. 79)

F

feature article (fē′ chər är′ ti kəl) A newspaper story that reports in detail on a person, subject, or event. (p. 194)

fertile (fûr′ təl) Good for growing crops. (p. 23)

folk art (fōk ärt) Things made by everyday people. (p. 205)

fossil (fos′ əl) An impression in rock left by a plant or an animal that lived long ago. (p. 13)

free enterprise (frē en tər prīz) Economic system in which people own and run their own businesses. (p. 177)

Freedmen's Bureau (frēd′ mənz byůr′ ō) An organization set up by Congress in 1865 to help former slaves in the South. (p. 138)

frontier (frun tîr′) The land lying along the border of a settled area. (p. 110)

G

General Assembly (jen′ ər əl ə sem′ blē) The legislative branch of the Arkansas government. (p. 186)

geography (jē og′ rə fē) The study of the earth and the way people live on it and use it. (p. 11)

global grid (glō′ bəl grid) A grid on a map or globe formed by lines of latitude and longitude. (p. 20)

gospel music (gos′pəl mū′ zik) A type of music that grew out of religious feelings of African Americans. (p. 207)

Great Depression (grāt di presh′ ən) The period during the 1930s when many businesses closed and millions of people were out of work. (p. 151)

grid (grid) A pattern of criss-crossed lines on a map or globe. (p. 18)

H

headline (hed′ līn) Sentences or phrases printed in large type at the top of a news story. (p. 194)

hemisphere (hem′ i sfîr) Half of a globe or sphere. (p. 19)

highland (hī′ lənd) A hilly or mountainous area. (p. 28)

historical map (his tôr′ i kəl map) A map that shows information about the past, such as the locations where past events took place. (p. 128)

history (his′ tə rē) Events of the past that have been preserved in written records. (p. 50)

husking bee (husk′ ing bē) A frontier party at which guests combined husking corn with the fun of gathering together with neighbors. (p. 113)

I

immigrant (im′ i grənt) A person who leaves one country in order to come and live in another. (p. 202)

industry (in′ də strē) A company or group of companies that all make a certain product or provide a certain service. (p. 142)

integration (in ti grā′ shən) The act of making something available to all racial groups. (p. 160)

interdependent (in tər di pen′ dənt) The condition of depending on others in order to help meet certain needs and wants. (p. 177)

irrigation (ir i gā′ shən) A method of bringing water to dry fields by use of ditches. (p. 24)

J

jayhawkers (jā′ hô kərz) Bands of thieves, supportive of the Union, who took advantage of the Civil War to rob people and destroy property. (p. 131)

jazz (jaz) A musical style with African rhythms that first appeared in the early 1900s. (p. 207)

Jim Crow laws (jim crō lôz) The laws passed in the late 1800s that kept African-Americans and whites apart. (p. 159)

judicial branch (jü dish′ əl branch) The part of a government that is related to courts and justice. (p. 188)

K

Ku Klux Klan (kü′ kluks klan′) A group that sought to bully and intimidate African-Americans during Reconstruction. (p. 139)

L

land bridge (land brij) A narrow area of land that connects two larger bodies of land. (p. 50)

landform (land′ form) A shape on the earth's surface, such as a valley or a mountain. (p. 11)

latitude (lat′ i tüd) The imaginary lines on a map or globe that measure degrees north or south of the equator. (p. 18)

legislative branch (lej′ is lā tiv branch) The part of a government that makes laws. (p. 186)

legislature (lej′ is lā chər) A group of people who have the power to make laws. (p. 100)

levee (lev′ ē) A large earthen wall built along the banks of a river to prevent flooding. (p. 33)

Little Dipper (lit′ əl dip′ ər) The bowl-shaped group of stars that includes the North Star. (p. 68)

livestock (līv′ stok) Animals such as cattle, pigs, and horses that are raised on a farm. (p. 171)

loess (les) Sandy, windblown soil. (p. 34)

longitude (lon′ ji tüd) The imaginary lines on a map or globe that measure degrees east or west of the prime meridian. (p. 19)

Louisiana Purchase (lü ē zē an′ ə pûr′ chəs) The treaty by which the United States bought Louisiana from France for $15 million. (p. 96)

lowland (lō′ lənd) An area of land that is lower than the surrounding areas. (p. 28)

M

manufacturing (man yə fak′ chər ing) Making products by machinery. (p. 142)

mayor (mā′ ər) The head of the executive branch of a city or town government. (p. 191)

meridian (mə rid′ ē ən) A line of longitude. (p. 19)

migrate (mī′ grāt) To move from one region to another in order to settle there. (p. 61)

mineral (min′ ər əl) A substance found in the earth that is neither plant nor animal. (p. 23)

mountain range (moun′ tən rānj) A series of mountains connected together. (p. 13)

mouth (mouth) The place where a river empties into another body of water. (p. 82)

municipal (mū nis′ ə pəl) Describing a town or city government. (p. 191)

N

natural resource (nach′ ə rəl rē′ sôrs) Something that is found in nature that is useful to people. (p. 22)

New Deal (nü dēl) President Franklin Roosevelt's programs for helping people during the Great Depression. (p. 153)

New Madrid Earthquake (nü mə drid′ ûrth′ kwāk) The violent earthquake that shook northeastern Arkansas in 1811. (p. 96)

New South (nü south) A plan for the South in which the economy would be built around manufacturing instead of farming. (p. 142)

GLOSSARY

news article (nüz är′ ti kəl) A story in a newspaper about an important event that has just taken place. (p. 194)

North Star (nôrth stär) A bright star that can be seen in the Northern Hemisphere and that can be used to find directions. (p. 68)

O

orient (ôr′ ē ənt) To line up a map with a compass. (p. 69)

P

Paleo (pā′ lē ō) Referring to a period in prehistory that took place about 12,000 years ago. (p. 51)

parallel (par′ ə lel) A line of latitude. (p. 18)

pioneer (pī ə nîr′) One of the first people to move into a region. (p. 110)

plantation (plan tā′ shən) A very large farm that usually grows only a single crop. (p. 102)

plateau (pla tō′) An area of flat land raised above the surrounding land. (p. 37)

point of view (point əv vū) The way a person looks at or feels about something. (p. 98)

pollute (pə lüt′) To make dirty or impure. (p. 218)

population (pop yə lā′ shən) The number of people living in a place. (p. 39)

poultry (pōl′ trē) Birds such as chickens and turkeys that are raised for their meat or eggs. (p. 172)

precipitation (pri sip i tā′ shən) The moisture that falls to the earth as rain, snow, hail, or sleet. (p. 15)

prehistory (prē his′ tə rē) A period in the past before writing was invented. (p. 50)

prime meridian (prīm mə rid′ ē ən) The meridian from which all other lines of longitude are measured. (p. 19)

professional (prə fesh′ ə nəl) A person who is paid to do a job. (p. 215)

profile (prō′ fīl) A side view of a part of the earth. (p. 31)

Progressive Era (prə gres′ iv îr′ ə) The period in American history between 1900 and 1920, during which many leaders tried to bring changes to our state and nation. (p. 144)

Q

quorum court (kwôr′ əm kôrt) The legislative branch of county government. (p. 190)

R

Reconstruction (rē kən struk′ shən) The process of returning the former Confederate states to the Union after the Civil War. (p. 136)

recreation (rek rē ā′ shən) Something that people do for relaxation or enjoyment. (p. 212)

region (rē′ jən) A large area with common features that set it apart from other areas. (p. 28)

religion (ri lij′ ən) The way a people worship the God or gods they believe in. (p. 89)

river basin (riv′ ər bā′ sin) The area drained by a river and by all the streams that flow into the river. (p. 13)

rural (rür′ əl) Having to do with the country or agriculture. (p. 203)

S

scalawag (skal′ ə wag) A white Southerner who worked with a Reconstruction government after the Civil War. (p. 137)

secede (si sēd′) To break away. (p. 123)

sediment (sed′ ə mənt) The rock, sand, or mud left behind by moving water, wind, or ice. (p. 23)

segregation (seg ri gā′ shən) Laws or practices that keep African-Americans and whites separate. (p. 158)

service industries (sûr′ vis in′ də strēz) Businesses that offer services rather than producing goods. (p. 175)

settlement (set′ əl mənt) A village or group of houses in a new area. (p. 64)

sharecropping (shâr′ krop ing) The system in which a farmer gives up a large share of his or her crop in exchange for being allowed to farm the land. (p. 138)

a cap; ā cake; ä father; är car; âr dare; ch chain; e hen; ē me; hw where; i bib; ī kite; îr pierce; ng song; o top; ō rope; ô saw; oi coin; ôr fork; ou cow; sh show; th thin; th those; u sun; u book; ü moon; ū cute; ûr term; ə about, taken, pencil, apron, helpful; ər letter, dollar, doctor

slavery (slāv ər ē) Practice of one person owning another. (p. 81)

speculators (spek′ yə lā tərz) People who make money buying land cheaply and selling it for a profit. (p. 97)

statehood (stāt′ hu̇d) The condition of being a state. (p. 101)

stocks (stoks) Shares of ownership in a company. (p. 151)

strait (strāt) A narrow waterway that connects two larger bodies of water. (p. 50)

subsistence farming (səb sis′ təns fär′ ming) The type of farming in which the farmer lives on the crop that he or she grows. (p. 170)

T

taxes (taks′ əz) The money that people pay to the government. (p. 185)

technology (tek nol′ ə jē) The use of new ideas and tools to meet people's needs. (p. 175)

temperature (tem′ pər ə chər) The measure of the heat or cold in the air. (p. 15)

timber (tim′ bər) Trees that may be used for buildings or to make wood products. (p. 22)

time line (tīm līn) A diagram that shows when events took place. (p. 86)

tourism (tu̇r′ iz əm) The business of providing services for people on vacation. (p. 149)

Trail of Tears (trāl əv tîrz) The name given to the route taken by the Cherokee to the Indian Territory after they were forced off their land. (p. 107)

Territory after they were forced off their land. (p. 107)

treaty (trē′ tē) A formal agreement. (p. 72)

tributary (trib′ yə ter ē) A river or stream that flows into a larger body of water. (p. 38)

U

unconstitutional (un kon sti tü′ shə nəl) Not allowed by the Constitution. (p. 159)

Union (ūn′ yən) The group of states that remained part of the United States during the Civil War. (p. 123)

urban (ûr′ bən) Having to do with cities. (p. 203)

V

veto (vē′ tō) To overrule or cancel a decision. (p. 187)

voyageurs (voi ə zhərz′) French hunters and trappers in Arkansas during the 1700s. (p. 91)

W

weather (weth′ ər) The condition of the air at a given time and place. (p. 15)

World War I (wûrld wôr wun) The war that broke out in Europe in 1914 between the Central Powers and the Allied Powers. (p. 147)

World War II (wûrld wôr tü) The war that involved most of the countries in the world, fought between 1939 and 1945. (p. 153)

a cap; ā cake; ä father; är car; âr dare; ch chain; e hen; ē me; hw where; i bib; ī kite; îr pierce; ng song; o top; ō rope; ô saw; oi coin; ôr fork; ou cow; sh show; th thin; th those; u sun; u̇ book; ü moon; ū cute; ûr term; ə about, taken, pencil, apron, helpful; ər letter, dollar, doctor

GLOSSARY

INDEX

Page references in italic type that follow an *m* indicate maps.
Those following a *p* indicate photographs, artwork, or charts.

INDEX

INDEX

CREDITS